The Life of

Johannes Brahms.

Second edition.

Volume 1.

Florence May

Travis & Emery

The Life of
Johannes Brahms.

Second edition, revised by the author,
with Additional Material and Illustrations.

First published, London, circa 1948.

Republished Travis & Emery 2010.

Volume 1 (of 2)

Published by
Travis & Emery Music Bookshop
17 Cecil Court, London, WC2N 4EZ, United Kingdom.
(+44) 20 7240 2129
neworders@travis-and-emery.com

Hardback: 978-1-84955-102-1 Paperback: 978-1-84955-103-8

Florence May (1845-1923), English pianist and author.

She studied with Clara Schumann and later under Brahms, which made her well positioned to write about them both.

Her biographies are well researched and also provide an insight to music of her time.

This edition was written in the 1910s but not published till 1948.

More details available from
- Stanley Sadie: The New Grove Dictionary of Music and Musicians.

THE LIFE OF JOHANNES BRAHMS

VOLUME I

THE LIFE

OF

JOHANNES BRAHMS

BY

FLORENCE MAY

**Second Edition revised by the Author, with
Additional Matter and Illustrations, and an
Introduction by Ralph Hill**

IN TWO VOLUMES. VOL. I

WILLIAM REEVES
BOOKSELLER LIMITED

83 CHARING CROSS ROAD,
— LONDON, W.C.2. —

1*

TO

THE MANY KIND FRIENDS

WHOSE SYMPATHY

HAS HELPED ME DURING THE WRITING OF THESE VOLUMES,

THEY ARE GRATEFULLY DEDICATED

Printed by The New Temple Press, London, S.W.16, Great Britain.

PREFACE TO THE SECOND EDITION.

THE task of preparing a second edition of my Life of Brahms, a German version of which was published in 1911, has been the more welcome to me since it has given me the opportunity of correcting a few trifling inaccuracies which found their way into the original version, as well as to determine certain doubtful points by the aid of the valuable additions to the previously existing Brahms literature that have appeared in recent years.

The publication especially of Brahms' correspondence with Joachim and Grimm, brought to light new details respecting the origin and growth of some of Brahms' early works, whilst the conclusion of Litzmann's "Clara Schumann," the second volume of which appeared in 1905—almost simultaneously with my Brahms biography—and the third volume in 1906 supplied incontrovertible chronological data as to the events with which it deals to which all future works dealing with the same matters must in future be referred.

The appearance of this monumental work not only affords opportunity, but makes it absolutely incumbent on Brahms' biographers to enter more in detail on the subject of the friendship between the composer and Clara Schumann than seemed to me appropriate in the first instance in my own case.

I have also introduced into the book some additional

scenes or incidents which throw new light on the master's individuality and have in a few cases partially revised and enlarged my remarks on the works.

· I have to add the following names to the list of friends who have helped me with information and sympathy :

> Herr Senator Brandt.
> Mrs. Brodsky.
> Herr F. Burg.
> Herr Dr. Georg Fischer.
> Herr Oskar Fux.
> Frau Dr. Nina Grieg.
> W. H. Hadow, Esq.
> Herr Geheimrath Dr. Oskar von Hase.
> Herr Kapellmeister Friedrich Hegar.
> George Henschel, Esq.
> Herr J. Marbach.
> Lady Thompson.
> Frau Professor Ellen Vetter.

PREFACE TO THE FIRST EDITION.

THE biographical materials from which I have written the following Life of Brahms have, excepting in the few instances indicated in footnotes, been gathered by me, at first hand, chiefly in the course of several continental journeys, the first of which was undertaken in the summer of 1902. Dates of concerts throughout the volumes have been authenticated by reference to original programmes or contemporary journals.

My aim in giving some account of Brahms' compositions has not been a technical one. So far as I have exceeded purely biographical limits my object has been to assist the general music-lover in his enjoyment of the noble achievements of a beautiful life.

I feel it impossible to ignore numerous requests made to me to include in my book some particulars of my own acquaintance with Brahms—begun when I was a young student of the pianoforte. I have not wished, however, to interrupt the main narrative of the Life by the introduction of slight personal details, and therefore place together in an introductory chapter some of my recollections and impressions, published a few years ago in the *Musical Magazine*. These were verified by reference to letters to my mother in which I recorded events as they occurred. Written before the commencement of the Biography, they are in no way essential to its completeness, which will not suffer should they remain unread.

I am indebted for valuable assistance and sympathy to:

> H.R.H. Alexander Friedrich, Landgraf of Hesse.
> Herr Carl Bade.
> Fräulein Berninger.
> Mrs. Jellings Blow (b. Finke).
> Fräulein Theodore Blume.
> Frau Professor Böie.
> Herr Professor Dr. Heinrich Bulthaupt.
> Herr Professor Julius Buths.
> The late Gerard F. Cobb, Esq.
> Frederic R. Comee, Esq.
> Herr Hugo Conrat.
> Fräulein Ilse Conrat.
> Fräulein Johanna Cossel.
> Frau Elise Denninghoff-Giesemann.
> Herr Geheimrath Dr. Hermann Deiters.
> Herr Hofcapellmeister Albert Dietrich.
> Herr k. k. Hofclavierfabrikant Friedrich Ehrbar.
> Herr Geheimrath Dr. Engelmann.
> Herr Professor Julius Epstein.
> Fräulein Anna Ettlinger.
> Frau Dr. Maria Fellinger.
> Herr Professor Dr. Josef Gänsbacher.
> Otto Goldschmidt, Esq., Hon. R.A.M., Member of Swedish A.M., etc.
> Herr Carl Graf.
> Dr. Josef Ritter Griez von Ronse.

Fräulein Marie Grimm.

Frau Grüber.

Herr Professor Robert Hausmann.

Fräulein Heyden.

Herr Professor Walter Hübbe.

Herr Dr. Gustav Jansen.

Frau Dr. Marie Janssen.

Frau Dr. Louise Langhans-Japha.

Herr Professor Dr. Joseph Joachim.

Mrs. Johann Kruse.

Herr Carl Lüstner.

J. A. Fuller Maitland, Esq., F.S.A.

Herr Dr. Eusebius Mandyczewski, Archivar to the Gesellschaft der Musikfreunde.

Carl Freiherr von Meysenbug.

Hermann Freiherr von Meysenbug.

Herr Richard Mühlfeld, Hofkammermusiker.

Herr Professor Dr. Ernst Naumann.

Herr Professor Dr. Carl Neumann.

Herr Christian Otterer.

Fräulein Henriette Reinthaler.

Herr Capellmeister Dr. Rottenberg.

Herr Kammermusiker Julius Schmidt.

Herr Fritz Schnack.

Herr Professor Dr. Bernhard Scholz.

Herr Heinrich Schröder.

Fräulein Marie Schumann.

Frau Simons (b. Kyllmann).

Herr Professor Josef Sittard.

Herr Dr. Julius Spengel.

Mrs. Edward Speyer.

Sir Charles Villiers Stanford, Mus.Doc.

Mrs. Edward Stone.

Frau Celestine Truxa.

Herr Superintendent Vogelsang.

Herr Dr. Josef Victor Widmann.

And others who prefer that their names should not be expressly
mentioned.

F. M.

SOUTH KENSINGTON,
September, 1905.

CONTENTS.

VOLUME I.

CHAPTER V.

1853.

CHAPTER VI.

1854-1855.

CHAPTER VII.

1855-1856.

CHAPTER VIII.

1856-1858.

CHAPTER IX.

1859.

CHAPTER X.
1859-1861.

CHAPTER XI.
1861-1862.

APPENDIX No. I.

APPENDIX No. II.

VOLUME II.
CHAPTER XII.
1862-1864.

CHAPTER XVII.

1872-1876.

CHAPTER XVIII.

1876-1878.

CHAPTER XIX.

1878-1881.

CHAPTER XX.

1881-1885.

CHAPTER XXI.

1885-1888.

CHAPTER XXII.

1889-1895.

CHAPTER XXIII.

1895-1897.

LIST OF ILLUSTRATIONS.

VOLUME I.

VOLUME II.

THE

LIFE OF JOHANNES BRAHMS

PERSONAL RECOLLECTIONS

BADEN-BADEN.

IT was to the kindness of Frau Schumann that I owed my
introduction to Brahms, which took place the very day of
my arrival on my first visit to Germany. I had had lessons
from the great pianist during her visit to London early in
the year 1871, and on her departure from England she
allowed my father to arrange that I should follow her, as
soon as I could possibly get ready, to her home in Lichtenthal, a suburb of Baden-Baden, in order to continue my
studies under her guidance.

I can vividly recall the bright morning in the beginning
of May on which I arrived at Baden-Baden, rather home-sick
and dreadfully tired, for owing to a railway breakdown
en route my journey had occupied fourteen hours longer than
it ought to have done, and my father's arrangements for my
comfort had been completely upset. It was too early to go
at once to Frau Schumann's house, and I remember to have
dreamily watched, whilst waiting at the station, a passing
procession of young girl communicants in their white wreaths
and veils, as I tried to realise that I was, for the first time in
my life, far away from home and from England. When the
morning was sufficiently advanced, I took an open Droschke,
and driving under the great trees of the Lichtenthaler Allée
to the door of Frau Schumann's house, I obtained the

2

address of the lodgings that had been taken for me in the
village.   Without alighting, I proceeded at once to my
rooms, where I was almost immediately joined by Frau
Schumann herself, who came round, as soon as she had
finished breakfast, to bid me welcome.

My delight at seeing the great artist again, combined with
her irresistible charm and kindness, at once made me feel
less strange in my new surroundings, and I joyfully accepted
the invitation she gave me at the close of a few minutes'
visit, to go to her house the same afternoon at four o'clock
and take coffee with her in her family circle.

On presenting myself at the appointed hour, I was at once
shown into a pleasant balcony at the back of the house,
overlooking garden and river.   In it was seated Frau
Schumann with her daughters, and with a gentleman whom
she presently introduced to me as Herr Brahms.   The name
awakened in my mind no special feeling of interest, nor did I
look at its owner with any particular curiosity.   Brahms'
name was at that time almost unknown in England, and I
had heard of him only through his arrangement of two books
of Hungarian dances for four hands on the pianoforte.   As,
however, from that day onwards I was accustomed, during
a period of months, to meet him almost daily, it may be
convenient to say at once a few words about his appearance
and manner as they seemed to me after I had had time to
become familiar with them.

Brahms, then, when I first knew him, was in the very
prime of life, being thirty-eight years of age.   Below middle
height, his figure was somewhat square and solidly built,
though without any of the tendency to corpulency which
developed itself at a later period.   He was of the blonde
type of German, with fair, straight hair, which he wore
rather long and brushed back from the temples.   His face
was clean-shaven.   His most striking physical characteristic
was the grand head with its magnificent intellectual forehead, but the blue eyes were also remarkable from their
expression of intense mental concentration.   This was

accentuated by a constant habit he had of thrusting the rather thick under-lip over the upper, and keeping it compressed there, reminding one of the mouth in some of the portraits of Beethoven. His nose was finely formed. Feet and hands were small, the fingers without "cushions."

"I have none," he said one day, when I was speaking to him about pianists' hands; and he spread out his fingers, at my request, to show me the tips. "Frau Schumann has them, and Rubinstein also; Rubinstein's are immense."

His dress, though plain, was always perfectly neat in those days. He usually wore a short, loose, black alpaca coat, chosen, no doubt, with regard to his ideas of comfort. He was near-sighted, and made frequent use of a double eyeglass that he wore hanging on a thin black cord round his neck. When walking out, it was his custom to go bare-headed, and to carry his soft felt hat in his hand, swinging the arm energetically to and fro. The disengaged hand he often held behind him.

In Brahms' demeanour there was a mixture of sociability and reserve which gave me the impression of his being a kindly-natured man, but one whom it would be difficult really to know. Though always pleasant and friendly, yet there was a something about him—perhaps it may have been his extraordinary dislike to speaking about himself—which suggested that his life had not been free from disappointment, and that he had reckoned with the latter and taken his course. His manner was absolutely simple and unaffected. To his own compositions he alluded only on the very rarest occasions, nor could he be induced to play them before even a small party. His great satisfaction and pleasure were evidently found in the society of Frau Schumann, for whom he displayed the most devoted admiration, an admiration that seemed to combine the affection and reverence of an elder son with the sympathetic camaderie of a colleague in art. He had established himself for the spring and summer months at Lichtenthal, in order to be near her, and was always a welcome guest at her house, coming and going as he liked. I met him there continually at the hour of afternoon coffee, as on the day of my arrival; and very often, when the coffee-cups were done with, it was my good fortune to listen to the two great artists playing duets; Brahms, the favoured, being always allowed to retain the beloved cigar or cigarette between his lips during the performance, and taking his turn in playing the treble part.

It was Frau Schumann's kind habit to invite me to her mid-day dinner on Sundays, and frequently to supper during the week. Brahms was rarely absent, and was sometimes accompanied by one or two of his friends. The talk on these occasions was more or less general, but natur- ally my chief interest was in listening to Frau Schumann and Brahms, who used to discuss all sorts of topics with great animation. Brahms' interest in politics was keen, and although he had been settled in Vienna for some years, and had become much attached to that city and to his friends and surroundings there, yet it was evident that he remained an ardent German patriot.

He was a great walker, and had a passionate love of nature. It was his habit during the spring and summer to rise at four or five o'clock, and, after making himself a cup of coffee, to go into the woods to enjoy the delicious fresh- ness of early morning and to listen to the singing of the birds. In adverse weather he could still find something to admire and enjoy.

" I never feel it dull," he said one day, in answer to some remark about the depressing effect of the long-continued rain, " my view is so fine. Even when it rains, I have only another kind of beauty."

He was considerate for others, even in trifles. I remember that one evening, before we had quitted the supper-table, someone produced a copy of " Kladderadatsch," and, point- ing out to Brahms a set of sarcastic verses dedicated to John Bull, begged him to read them aloud for the entertainment of the assembled party. Brahms, after glancing down the column, playfully declined to do as he was asked, indicating, with a wave of the hand, his English *vis-à-vis* as his reason for objecting; and it was not until I had laughingly and repeatedly expressed my earnest wish to hear whatever might be in store for me as Mr. Bull's representative, that he at length, and still reluctantly, complied with the request.

Frau Schumann often spoke to me of his extraordinary genius and acquirements both as composer and executant, as well as of his general intellectual qualities, and especially of his knowledge and love of books. She wished me to hear him play, but said it was no easy matter to do so, as he was extremely dependent on his mood, and not only disliked to be pressed to perform, but was unable to do justice either to himself or his composer when not in the right humour. The first time, indeed, that I heard him, at a small afternoon gathering at Frau Schumann's house, I was utterly disappointed. After a good deal of pressing, he crossed over to the piano and gave the first movement of the G major Fantasia-Sonata and the first movement of the A minor Sonata, Op. 42, both of Schubert, but his playing was ineffective. It appeared to me to be forced and self-conscious, and he himself seemed to remain, as it were, outside the music. I missed the living throb and impulse of feeling by which I had been accustomed to be carried away when listening to Frau Schumann, and he left one of his audience, at all events, cold and unmoved. When I told this to Frau Schumann afterwards, she answered that I had not yet really heard him; that he had not wished to play, but had yielded to over-persuasion, and that I must wait for a better opportunity of judging before forming an opinion.

The opportunity came the very next evening, when the same friends were assembled and Brahms played again. The next day I wrote home as follows:

" . . . . Then Brahms played. It was an entirely different thing from the day before. Two pieces were by some composer whose name I can't remember, and then he played a wild piece by Scarlatti as I never heard anyone play before.

He really did give it as though he were inspired; it was so mad and wild and so beautiful. Afterwards he did a little thing of Gluck's. I hope I shall hear him often if he plays as he did last night. The Scarlatti was like nothing I ever heard before, and I never thought the piano capable of it.''

Such were the general impressions I formed of Brahms during the first seven or eight weeks of my stay at Lichtenthal. To say the truth, I thought but little about him at the time, my whole attention being absorbed in my studies and in the charm of my new experiences of life. To me he seemed a very unaffected, kind-hearted, rather shy man, who appeared quietly happy and content when under the influence of Frau Schumann's society. As yet I had had scant opportunity of testing my own capacity for appreciating his musical genius, and next to none of individual personal intercourse with him. Frequently, when my landlady's servant came to attend me to my lodgings after an evening spent at Frau Schumann's house, and Brahms and I took our leave at the same moment, he would say, "I am coming, too," and, our ways lying partly in the same direction, would walk the short distance by my side; but these occasions did not add much to my knowledge of him. He would make a few casual remarks, often playful, always kindly, on any topics of the hour, but did not touch on musical subjects. One evening, however, I asked him if he intended to visit England. "I think not," he immediately replied, as though his mind were definitely made up on this point. I ventured to pursue the subject, telling him he ought to come, in order to make his compositions known. "It is for that they are printed," he said rather decidedly, and with these words he certainly gave me some real insight into his character. The composer of a long series of works which included such masterpieces as the second serenade, the two string sextets, the first and second pianoforte quartets, the inspired German Requiem, and a host of others already before the world (but of which I then knew nothing), could, of course, do no otherwise than allow his compositions to rest quietly on their merits; and doubtless the intense pride which is equally inherent with intense modesty in the higher order of genius had its share in causing Brahms' reticence about all things concerning himself.

From his determination not to visit England I do not believe he ever seriously wavered. Only on one occasion— a few years before his death—did I ever hear him speak doubtfully on the subject, and then I felt sure that he was only playing with the idea of coming. Of when or why he formed his resolution I cannot speak with absolute certainty; it had become fixed before I made his acquaintance. His want of familiarity with our language may have had something to do with it; he could read English a little, but I never heard him attempt to speak it. He had a horror of being lionized and of involving himself in an entanglement of engagements; perhaps, also, he was possessed with an exaggerated notion of the inflexibility of English social laws, especially as to the wearing of dress-clothes and the restrictions with regard to smoking. Before and behind all such superficial considerations, however, I suspect that early in his career the idea had taken root in him, right or wrong as it may have been, that to visit England would not further his artistic development. Brahms had certainly formed the clearest conception not only of his purpose in life, but of the means by which he felt he could best pursue and achieve it, and from first to last he inflexibly adhered to the conclusions he had come to on these points. If his aim was to give the most complete possible expression in his musical creations to the very best that was in him, his method, while it satisfied an inner craving of his being, was yet, as I believe, deliberately adopted; and it was to lay himself open to every kind of influence which could healthily foster the ideal side of his nature, and more or less completely to eschew all others. It would be ridiculous, at the present time, to touch upon the completeness of his technical musical equipment, to dilate on his easy grasp of all the

resources of counterpoint, on his mastery of form, of harmonic and rhythmic combinations, and the like. These
things are matter of course. But Brahms knew that not
alone his intellect, but his mind and spirit and fancy, must
be constantly nurtured if they were to bring forth the highest of which they were capable, and he so arranged his life
that they should be fed ever and always by poetry and literature and art, by solitary musing, by participation in so
much of life as seemed to him to be real and true, and,
above all and in the highest degree, by the companionship
of Nature.

"How can I most quickly improve?" I asked him one
day later on. "You must walk constantly in the forest,"
he answered; and he meant what he said to be taken literally. It was his own favourite prescription that he advised
for my application. For such a man, with a name practically unknown in England, life in London, and especially
during a concert season, would have been not only uncongenial, but impossible. It would only have been a hindrance to him for the time being. It was not his business to
push his works before either conductors or the public, and,
after early successes and failures in this direction, he had
almost entirely given up planning for the future of his compositions, and had yielded himself wholly to his destiny,
which was to create.

In adopting this attitude, there was nothing whatever of
outward posing. He simply did faithfully what he found
lying before him to do, and did not look beyond.

Life at Lichtenthal passed quickly onwards, and the time
approached when Frau Schumann would pay her annual
visit to Switzerland. At the close of one of my lessons she
said to me:

"I have been thinking that perhaps you might like to
have some lessons from Herr Brahms whilst I am away. It
would be a very great advantage for you in every way,
and he would be able to help you immensely with your
technique. He has made a special study of it, and can do

anything he likes with his fingers on the piano. He does not usually give lessons, but if you like I will ask him, and I think he would do it as a favour to me."

I must here explain that my visit to Germany had been undertaken with the special object of correcting certain deficiencies in my mechanism which Frau Schumann had pointed out, she having advised me to study for a year with this aim particularly in view.

It need hardly be said that I now eagerly accepted her proffered kindness, and it was decided that she should sound Herr Brahms on the question of his willingness to give me lessons. If he should show himself favourable to the project, the arrangement was to be considered as decided, subject only to the approval of my father, who was on the point of starting from London to join me at Lichtenthal. The next morning Frau Schumann informed me that Brahms had consented to the plan, and a few days later, on my receiving my father's ready assent to my request, all preliminaries were settled, and it was arranged that I should have two lessons every week from Brahms.

"You must ask him to play to you," Frau Schumann said; "and if he will do it, it will give you a real opportunity to hear him. And now, now you will begin to know Brahms."

BRAHMS AS TEACHER OF THE PIANOFORTE.

Brahms united in himself each and every quality that might be supposed to exist in an absolutely ideal teacher of the pianoforte, without having a single modifying drawback. I do not wish to rhapsodise; he would have been the first to object to this. Such lessons could only have come from such a man. I have never to this day got over the wonder of his giving them, or the wonder and the joy of its having fallen to my lot to receive them.

He was strict and absolute; he was gentle and patient and encouraging; he was not only clear, he was light itself;

he knew exhaustively, and could teach, and did teach, by
the shortest possible methods, every detail of technical
study; he was unwearied in his efforts to make his pupil
grasp the full musical meaning of whatever work might be
in hand; he was even punctual.

I cannot hope in what I may say to convey more than a
faint impression of what his lessons were to me. From the
very first hour of coming under his immediate musical influence I felt that it was a power which would continue to
act upon and develop within me to the end of life. Perhaps,
however, I may succeed in helping lovers of his music to
add to their conception of his character and his gifts, by
writing of him as he was in a capacity in which, so far as
I know, he has not hitherto been described. Such personal details as I may introduce will be given with the
object of illustrating that side of Brahms' character which
I once knew so well; of exhibiting him as the all-capable,
single-hearted, encouraging, inspired and inspiring teacher
and friend.

Remembering what Frau Schumann had said of his
ability to assist me with my technique, I told him, before
beginning my first lesson, of my mechanical difficulties, and
asked him to help me. He answered, "Yes, that must come
first," and, after hearing me play through a study from
Clementi's "Gradus ad Parnassum," he immediately set to
work to loosen and equalise my fingers. Beginning that
very day, he gradually put me through an entire course of
technical training, showing me how I should best work, for
the attainment of my end, at scales, arpeggi, trills, double
notes, and octaves.

He not only showed me how to practise: he made me, at
first, practise to him during a good part of my lessons,
whilst he sat watching my fingers; telling me what was
wrong in my way of moving them, indicating, by a movement of his own hand, a better position for mine, absorbing
himself entirely, for the time being, in the object of
helping me.

He did not believe in the utility for me of the daily practice of the ordinary five-finger exercises, preferring to form exercises from any piece or study upon which I might be engaged. He had a great habit of turning a difficult passage round and making me practise it, not as written, but with other accents and in various figures, with the result that when I again tried it as it stood the difficulties had always considerably diminished, and often entirely disappeared. "How must I practise this?" I would ask him, with confidence, which was never disappointed, that some short-cut would be found for me by which my way would be effectually smoothed.

His method of loosening the wrist was, I should say, original. I have, at all events, never seen it or heard of it excepting from him, but it loosened my wrist in a fortnight, and with comparatively little labour on my part.

How he laughed one day, when I triumphantly showed him that one of my knuckles, which were then rather stiff and prominent, had quite gone in, and said to him: "You have done that!"

It may seem incredible, but it is none the less true, that after a very few weeks of work with him the appearance of my hands had completely changed. My father says, writing to my mother:

"Her hand has an entirely different conformation from what it used to have; it has lost all its angular appearance, and it really is the case, as she says, that her knuckles are disappearing. I have given up all idea of inducing her to go anywhere with me; she will allow nothing to interfere with her practising. She is enthusiastic in her admiration of Brahms, and says his patience is wonderful. He keeps her strictly to finger-work."

He was never irritable, never indifferent, but always helped, stimulated, and encouraged. One day, when I lamented to him the deficiencies of my former mechanical training and my present resultant finger difficulty, "It will come all right," he said; "it does not come in a week nor in four weeks."

Perceiving at once the extraordinary value of my technical . studies with him, I was desirous of not being hampered by feeling obliged, at first, to get up many pieces to play through. That, he said, was quite right; I must practise a great deal in little bits for a time. Here is an extract from one of my letters. I copy it exactly as it stands, without altering the careless wording of a girl's letter hastily penned for home perusal in an interval between practice times:

" My lessons with Brahms are too delightful; not only the lessons themselves, but he makes me feel I must practise all day and all night. I have begun to eat a great deal for the mere purpose of being able to practise! He is so patient, and takes such pains, and I ask all sorts of questions, and the lessons are too delightful. I can't understand his giving lessons, and yet he is never angry at any sort of foolishness, only says, 'Ah! that is so difficult.' As for an hour's lesson, that is nothing. He systematically arranges for an hour and a half. I absolutely revel in my lessons. He makes the saraband sound on the piano just as on a violin. Then he never expects too much, and does not give much to learn, but is always satisfied with little if one is really trying."

He was extremely particular about my fingering, making me rely on all my fingers as equally as possible. One day whilst watching my hands as I played him a study from the " Gradus," he objected to some of my fingering, and asked me to change it. I immediately did so, but said, knowing there was no danger of his being offended by the remark, that I had used the one marked by Clementi. Brahms, not having had his eyes on the book at the moment, had not perceived this to be the case. He at once said I must, of course, not change it, and would not allow me to adopt his own, as I begged him, saying: "No, no; he knew."

I had with me at Lichtenthal my own copies of Bach, which I had brought from England, but the edition was unfingered, and Brahms desired me to get copies with Czerny's fingering, and always to use it. The other indications in the edition I was not to adopt.

A good part of each lesson was generally devoted to Bach, to the "Well-tempered Clavier," or the English Suites; and as my mechanism improved Brahms gradually increased the amount and scope of my work, and gave more and more time to the spirit of the music I studied. His phrasing, as he taught it me, was, it need hardly be said, of the broadest, whilst he was rigorous in exacting attention to the smallest details. These he sometimes treated as a delicate embroidery that filled up and decorated the broad outline of the phrase, with the large sweep of which nothing was ever allowed to interfere. Light and shade, also, were so managed as to help to bring out its continuity. Be it, however, most emphatically declared that he never theorised on these points; he merely tried his utmost to make me understand and play my pieces as he himself understood and felt them.

He would make me repeat over and over again, ten or twelve times if necessary, part of a movement of Bach, till he had satisfied himself that I was beginning to realise his wish for particular effects of tone or phrasing or feeling. When I could not immediately do what he wanted, he would merely say, "But it is so difficult," or "It will come," tell me to do it again till he found that his effect was on its way into being, and then leave me to complete it. On the two or three days that intervened between my lessons, I would, after practising at the pianoforte, sometimes take my music into the forest to try to think myself more completely into his mind, and if, when he next came, I had partially succeeded, he took delight in showing his satisfaction. His face would light up all over, and he would be unstinting in his praise. "Very good, quite right; Frau Schumann would be very surprised to hear you play like that," or, "That will make a great effect with Frau Schumann."

In spite of his extraordinary conscientiousness about detail, Brahms was entirely free from pedantry and from the tendency to worry or fidget his pupil. His great pleasure was to commend, and if I played anything to him for the first time, in the way he liked, nothing would induce him to suggest, with one word, any change at all. "That is quite right; there is nothing to say about it," he would say; and though I have felt disappointed not to get any remark from him, and have entreated him to make some suggestions, he would remain firm. "No, it must be like that; we will go on," and there was an end of the matter.

One morning my father, coming into the room at the close of my lesson, asked Brahms: "Has she been a good girl to-day?" "Sehr fein,"* answered he, and suddenly turning to me added imperatively: "Tell your father that." I was equal to the occasion, however, and promptly translated: "Herr Brahms says he is not very satisfied to-day, papa." My father's face fell a little. Brahms looked straight before him, displeased and impassive. "I have told him," said I. "No, you have not told him." "But you don't know that; you don't understand English." "I understand enough to know that"—stonily. "Herr Brahms says I have done pretty well," I reassured my father; then to Brahms: "Now I have." "Yes, now," he admitted, with relenting countenance.

Another day, in the middle of my lesson, the door of my sitting-room opened, and my landlady begged to speak to me. "No, Frau Falk," I said; "I am engaged and can see no one; you must please go away." "One moment, gnädiges Fräulein," she said, and persisted, to my displeasure, in coming in. I then perceived she had with her a pretty little girl of about five years old, who held some beautiful yellow roses in her hand. Frau Falk led the child straight up to the piano and made her little speech. The small maiden was the daughter of the gentleman living in the neighbouring villa, and, being with her father in his

---

* An expression of commendation peculiarly German.

beautiful rose-garden, had begged him to let her carry some of his roses to the Fräulein to whose playing they had been listening. The little one, seeing I was not alone, became suddenly shy as she handed me the lovely flowers, and, turning away her face, looked downwards with very red cheeks as she stood quietly at Brahms' knee. But this was not the kind of interruption to displease him. "Na," he said, coaxing her, "you must look at the Fräulein, and let her thank you. Look at her; she wants to thank you." Between us we reassured the little one, who held up her face to me to be kissed, and sedately allowed Frau Falk to lead her away.

Soon after beginning my work with Brahms, I asked him at the end of my lesson if he would play to me, telling him I did so by Frau Schumann's desire. There was an instant's hesitation; then he sat down to the piano. Just as he was about to begin, he turned his head round, and said almost shyly: "You must learn by the faults also." That was the beginning. From that day it became his regular habit to play to me for about half an hour at the close of the hour's lesson, which he never shortened. Oftenest he chose Bach for his performance. He would play by heart one or two of the preludes and fugues from the "Well-tempered Clavier," then take up the music and continue from book as the humour took him. When he reached the end of a composition, I would say little or nothing beyond "Some more," for fear of stopping him, and he would turn over the leaves to find another favourite. I do not remember his ever making a remark to me either between-whiles or after he had finished playing, beyond, perhaps, telling me to get him another book. Once, and once only, he resisted. I had made my usual request at the end of the lesson, when he quaintly and unexpectedly replied: "Not every time; it is silly. Frau Schumann would say it is silly to play every time." "It is so disappointing," I wished to say, but was uncertain of the right German word. He, as was his wont on similar occasions, made me show it him in the dictionary.

There was some little argument between us, and he returned to the piano and took his place there. It was of no use, however. He could not play that day, and almost seemed to take pleasure in doing as badly as possible. Every time he was conspicuously faulty he turned round to me with a sardonic smile, as though he would say : " There! you have got what you wanted; how do you like it?" " Very un-kind," I murmured, and he soon rose. "I will *not* play next time," he angrily declared as he took leave. "I will *never* ask you again," I rejoined. A shrug of the shoulders was his only answer, and, with the usual "good-day," he left the room.

After two days came my next lesson. It passed off de-lightfully, as usual, and at the close Brahms departed, without a word about his playing being said on either side; but I was left with a feeling of something having been very much wanting. In the middle of the following lesson, giving way to a sudden impulse which I could not have ex-plained, but which, perhaps, arose from the fear of renewed disappointment, I abruptly ceased playing in the middle of my piece, saying, "I cannot play any more to-day." Brahms glanced at me with rather an inquiring expression, and asked, "Why?" "I don't know; I cannot," I replied. There was an instant of dead silence, during which I did not look round. Then Brahms spoke. "I will play to you," he said quietly, "in order that you may have some-thing." We immediately changed places, and he never refused me again.

My father, writing to my mother, says :

"Brahms is recognised in Germany as the greatest musi-cian living. It is said to be most difficult to get him to play; however, after every lesson he plays piece after piece. He is a delightful man—so simple, so kind and quiet. He lives in a beautiful situation among the hills, and cares only for seclusion, and time to devote himself to composition. He was pleased the other day by F.'s asking him about a passage in Goethe that she could not comprehend, and went into it in a way which delighted her. With all his genius he is thoroughly practical. Punctual to a minute in his lessons, and of extreme delicacy."

It was my happiness to hear, amongst other things, his readings of many of the forty-eight preludes and fugues, and his playing of them, and especially of the preludes, impressed me with such force and vividness that I can hear it in memory still. His interpretation of Bach was always unconventional and quite unfettered by traditional theory, and he certainly did not share the opinion, which has had many distinguished adherents, that Bach's music should be performed in a simply flowing style. In the movements of the suites he liked variety of tone and touch, as well as a certain elasticity of *tempo*. His playing of many of the preludes and some of the fugues was a revelation of exquisite poems, and he performed them, not only with graduated shadings, but with marked contrasts of tone effect. Each note of Bach's passages and figures contributed, in the hands of Brahms, to form melody which was instinct with feeling of some kind or other. It might be deep pathos, or light-hearted playfulness and jollity; impulsive energy, or soft and tender grace; but sentiment (as distinct from sentimentality) was always there; monotony never. "Quite tender and quite soft," was his frequent admonition to me, whilst in another place he would require the utmost impetuosity.

He loved Bach's suspensions. "It is here that it must sound," he would say, pointing to the tied note, and insisting, whilst not allowing me to force the preparation, that the latter should be so struck as to give the fullest possible effect to the dissonance. "How am I to make this sound?" I asked him of a few bars of subject lying for the third, fourth, and fifth fingers of the left hand, which he wished brought out clearly, but in a very soft tone. "You must think particularly of the fingers with which you play it, and by and by it will come out," he answered.

The same kind of remarks may be applied to his concep-

3

tion of Mozart. He taught me that the music of this great master should not be performed with mere grace and lightness, but that these effects should be contrasted with the expression of sustained feeling and with the use of the deep legato touch. Part of one of my lessons was devoted to the Sonata in F major—

etc.

Brahms let me play nearly a page of the first movement without making any remark. Then he stopped me. "But you are playing without expression," said he, and imitated me, playing the same portion, in the same style, on the upper part of the piano, touching the keys neatly, lightly, and unmeaningly. By the time he left off we were both smiling at the absurd performance.

"Now," he said, "with expression," and he repeated the first few bars of the subject, giving to each note its place as an essential portion of a fine melody. We spent a long time over the movement that day, and it was not until the next lesson, after I had had two, or perhaps three, days to think myself into his conception, that I was able to play it broadly enough to satisfy him. At the close of the first of these two Mozart lessons I said to him: "All that you have told me to-day is quite new to me." "It is all there," he replied, pointing to the book.

Brahms, in fact, recognised no such thing as what is sometimes called "neat playing" of the compositions either of Bach, Scarlatti, or Mozart. Neatness and equality of finger were imperatively demanded by him, and in their utmost nicety and perfection, but as a preparation, not as an end. Varying and sensitive expression was to him as the breath of life, necessary to the true interpretation of any work of genius, and he did not hesitate to avail himself of such resources of the modern pianoforte as he felt helped to impart it; no matter in what particular century his composer may have lived, or what may have been the peculiar excellencies and limitations of the instruments of his day.

Whatever the music I might be studying, however, he would never allow any kind of "expression made easy." He particularly disliked chords to be spread unless marked so by the composer for the sake of a special effect. "No apége," he used invariably to say if I unconsciously gave way to the habit, or yielded to the temptation of softening a chord by its means. He made very much of the well-known effect of two notes slurred together, whether in a loud or soft tone, and I know from his insistence to me on this point that the mark has a special significance in his music.

Aware of his reluctance to perform his compositions, I let some weeks pass before I asked him to play me something of his own. When I at length ventured to do so, he objected: "Not mine; something by another composer." But I had resolved to carry my point. "No, no," I insisted; "a composition played by the composer himself is what I wish to hear," and my importunity gained the day. He gave me a splendid performance of a splendid theme with variations, which, as I found out some months afterwards, was from the now familiar string Sextet in B flat. It was the first time I had heard anything of Brahms' composition with the exception of one or two songs, and it raised in me a tumult of delight. Probably I said to him little beyond thanks, but the power of the music and the performance must have worked itself in me to some manifest effect, for on my taking my seat directly after the lesson at the *table d'hôte* of the Hôtel Bär, the village inn where my father and I used to dine, a lady of our acquaintance exclaimed: "What is the matter with you to-day that you look so excited?" I remember answering her: "Brahms has just played me something quite magnificent—something of his own—and it keeps going in my head."

Since then I have heard the movement times innumerable
in England and on the Continent, performed by various
combinations of artists, but I never listen to it without being
carried back in thought to the gardener's house on the slope
of the Cäcilienberg where, in my blue-papered, carpetless
little room, Brahms sat at the piano and played it to me.
The scent of flowers was borne in through the open lattice-
windows, of which the green outside sun-shutters were
closed on one side of the room to keep out the blazing
August sun, and open on another to views of the beautiful
scenery.

The merits of our respective views had been the subject
of some friendly argument soon after my arrival at Lichtenthal. Brahms had declared that no prospect from any
windows in the village could possibly be as fine as his,
whilst I was equally sure that mine must be quite unrivalled.
Two of my windows looked right across the valley of the
Oos as far as the plain of Strassburg, and showed, in fine
weather, the distant peaks of the Vosges glimmering in the
sunlight. Two others commanded a prospect of the pine-
covered ranges of Black Forest hills. The first time Brahms
came to my rooms, in order to give me a lesson, the variety
and loveliness of my view drew from him an exclamation of
delight. "But yours is really grander and sterner, is it
not?" I magnanimously asked. "This is more suitable for
a girl," he prettily replied.

On the next occasion after the day when he had performed
his own work, I reminded Brahms that he had promised he
would allow my father, who was anxious to hear him play
to better advantage than from the room overhead, to share
with me this great pleasure some time. "But he is not
here," he said, and taking this as a token of assent, I quickly
called my father, who was writing letters above, to come
down. When we were all three seated, I told Brahms I
wished to have the piece he had played to me two or three
days before, but he said he would not play anything of his
own—"something else." "No," I said, "something of

yours, and the same; my father wishes to hear the same."
"Ah, I forget what it was; I have composed a great many
things. I will play something else." "But no, no, no!"
l urged. "I know what it was. I must have the same.
Play the first two or three chords." "Well, then, I think it
was this," said he, giving way; and he repeated the movement from beginning to end, carrying us both completely
away.

Brahms' playing at this period of his life was, indeed,
stimulating to an extraordinary degree, and so *apart* as to
be quite unforgettable. It was not the playing of a virtuoso,
though he had a large amount of virtuosity (to put it mod-
erately) at his command. He never aimed at mere effect,
but seemed to plunge into the innermost meaning of whatever music he happened to be interpreting, exhibiting all
its details and expressing its very depths. Not being in
regular practice, he would sometimes strike wrong notes—
and there was already a hardness, arising from the same
cause, in his playing of chords; but he was fully aware of
his failings, and warned me not to imitate them.

He was acutely, though silently, sensitive to the sus-
ceptibility or non-susceptibility of his audience. As I have
already mentioned, but few words passed between him and
myself during the momentary intervals between his playing
of one piece and another, but he would now and then suddenly turn his head round towards where I sat and give
me a swift, searching glance, as though to satisfy himself
that I understood and followed him. Once only he refused
to go on. It was soon after his performance before my
father. I had begged for another of his compositions, and
he had begun to play one. I was sitting rather behind
him, listening intently and trying to follow, but I knew I
did not understand. Very soon he turned to give his usual
scrutinising look, and immediately ceased playing, saying:
"No, really I can't play that." I did not attempt to make
him think I had entered into the meaning of the music, but
only entreated him to begin it again and give me one more

chance, as it was difficult to follow. Nothing would induce
him, however, to play another note of it, and he went on
to something by another composer, much to my disappointment and mortification.

Brahms disliked to hear anything said which could possibly
be interpreted as depreciation of either of the great
masters. Once, when two or three people were present, a
remark was made on the growing indifference of the younger
musicians to Mendelssohn, and particularly on the neglect
with which his once popular "Songs without Words" had
for some time been treated. "If it is the case, it is a great
pity," observed Brahms, "for they are quite full of beauty."

He especially loved Schubert, and I have heard him declare that the longest works of this composer, with all their
repetitions, were never too long for him.

He greatly admired my copy, which was of the original
edition and in good preservation, of Clementi's "Gradus,"
and asked me to lend it him for a day or two to compare
with his own. I did not at that time attach much value
to original editions; and, fancying he merely wished to
prevent me from overworking, against which he often
cautioned me, I said I could not spare it. "You won't
lend it me!" he exclaimed, very much astonished indeed.
I answered that if he did take it away it would make no
difference, as I could practise as well without it. Finding,
however, that he really wished to examine the copy, I said
it was too hot for him to carry so large a book in the middle
of the day, and that I would send it in the evening. "I
am not so weak!" he replied, but consented to the proposal. He sent it back after a few days, strongly scented
with the odour of his tobacco, which it retained through
many a long year, and which rather enhanced its value
to me.

Rather curiously, he liked the scent of eau-de-Cologne.
My father brought me a case from Cöln, and if, on my lesson
day, I had an open bottle near at hand, and offered some
to Brahms, he would place his hands together, palm up-

wards, for me to pour into, and dipping his head, would rub the scent over his forehead, protesting as he did so, "But it really does not become a man." Seeing that he liked it, I used it sometimes to wash the keys of the piano when he was coming, but I do not think he ever found me out.

He delighted in the music of Strauss' band, which was engaged to play daily at Baden-Baden through some weeks of the season. It was then conducted by the great Johann Strauss, Brahms' particular friend, and he used to walk over every evening to hear it. "Are you so engrossed?" said a voice behind me one evening as I was standing in the Lichtenthal village street with a friend, looking at the performances of a dancing bear. On turning round I found Brahms, hat in hand, smiling with amusement at our pre-occupation, himself on his way, as usual at that hour, to listen to the delicious music of the Vienna waltz-king.

Brahms disliked mere compliment, but he had a warm appreciation of the genuine expression of friendly feeling towards himself, and did not try to hide the pleasure it gave him. His countenance would change, and he would answer in a simple, modest way that was almost touching. One day when I told him how I valued his teaching, and felt it was something for my whole life, "You ought to tell Frau Schumann," replied the composer of the German Requiem, as though he were asking me to give a good report of him. On my assuring him that I had already done so by letter, he added hastily: "You will make Frau Schumann angry with me. But not too much"; and he added, "never praise too highly; always keep within bounds."

Shortly before Frau Schumann's return I said to him that I hoped he would not lose all interest in my music at the termination of my lessons with him, and that I should like, if it were possible, to make some additional arrangement by which it might be maintained. He did not give me any definite reply at the moment one way or the other, but on my saying the same thing to him another day he replied:

"It is very nice and very kind of you, but I don't think it can be done. You must, however, play to me very often. Everything you learn with Frau Schumann you must play to me."

About this time, however, my father, who was about to start on his homeward journey, persuaded me to go away with him for a week's holiday before his departure for England, and on my return to Lichtenthal Frau Schumann arranged that I should continue my studies under Brahms for the remainder of my stay, saying I had become more his pupil than hers. There were, indeed, but few more lessons to look forward to. Autumn had set in, and everyone was thinking of departure. Brahms had to go sometimes to Carlsruhe, where he was occupied with rehearsals, but he punctually kept his remaining appointments with me. His concluding lessons were as magnificent as the earlier ones, and when I went back to England my ground was clear. I do not mean to assert that my hand was already completely developed from a pianist's point of view, or my technique as yet fully in my possession. These things were physically impossible; but Brahms had shown me the path which led straight to my goal, and had himself brought me a considerable distance on my way. A cast of one of my hands taken on my return to England, when compared with one that had been done shortly before I left, could not have been recognised as being from the same person.

Those were, indeed, golden days, when Brahms sat by my side, and taught me; memorable to me no less for their revelation of an exquisite nature than for the musical advantages they brought. I have often been told that there was another side to his character, and that he could, even at that time, be bitter and rough and satirical. I dare say he was not faultless, but I do not think that he can at any period of his life have been bitter in the sense of being soured. He no doubt had a strong feeling about the indifference and downright antagonism against which his works long had to struggle; but if it had ever been a feeling even of disappointment, I am sure this had mellowed, before I knew him, into a firm though silent belief in the future of his compositions, and had only served to intensify, if possible, his determination to put into them of his very best.

Rough he may have been sometimes, and in later years I had occasional opportunity of perceiving that he was not always gentle, though he was never otherwise with me. His roughness was, in certain instances, no doubt caused by his resolution in protecting his time from celebrity-hunters, and even from friends. It may have been partly traceable, also, to the circumstances of his youth, when he must often have been placed amid surroundings where rough-and-ready frankness of speech was more cultivated than conventional polish of manner. It is, however, certain that during the latter part of his life he sometimes availed himself of the privilege of the *enfant gâté* to yield to the caprice of the moment, and that he now and again said things which could not but wound the feelings of others. This was to be regretted, and it hardly excused him that his pungent words came from the lips only, and not from the heart. I am, however, quite certain that many of his acerbities were assumed to cover his naturally acute sensibility of temperament, of which he stood a little in dread, and which he liked to conceal even from himself. He was a firm believer, for himself and for others, in the salutary process of bracing both mental and physical energies.

A year or two before Brahms' death I revisited Lichtenthal, staying a night at the Hôtel Bär, where I used to dine in the old days. I looked up old acquaintances, and amongst them the former mistress of the dear old inn, whom I found retired and living in a charming villa close by, her brother being still the proprietor of the hotel. She, of course, had known Brahms well, and during the hour or two that I spent with her we talked chiefly about him. She repeated the verdict given by everyone really acquainted

with him : "So simple and natural, so kind and cheerful,
able to take pleasure in trifles. He was such a simple-
hearted man." A tease, certainly, but his teasing was
never unkind, never more than mere raillery. He would
often bring a friend to dine at the Bär in the old days, and
she always had the cloth laid for him in a private room or
in the back part of the garden, so that he should not be
worried by the visitors. "He never minded what he did.
He would sometimes drop in, if he were passing, to say
good-morning to us, and if we were very busy he would
make a joke of sitting down and amusing himself by helping us cut up the vegetables for dinner. Only he could not
bear to go into formal society, or to have to wear his dress-
clothes. I have not seen him now for several years. The
last time was in September, 1889, when he paid a flying
visit to the Bär. He was very angry to find that three
pine-trees had been cut down near the house where he used
to lodge, thinking the poetry of the view had been impaired,
and he said he would never stay in the place again. What
a warm heart he had! He liked to know all the country
people of the neighbourhood, and took a pride in feeling
that every man, woman, and child whom he met in his early
morning walks interchanged greetings with him. I begged
for his autograph the last time he was here. You would
like to see what he wrote"; and my old friend sent for the
album in which the master had written :

"Johannes Brahms.   ("J. B.
    eines schönen Tages   one fine day
    im schönen Baden   in beautiful Baden
    im lieben Bären."   at the dear Bear.")

BERLIN.

Years were destined to elapse before my next meeting
with Brahms. After my return to England I worked un-
remittingly on the lines he had indicated, and found that by
the observation and practice of his principles I was guided
straight onwards in the path of progress. His teaching

had been of such a kind that its development did not cease with the actual lessons. As the weeks and months went by I found myself growing continually into a clearer perception of the aims and results it had had in view. It caused me no surprise to find, on becoming acquainted with his pianoforte compositions, that I must postpone for a time the delightful task of getting them up. Brahms himself had prepared me for this. He had always been extremely careful, when selecting music for me to work at, to choose what would develop my technical powers without straining my hands, and when I had wished to study something of his had answered that his compositions were unfit for me for the present, as they required too much physical strength and grasp. He fancied, indeed, at that time that nearly all of them were beyond a woman's strength. When I asked why it was that he composed only such enormously difficult things for the pianoforte, he said they came to him naturally, and he could not compose otherwise ("Ich kann nicht anders").

In the winter of 1881-82 I found myself in Berlin. It is difficult to describe the feelings with which I one day read the announcement that von Bülow, in the course of a *tournée* with the Meiningen Orchestra, of which he was conductor, would shortly visit the city to give a three days' series of concerts in the hall of the Singakademie; that Brahms' compositions would figure conspicuously in the programmes; that Brahms himself would be present, and that he would probably take part in one or more of the performances. The life at Lichtenthal had come to seem to me a sort of far-away fairy-tale impossible of any sort of renewal, and I could hardly realise that I should soon see Brahms again. Finding, however, from subsequent announcements, that the concerts were really to take place, I lost no time in securing a subscription ticket for the series.

Feeling sure that every moment of Brahms' short stay in Berlin would be occupied, I decided that my only chance of getting a word or two with him would be to gain admission to one of the rehearsals, and to watch for a favourable moment in which to make myself known to him. As ill luck would have it, I was claimed on the first day by engagements that could not be postponed. I was, however, the less inconsolable since Brahms was to take an active part only in the second and third concerts. Their respective programmes included a new pianoforte concerto still in MS. (No. 2 in B flat), to be played by the composer, with von Bülow as conductor; and the first pianoforte concerto, with Bülow as pianist and Brahms at the conductor's desk.

Betaking myself to the Singakademie in good time for the rehearsal on the second morning of the series, I explained, to the friendly custodian at the entrance-door, my claims to admission. He allowed me to enter the hall and to take my place amongst the small audience of persons privileged to attend.

The members of the orchestra were already assembled, and after some moments of waiting von Bülow came in with several gentlemen. Lusty applause broke forth from platform and stalls, and a small stir of greetings took place. But where was Brahms? I could perceive him nowhere at first, and it was only as the rehearsal proceeded, and he took his place on the platform, that I felt certain he was really present. I had prepared myself to find him looking changed and older, but not beyond recognition. It is, however, no exaggeration to say that as I gazed at him, knowing him to be Brahms, I was utterly unable to recognise the man I had known ten years previously. There, indeed, was the great head with the hair brushed back as of old, though less tidily than in former days; but his figure had become much heavier, and both mouth and chin were hidden by a thick moustache and shaggy, grizzled beard that had completely transformed his appearance. When I first knew him at the time of his early middle age, one might fancy that his countenance and expression had retained more than a trace of his youthful period of *Sturm und Drang*, but this had now quite vanished. I felt, with a shock, that my foreboding that I should never see my old friend again had been realised, though in a way different from that anticipated by me.

Brahms received an ovation when he had finished his performance of the new concerto, and as he was retiring from the platform Bülow, unable to restrain his excitement, darted forward and gave him a kiss. It seemed to take him rather aback, but he submitted passively.

At length the rehearsal came to an end, and Brahms was immediately surrounded by friends eager to offer their congratulations and to receive a word of greeting from him. "Now or never," I thought, and taking my courage in my hand, I managed to get near, though a little behind him. "I, also, should like to say a word of thanks to you, Herr Brahms," I said. Brahms turned his head. "Are you here in Berlin, then?" he rejoined instantly, answering as he might have done if we had met the previous week. Someone else pressed forward to claim his attention as I was replying, and I fell behind again. I did not like to wait for a second opportunity, feeling there was no chance of his being free, so I straightway departed and went back to my lodgings.

Thinking things over on my road, I came to the conclusion that Brahms had not recognised me, but that when my words caught his ear he had uttered the first casual reply that rose to his lips, and which might be appropriate to any acquaintance whom he did not at the moment remember. However exceptional his memory for faces might be, it appeared to me incredible that, after the lapse of so many years, he should have known me without the hesitation of a second at a moment when his attention was preoccupied by the concert business of the day and by the claims of his Berlin friends.

It was in this frame of mind that I took my seat in the evening to hear the concert. Having got over the first

excitement of seeing Brahms again, and knowing what I
had to expect in regard to his personal appearance, I was
able to listen to the music in a more composed mood than
had been possible to me in the morning. My pleasure in
the performance of the concerto was, of course, in some
measure impaired by the circumstance that the long,
intricate work was quite new. I think, however, that I
should have enjoyed it more if Brahms had conducted and
Bülow performed the solo. I did not think Brahms' playing what it had been. His touch in *forte* passages had
become hard, and though he might, perhaps, be said to
have mastered the difficulties of his part, he had not sufficiently surmounted them to execute them with ease. It
could not, in fact, have been otherwise. No composer
having attained to the height of Brahms' greatness could
have kept his technical command of the pianoforte unim-
paired; life is too short for this. I knew, however, that
I had listened to a magnificent work of immense propor-
tions, and longed for opportunity to hear it again that I
might assimilate it.

There was a scene of tumultuous enthusiasm at the close
of the work. The public applauded wildly, and shouted
itself hoarse; the band joined in with its fanfare of trumpet
and drum; Brahms and von Bülow were recalled again and
again separately and together; and in the moment of the
great composer's triumph I saw the earlier Brahms once
more standing before me, for, whilst his eyes shone and
his face beamed with pleasure, I recognised in his bearing and expression the old familiar look of almost
diffident, shy modesty which had been one of his characteristics in former days.

I did not, of course, seek for a further opportunity of
speaking to Brahms on the evening of which I am writing,
but I laid my plans for the next morning, and at the proper
hour again made my way to the Singakademie and successfully begged for admission to the rehearsal.

During the first part Brahms sat as one of the audience

in the front row of stalls, and in a convenient break between the pieces I sent my English visiting-card to him, having written on it a few lines recalling myself to his remembrance. He read it and looked round. "I know that already," he said coldly, but rising and coming towards me. "I saw you yesterday." "But you did not know who I was?" I returned, still sceptical. "Yes, I knew." "It seemed to me quite impossible you could have recognised me!" I ejaculated. "Oh yes, yes—*oh* yes!" said Brahms in quite a different tone, and for a couple of seconds I forgot to look up or say anything.

"Are you taking notes?" he asked by way of recalling me to myself, touching my pencil. But the rehearsal had to proceed, and Brahms presently took his place on the platform with Bülow for the performance of the Concerto in D minor. When the rehearsal was over, I did not leave the hall so quickly as on the previous day, but waited in the hope of getting another word with Brahms, and was rewarded by having a good many.

In the evening, as he faced the audience, before the commencement of the concerto, catching sight of me in the third row of stalls, he was at the pains to bestow upon me a kind bow and smile of recognition. He glanced slightly at me again once or twice during the evening, and I knew, though his appearance still seemed a little strange to me, that Brahms was in the world after all.

The execution of the D minor Concerto was one of those rare performances that remain in the memory as unforgettable events. Brahms, when conducting, indulged in no antics, and was sparing of his gestures, often keeping his left hand in his pocket, or letting it hang quietly at his side; but he cast the spell of his genius over orchestra and pianist alike. The performance was remarkable for its power and grandeur, but not chiefly so, for these qualities were to be expected. It was made supremely memorable by the subtle imagination that touched and modified even the rather hard intellectuality of von Bülow's usual style. Good per-

formances of Brahms' orchestral works may not seldom be
heard, and great ones occasionally; but the particular
quality of his poetic fancy, by which, when conducting an
orchestra, he made the music sound from time to time as
though it were floating in some rarefied atmosphere, vibrating now with fairy-like beauty and grace, now with ethereal
mystery, was, I should say, peculiar to himself, and is
hardly to be reproduced or imitated.

As soon as Brahms had finished his share in the evening's
programme I quitted the hall, for I was thoroughly exhausted by the excitement of the past two days, and felt I
could bear nothing more. Early the next morning he left
Berlin to fulfil engagements in another town.

VIENNA.

During the next four years much of my time was passed
in Berlin. I delighted in the concerts and general musical
atmosphere of the German capital, and did not allow my
plans to be disturbed by a vague invitation to visit Vienna
which Brahms had given me in the course of our short interview in the hall of the Singakademie. I felt that however
kind and friendly his recollection of me might have remained, yet I could not hope to derive direct musical benefit
from one absorbed in the intense thought and brooding to
which the life of a really great composer must be largely
devoted.

It was not until December, 1888, that I paid my first
visit to Vienna. I arrived there towards the end of the
month, armed with letters of introduction which met with a
kind response and obtained for me immediate admission
into those English and Austrian circles to members of
which they were addressed. I waited for a week before
letting Brahms know of my arrival, as I wished not only to
be settled before calling on him, but also to be in such a
position in regard to my acquaintance as would make it

impossible for him to suspect that I could want anything whatever of him beyond the delight and honour of seeing him again, and of recalling myself to his remembrance.

Meanwhile I gathered, from all I heard, that his dislike of anything approaching to general society had steadily grown upon him. Some, even, of his old friends spoke of the increasing rarity of his visits. A lady at whose house he had been intimate for many years told me it had once been his custom to announce himself for the evening from time to time at a few hours' notice, with the proviso that he should find her and her husband alone in their family circle, or at most with one or two chosen friends. On these occasions he had been used to play to them one after another of his newest compositions. This habit, however, he had almost entirely given up.

I heard but one opinion, both from friends and outsiders, as to his essentially high character and sterling qualities of nature; but his manners were described with unanimity, by those not within his immediate circle, as difficult, sarcastic, and arrogant. I was, indeed, so repeatedly assured that I should do no good by trying to see him that I almost began to fear I should find he had become rude and impossible, if not hopelessly inaccessible. To all that was said to me on the subject I answered merely that I had once known him well, and had never found him otherwise than kind and simple, but that I had prepared myself to find him changed and rough in his behaviour to me.

At length, on a dark afternoon of one of the closing days of the year, I made my way to the Wieden, the quarter of Vienna inhabited by Brahms, and, turning in at the doorway of No. 4, Carlsgasse, I ascended the worn stone staircase as far as the third *étage*. Here I pulled the shining brass handle of the old-fashioned door-bell, and the feeling of doubt which had possessed me changed to one of positive alarm as I listened to the prolonged peal I had awakened. I thought it must sound to Brahms like the announcement of a most daring and determined intruder, and that it would inevitably prove the death-knell of any chance of my admission.

The door was soon opened by a friendly maid-servant, who told me, indeed, that the Herr Doctor was not at home, but satisfied me that I was not being put off with a mere phrase by adding that she thought he would probably be back by six o'clock, and that she advised me to return about that hour if I particularly wished to see him, as he was to start on a journey early the next morning. I thanked the girl, said I would follow her suggestion, and, without leaving my name, returned to my rooms to wait for the evening.

The second visit was again unsuccessful, but on trying a third time, at seven o'clock, I found that Brahms had returned. "Please to walk in," said the landlady, who this time opened the door. But this unexpected facility of access to the master was even more embarrassing than would have been the conflict of argument I had anticipated. "Please take my card," said I, "to the Herr Doctor, and ask if he will see me." "Oh, it is not necessary," she said; but took it in, returning immediately and asking me to enter. As I advanced, the formidable and overbearing Brahms hastened to meet me. "Why did you not leave your address? I should have come to find you out," he said, giving me his hand. And returning with me to the sitting-room, he bade me take a seat on the sofa, whilst he placed himself on a chair opposite.

He did not try to hide that he was pleased to see his old pupil. He evidently wished me to understand that our acquaintanceship was to be taken up from the exact point at which it had been last left, and reminded me, when I alluded to his lessons at Baden-Baden, that he had seen me since those early days. "Oh, for a moment at the rehearsals at Berlin," I answered. "But since then," he insisted. "Only at the concert," said I, rather surprised. "Yes, at the concert," he agreed, "and you sat downstairs, I remember."

I told him I had lately been getting up the same B flat Concerto which he had played at the time, and had performed it in London before a private audience. He was interested in hearing the particulars of the occasion, and when I said, laughingly, that the fatigue entailed by the practice of its enormous difficulties had given me all sorts of aches and pains, and made it necessary for me to go into the country for change of air after the performance was over, he replied in the same vein: " But that is very dangerous; one must not compose such things. It is too dangerous!"

He informed me rather slyly, "I am the most unamiable of all the musicians here," as though he would like to know if I had heard of his reputation for cross-grained perversity, and was frankly gratified when I answered: "That I will never believe, Herr Brahms—never!" He was to be absent at the longest for ten days only, and when I took leave of him it was with the pleasant consciousness that he would be glad to find me still in Vienna on his return.

In appearance, Brahms had again greatly altered since our meeting in Berlin. Though not fifty-six, he looked an old man. His hair was nearly white, and he had grown very stout. I had a good opportunity of observing him, myself unnoticed, soon after his return from his journey. The first public performance in Vienna was given of his newly-published Gipsy Songs, at the concert of a resident singer, one of his friends. Brahms had not been announced to take part in the performance, but when the evening came, he walked quietly on to the platform as the singers were arranging themselves in their places and took his seat at the pianoforte as accompanist. Of course his appearance was the signal for an outburst of enthusiastic welcome from the crowded audience, some hopes, but no certainty, having been entertained that he would show himself.

As I sat in my corner and watched, I was aware that both his general aspect and his expression had undergone another and a curious change during the last years. He now wore the happy, sunshiny look of one who had realised his purpose, and was content with his share in life; of one to whom the complete measure of success had come, and not too late to be valued. If in Baden-Baden he had made upon me the impression of a man awaiting full recognition, who had already waited long for it; if in Berlin, the impression of one who, having attained a glorious pinnacle of fame, whilst still in the plenitude of his powers, was untiringly pressing onward towards higher summits of fulfilment—I had the feeling, when I looked at him in Vienna, that the second phase, too, was more or less belonging to the past, and that he had entered upon a period of reward, and perhaps of less strenuous exertion.

One of the very few opportunities I ever had of seeing Brahms avail himself of a great man's licence to follow his whims regardless of convention, and, perhaps, of due respect to others, was afforded me at a meeting of the Vienna Tonkünstlerverein, the musicians' club, of which he was honorary president. It was one of the special social evenings of the society, when the members supped together. Brahms was late in coming, and when he arrived supper was proceeding. He allowed himself to be conducted to the place, at the top of a long table, which had been reserved for him as president, but did not sit down. Leisurely scanning the assembled company, he picked out the position he preferred, which happened to be at the side near the bottom. A slight space was certainly there, but not enough for a seat. "There," he said, pointing to it, and he sauntered down the room, apparently quite unconcerned at the disturbance and inconvenience which he caused, a bench having to be moved and several people being obliged to shift their places to make room for him. When once in occupation of the seat he fancied, he contributed his share to the cordiality of the evening, and was in no hurry to leave.

Another occasion was very similar. He was again dissatisfied with a place that had been assigned him at a supper-party. This time it was at a private house, and, as he could not have declined the seat without making himself unbearably rude, he submitted, with a kind of half-protest, to occupy it. During the greater part of the entertainment, however, he was not only in a wayward mood, but in a thoroughly bad temper, which he could not control. There was, when all is said, certainly no ill-natured intention in what he did on either occasion, but at the worst a mere childish petulance and over-excitability under slight disappointment.

I discovered, though Brahms had no fixed hour, that the right time to call upon him was about eleven o'clock. Always an early riser, he had then completed his morning's work, and if at home, as was generally the case, was ready to receive a visitor. He was sometimes to be found seated at the piano with an open volume (often Bach) on the music-stand, which was placed on the closed top lid of the instrument, playing softly, or silently studying the work in front of him. I have never felt that I was disturbing him when I called. It is true that I only went occasionally, and when provided with a legitimate excuse. Still, I do not altogether understand how he acquired such a reputation for incivility. He was, in his own way, of a sociable disposition.

One day when I was with him, some terrible pianoforte strumming was going on in the flat above him. I commented on the strange constitution of people who could deliberately plant themselves in his immediate neighbourhood—for he had occupied the same rooms for years—and then worry him with such noise. He said there was sometimes bad singing and violin-playing, both of which he found harder to bear than the piano, but added: "They have their rights, and I know how to help myself"; and he held out his hands in keyboard position, to indicate that when too much disturbed to do anything else, he shut out the sounds and employed his time by playing.

Brahms generally went out at about a quarter to twelve

at latest, and would arrive before one o'clock at his favourite restaurant, Zum Rothen Igel. After his early dinner he walked, finding his way to a café in another part of the town, where he would read the papers over a cup of black coffee. After this was his best time for paying visits, and about six o'clock he often returned to his rooms to write letters or do other work. Later on he would go out again to fulfil his evening engagements. Sometimes it happened that he did not go home, after leaving in the morning, until after supper. These details I learnt incidentally in the course of my stay in Vienna.

Brahms made a great point of being polite to ladies on the question of smoking, and was very particular in asking permission before lighting his cigar. Of course, if I found him alone, he never smoked. One day, however, when I had been with him only a very few minutes, the door-bell rang, and two gentlemen appeared, one a friend of Brahms, the other a youth whom he had brought to introduce to the master. Brahms wished me to remain, and I therefore kept my seat. Very soon he produced his box of cigars, according to Continental custom, and handed it to his visitors, saying, however: "But I do it unwillingly, as a lady is present." The elder of the two gentlemen put his cigar into his breast-pocket, the younger lighted his and vigorously puffed away alone, from sheer confusion, I think, at finding himself in the presence of the master. Brahms returned to his seat without taking one. "But won't you smoke, Herr Brahms?" I said, after a few seconds. "If you allow it," he answered, making as much as possible of the few words, and taking a cigar.

Though Brahms was not, during the latter part of his life, a frequenter of concert-rooms, he nearly always attended the concerts of the Philharmonic Society and of the Gesellschaft der Musikfreunde in Vienna, sitting usually, in the "artists' box" in the gallery. In the intervals between the pieces he would lean forward, both arms on the front, with his opera-glasses to his eyes, spying out his acquaintances in different parts of the hall.

When I called to say good-bye to him at the close of my first visit to Vienna, I happened to mention that I had made a small collection of works written for the keyed instruments of the seventeenth and eighteenth centuries, and had picked up one or two rather valuable first editions. He was greatly interested, and saying, "We have done the same thing," took down from the bookcase one or two of his own old music-books to show me. I especially remember an original edition of Scarlatti's Sonatas, in first-rate preservation, but without the title-page, of which he was particularly fond and proud. He asked if I would bring one or two of mine to show him on my next visit, and I told him that I happened to have one with me—an original Rameau—and that if he had not got a copy I would send it him at once.

"No," he answered; "it is too late now—you are going away to-morrow—but next year when you come again." "But I mean," I rejoined, "that I will give it you." Brahms did not immediately answer, and I added: "Would you rather not? If so, I will not do it." "No, I would *not* 'rather not,' but you must not immediately give your things away," he replied. "Then I will do it," I declared, delighted that I possessed something he would like to have, and to accept from me. Later in the day I sent him the book, with a few lines telling him how much pleasure it would give me if I might leave it with him as a remembrance. Early the next morning I left Vienna. I was not to arrive in London for another week, having engagements *en route*, and this Brahms knew. On the evening of my return home, as soon as my mother's first greetings were over, she said: "There is a letter for you from Brahms; it arrived this morning." "From Brahms! How do you know?" I answered. "From his having written his name on the outside," she returned, handing me the precious missive.

On the outside of the envelope, above the adhesive, he

had written " J. Brahms, Vienna, Austria,'' and, opening
the envelope, I read as follows :

"VERY ESTEEMED AND DEAR FRÄULEIN,

"It was too late the other evening for me to be able
to do as I wished, and come and express my thanks to you
in person.

"Let me, therefore, send them very heartily after you, for
your so kind and valuable gift.

"It was indeed much too kind of you to part with the
pretty treasure in order to give me pleasure, and it shall still
be at your disposal next year !

"In the hope of seeing you here again next year, and of
being able to repeat my hearty thanks,

"Yours very sincerely,

"J. BRAHMS."*

On my first visit to Brahms in the following winter, he
led the way to his bookcase and showed me the Rameau,
saying : "I shall die in ten years, and you will get it back
again." I told him that should I outlive him I should prefer not to have it back, but to let it go with his collection,
and thus the matter remained.

The success of my first visit to Vienna induced me to pay
several subsequent ones, the last of which took place rather
more than a year before Brahms' death. A minute account

---

* "SEHR GEEHRTES UND LIEBES FRÄULEIN,

"Es war neulich zu spät am Abend geworden als dass ich, wie
ich wünschte, Sie selbst noch hätte aufsuchen u. Ihnen meinen Dank
aussprechen können.

"So lassen Sie mich denn nachträglich diesen sehr herzlichen sagen
für Ihr so freundliches u. werthvolles Geschenk.

"Es war in der That gar zu liebenswürdig von Ihnen sich mir zu
gefallen von dem hübschen Schatze zu trennen u. es soll Ihnen im
nächsten Jahre auch noch zur Verfügung stehen !

"In der Hoffnung Sie aber im nächsten Jahre wieder hier zu sehen
u. Ihnen meinen herzlichen Dank wiederholen zu können,

"Ihr sehr ergebener,

"J. BRAHMS."

of each would be wearisome, and I will only allude, therefore, to the opportunity that I had, in the course of two
separate winters, of hearing the concerts of the Joachim
Quartet in Vienna, and of seeing Brahms as one of the audience. On one of these enchanting evenings the Clarinet
Quintet was given, with Mühlfeld as clarinettist. Brahms
had his seat downstairs, at the end of the room reserved for
resident and other musicians, and separated from the
general audience by the performers' platform. My place
was only two or three away from his, and so situated that
I could see him all the time the work was being played.
His face wore an unconscious smile, and his expression was
one of absorbed felicity from beginning to end of the performance. When the last movement was finished, he was
not to be persuaded to come forward and take his part in
acknowledging the deafening clamour of applause, but, as
it were, disclaimed all right in it himself by vigorously
applauding the executants. At the last moment, however,
as the noise was beginning to subside, up he got, and
stepping on to the platform, in his loose, short, shabby
morning-coat, made his bow to the audience. Another
item in the programme was the Clarinet Trio, played by
himself, Mühlfeld, and Hausmann. Joachim, sitting on the
right-hand side of the piano, turned over for him. I
changed my seat during the performance of this work,
taking the place that Brahms had vacated, which was close
to the piano and gave me a full view of the keyboard. In
spite of my several experiences of the master's tenacious
memory for small things, I confess that I felt a thrill of surprise at the end of the first movement, and again at the
end of the second, when he turned his head suddenly round
and glanced straight at me in the very same quick, searching
way to which I had been accustomed in the old Lichtenthal
days, as though to satisfy himself as to whether or not I
had understood.

ISCHL.

I spent several weeks at Ischl during the summers of 1894 and 1895, and was much interested in observing the life of my old friend in surroundings that were new to me. His habits, during these closing years of his life, were in all essential respects the same as when I had first known him in Baden-Baden. Rising soon after four o'clock, his days were passed in the same simple, natural routine of walking, studying and composing, in the enjoyment of the society of his friends and of the cordial relations which he maintained with the people of the country, between whom and himself a perfect understanding existed.

His love of children has often been recorded. I have seen him sitting reading on the bench of the little garden of his lodgings, apparently quite undisturbed by his landlady's boys, who romped round and about him, jumping on and off the bench, playing hide-and-seek behind his back, and the like. Now and then he would interrupt his studies to caress a couple of kittens that were taking part in the frolics.

"I know this man," said a droll, tiny boy of five or six, in a funny red suit, who, taking a stroll along the promenade one afternoon with some companions, came upon Brahms sitting under the trees before Walter's coffee-house, the centre of a large group of musicians and friends. The great composer was quite ready to acknowledge the acquaintanceship, and called his small friend to his table to receive a spoonful of half-melted sugar from his coffee-cup.

"My Katie knows Brahms," said a village dressmaker to me, alluding to her pretty little fair-haired daughter of eight. "We have met him out walking very early in the morning, but Katie was frightened the other day and cried because he ran round her and pretended he wanted her piece of bread."

"The Herr Doctor has already seen him," a young peasant mother observed to me as she showed me her three-months-old son, "and says he is a strapping boy."

One morning when I called on Brahms to say good-bye, I found him in the midst of preparations for his own departure. An open portmanteau, in process of being packed, was in the sitting-room, and there was a litter of small things about. Brahms invited me to take a seat on the sofa. A book which he had been reading lay open, face downwards. I ventured, with an apologetic glance at him, to take it up and look at it. This he did not at all mind. He had been amusing himself with an essay on Bismarck. After we had chatted a little while, as I rose to say farewell, my eye was caught by a table on which were a number of cheap German playthings—small boxes of puzzles, toy knives and forks, etc., evidently destined for parting or returning gifts to quite poor children.

"What is this?" I involuntarily exclaimed, taking up, before I knew what I was doing, a toy fork of most ungainly make, broad, squat, and almost without handle. An inquisitiveness, however, which seemed to hint at the soft side of Brahms' nature could not be allowed. "What does that matter to you?" he cried. Then, instantly, as though afraid he had been rough, he added: "It is for small things —fruit, fish, or the like." Only I, having seen the clumsy toy, can quite appreciate the comicality of the answer, which of course simply meant: "No allusion, if you please." Brahms, however, had saved appearances, and without being hard on me, had drawn a thin veil over his kind intentions to his little friends. I held the fork another instant, and then replaced it on the table, saying with gravity: "I thought it was a plaything, Herr Brahms."

A young lady, an inhabitant of Ischl, who taught singing, and gave an annual concert there, and who, during the season, presided over a milliner's business on the Promenade, was a great ally of Brahms', and never omitted to stand outside the door of her atelier as the hour approached for him to pass to his café, in order to get a greeting from him. The little ceremony was duly honoured by the great composer, who was always ready with, at the least, his genial "Good-day."

Fräulein L. talked of him to me in just the same way as all others did who were content to be natural and unostentatious in their manner towards him. He was so good-natured and bright, she remarked, and though he loved to tease, his teasing was so kindly. He made a point of calling on her formally once every season. Taking advantage of this ceremony, she one day placed before him a cabinet photograph of himself, and asked if he could do her the honour of writing his name underneath.

"Yes, I can do that," he answered in his cheerful tone, "I learned that at school. But why do you keep this ugly old face? Why not have a handsome, curly-haired one? Ah, what have we here?"—catching sight of a little saucer containing cigar-ash. "*You smoke!*"

Fräulein L. laughingly assured him that neither she nor her assistant had been guilty of the cigar. "So much the worse!" he retorted. "Who was it? Is he dark or fair?"

By such genial intercourse and harmless banter, Brahms endeared himself to all the towns-people with whom he came in contact, and his preference for Ischl was a source of pride and gratification to them. His sociability had in it no suggestion of patronage; it was that of a friend with friends, and was valued accordingly.

A few words spoken to me by his landlady at Ischl are not without their value, coming, as they do, from one who had the opportunity of knowing him in small things. The occasion was as follows. My lodging was opposite to Brahms' on the other side of the valley, but on a much higher mountain slope. I could see his house from my balcony and windows, but was too far away to have the least apprehension that he could be disturbed by hearing anything of my piano. Someone suggesting to me, however, that, with the wind in a certain direction, the sound might possibly reach his windows, I went across one afternoon, when I knew he would be out, to interview his landlady on the subject. She assured me nothing had ever been heard, and added: "You can play quite without fear, gnädiges Fräulein, nothing is heard here—the water makes too much noise. And even if a tone were to be heard now and then —it could not be more—the master is not so particular: it would not disturb him. He is not capricious: no one can say that of him."

That Brahms had his little prejudices and limitations, however, cannot be denied, and these grew more pronounced as he advanced in years and became less pliable. The mere circumstance of his having inflexibly adhered to the particular method of life adopted by him as a young man, by which he shut himself away as much as possible from whatever was at all distasteful to him in ordinary social intercourse, contributed, as time went on, to increase his sensitiveness and make him impatient of contradiction. He became rather too prone to suspect people to whom he did not take a fancy, of conceit and affectation; and, without knowing it, he acquired a habit, which sometimes made conversation with him difficult, of dissenting forcibly from trifling remarks made more with the object of saying something than for the sake of asserting a principle. He had his own particular code of polite manners, and was rigorous in expecting others to adhere to it, yet he was apt, in his latter years, to be intolerant of those whose ideas of what was due to the amenities of life were more extended than his own, or somewhat differed from them.

What, however, were his prepossessions, his little sarcasms, and occasional roughnesses, but as the tiniest flecks on the sun? We may well be thankful, we musicians and music-lovers of this generation, to have passed some part of our lives with Brahms in our midst—Brahms the composer and Brahms the man. As his music may be searched through and through in vain for a single bar that is not noble and pure, so also in his mind dwelt no thought which was otherwise than good and true. We may even be glad that he was not perfect, but human, the dear, great tender-hearted master, whose lofty message, vibrating with the pulsations of the nature he so loved, was of such rare beauty and consolation.

The few lines with which I conclude these slight personal reminiscences were the last I ever received from Brahms. They were written on his card and sent, enclosed in an envelope, when I was at Ischl. I had been expecting him to come to see me, and he had not appeared.

"ESTEEMED FRÄULEIN,

"Prevented by many things, I venture to ask if it is not possible for you to call on

"Yours most sincerely,

"JOHANNES BRAHMS."*

---

* "GEEHRTES FRÄULEIN,

"Mannichfach abgehalten, erlaube ich mir die Anfrage ob es Ihnen nicht möglich ist vorzusprechen bei

"Ihrem ergebensten,

"JOHANNES BRAHMS."

CHAPTER I

1760-1845

JOHANNES BRAHMS came of a race belonging to Lower
Saxony. This is sufficiently indicated by the family name,
which appears in extant church records variously as Brahms,
Brams, and Brahmst. The word Bram belongs to the old
Platt-Deutsch, the near kin to the Anglo-Saxon and English
languages. It is still the common name in some of the
Baltic districts of Germany, the Hanoverian provinces, and,
with a modified vowel, in England, for the straight-growing
Planta genista, the yellow-flowering broom, and is pre-
served in its original form in the English word "bramble."

The letter *s* at the end of the name has the same meaning
in German as in English, and just as "Brooks" is a
contraction of the words "son of Brook," so "Brahms"
signifies, literally, "son of Bram," or "Broom."

Peter Brahms, the great-grandfather of the composer, and
the first of his family of whom there is authentic record,
was a child of the people. He trekked across the mouth of
the Elbe from Hanover into Holstein, and settled down to
ply his trade of joiner at Brunsbüttel, a hamlet or small
township situated in the fertile fen-country which lies along
the shore of the North Sea between the mouths of the Elbe
and the Eider. This district is remembered as the land of

the Ditmarsh Peasants, who were distinguished, some centuries ago, by their fierce and obstinate struggles for the maintenance of their independence, but who finally settled down about the year 1560 under the dominion of the Princes of Holstein. They are said to have been pre-eminent amongst neighbouring peoples, not only in courage, but in a simple untaught genius for the arts of poetry and music. They loved to turn their various adventures into verse, which they afterwards sang to the most expressive and appropriate melodies of their own invention, and their war-songs and ballads, though now forgotten, were long a cherished possession of their children's children. The little country has in recent times proved not unworthy of its former reputation. Niebuhr the traveller, and his son, the celebrated historian, both belonged to Meldorf. Claus Groth, the Low-German poet, was a native of Heide, where his grandfather and father were millers living on their own land in patriarchal fashion. Groth has drawn, notably in his volume "Quickborn," pathetically naïve pictures of his beloved Ditmarsh; of its homely scenery, its changing cloud-effects, its sudden bursts of storm, its simple, hard-working, honourable peasant life; and it is a striking circumstance that he should have been in a position to describe, as old family friends and neighbours, living amongst the memories of his childhood, the great-grandfather, grandfather, father, and uncle of Johannes Brahms.*

Old Peter the trekker was respected as a thoroughly well-mannered, orderly citizen. He was short and robust, and lived to a ripe old age. He passed the closing years of his life at Heide, where he spent most of his time sitting on a bench in front of his house, smoking a long pipe, and was wont to startle the dreamy Claus Groth, as he passed by every morning on his way to school, with a loud, jocular greeting.

Johann his son, who was tall and handsome, with straight,

---

* "Brahms Erinnerungen," in *Die Gegenwart*, No. 45.

No. 60 Speckstrasse, Hamburg.

yellow hair and fair complexion, combined the callings of innkeeper and retail dealer first at Wöhrden and afterwards at Heide. He married Christiana Asmus, a daughter of the country, and who knows what strain of latent poetic instinct, inherited from some old minstrel and patriot ancestor, may have been transmitted, through her veins, into the sturdy Brahms family? There is some presumption in favour of such a conjecture.

Two sons were born of her marriage with Johann, each of whom had a marked individuality. Peter Hinrich, the eldest, married at the age of twenty, and settled down as his father's assistant and future successor. Groth has described his adventure in the fields one memorable Sunday afternoon. Accompanied by his little son, he carried a huge kite, taller than himself, with a correspondingly long, thick string, which he successfully started. A strong north-west wind carried it along, and, to the delight of a crowd of small spectators, he tied to it a little cart of his own manufacture, in which he placed his boy. The cart began to move, drawn by the kite, slowly at first, then more quickly. Faster and higher flew the monster, quicker and quicker rolled the wheels, the child in the carriage, the father by its side. Then a scream, a crash! The terrified Claus knew no more till next day, when he heard that the little carriage had been dragged over a wall and upset, that the child had fallen out unhurt, and the kite been found on a high post a mile or two distant.

This Peter Hinrich added to the vocations of his father that of pawnbroker, and gradually acquired a large business as a dealer in antiquities. In the end, however, his delight in his possessions gained decided predominance over his business instincts. Becoming partially crippled in old age, he would sit in a large armchair for which there was barely space, surrounded by his beloved pots and pitchers, weapons and armour, and point out desired objects to would-be purchasers with a long stick. Often, however, he could not persuade himself to part with his curiosities, and would

5

send his customers away empty-handed, satisfied with the mere pleasure of showing the treasures with which he packed his house quite full.   His children and grandchildren remained and spread in the Ditmarsh, where some of them prosper to this day.

Johann Jakob, the second son of Johann and Christiana, destined to become the father of our composer, was his brother's junior by fourteen years, and was born on June 1, 1806. From his early boyhood he seems to have had no doubt as to his choice of a vocation. He could by no means be persuaded to settle down to the routine of school-work, to be followed in due course by the humdrum existence of a small country innkeeper or tradesman, such as had sufficed for his father and grandfather, and was contentedly accepted by his elder brother. He was upright, good-natured, and possessed of a certain vein of drollery, which made him throughout life a favourite with his associates; he was born, also, with a quietly stubborn will. He had an overmastering love of music—music of the kind he was accustomed to hear at neighbours' weddings, at harvest merry-makings, in the dancing-rooms of village inns. A musician he was resolved to be, and a musician, in spite of the determined opposition of parents and family, he became.

There existed, not far from his home, a representative of the old "Stadt Pfeifereien," establishments descended directly from the musicians' guilds of the Middle Ages, whose traditions lingered on in the rural districts of Germany for some time after the original institutions had become extinct. The "Stadt Pfeiferei" was recognised as the official musical establishment of its neighbourhood, and was presided over by the town-musician, who retained certain ancient privileges. He held a monopoly for providing the music for all open-air festivities in the villages, hamlets, and small townships within his district, and formed his band or bands from apprenticed pupils, who paid a trifling sum of money, often helped with their manual labour in the work of his house and the cultivation of his garden or farm, and, in return, lived with him as part of his family and received musical instruction from himself and his assistants.   At the termination of their apprenticeship he provided his scholars with indentures of character and efficiency, according to desert, and dismissed them to follow their fortunes.   Country lads with ambition, who desired to see something of the world, or to attain a better position than that of a peasant or journeyman, would persuade their parents to place them in one of these establishments.   They were expected to acquire a practical knowledge of several instruments, so as to be able to take part upon either as occasion might demand, and the bands thus formed were available for all local functions.   Johann Jakob would readily have applied himself to learn, from the nearest town-musician, all that that official was able to teach him, but his father could not be brought to consent to his exchanging the solid prospects of a settled life in the Ditmarsh for the visionary future of an itinerant performer. The boy's inclination was, however, unconquerable, and he settled the matter in his own fashion.   He ran away from home several times and made his own bargain with his musical hero.   Twice he was recalled and forgiven, and after the third escapade was allowed to have his own way, and bound over to serve his time in the usual manner.   "I cannot give such proofs of my devotion to music," wrote his son Johannes to Claus Groth many years afterwards.   Five years of apprenticeship were spent, the last three at the more distant town of Wesselbüren, in the study of the violin, viola, 'cello, flute, and horn, and, in the beginning of the year 1826, the quandam musical apprentice obtained his indentures, which testified to his faithfulness, desire to learn, industry, and obedience,* and quitted the old home country to try his luck at Hamburg.

It is not easy to imagine the feelings of this youth of nineteen or twenty on his arrival, fresh from the simple life

---

* Printed verbally in Max Kalbeck's " Johannes Brahms," p. 4.

of the Ditmarsh peasants, in the great commercial fortress
city, still the old Hamburg of the day, with its harbour
and shipping and busy river scenes; its walls and city gates,
locked at sunset; its water-ways and bridges; its churches
and exchange; its tall gabled houses; its dim tortuous
alleys. Refined ease and sordid revelry were well represented there; the one might be contemplated on the
pleasant, shady Jungfernstieg, the fashionable promenade
where rich merchants and fine ladies and gay officers sat
and sipped punch or coffee, wine or lemonade, served to
them by the nimble waiters of the Alster Pavilion, the
high-class refreshment house on the lake hard by; the other,
in the so-called Hamburger Berg, the sailors' quarter,
abounding in booths and shows, small public houses, and
noisy dancing saloons, in which scenes of low-life gaiety
were regularly enacted. Johann Jakob Brahms was destined
to appear, in the course of his career as a musician, in both
localities. He made his debut in the latter.

Thrown entirely on his own resources, with a mere pittance
in his pocket for immediate needs, he had to pick up a
bare existence, as best he could, in the courtyards and
dancing-saloons of the Hamburg Wapping. He seems to
have preserved his easy imperturbability of temper throughout his early struggles, and to have kept his eyes open for
any chance opportunity that might occur. Helped by his
natural gift for making himself a favourite, he managed, by-
and-by, to get appointed as one of the hornists of the Bür-
ger-Militair, the body of citizen-soldiers, or town-guard, in
which, with a few exceptions, every burgher or inhabitant
between the ages of twenty and forty-five was bound to
serve. Each battalion of the force had its own band, and
each band its own uniform, the musicians of the Jäger corps,
to which Johann Jakob was attached, wearing a green coat
with white embroidered collar, headgear decorated with a
white pompon, and a short weapon called a Hirschfänger.
This was a distinct rise in the fortunes of the wanderer.
He won for himself a recognised place in the world, obscure

though it might be, when he acquired the right to wear a uniform of the city of Hamburg, and in due time he enrolled himself as one of its burghers. The document of his citizenship has been preserved, and will be mentioned again near the close of our narrative.* It cannot be said that his further advancement was rapid. His partiality for the music he knew of is suggestive rather of a struggling instinct than an actual talent. His professional acquirements were slender, and of general education he had none; but he was not without shrewdness, was upright and diligent, and he made gradual progress. He and his colleagues used to form themselves into small brass bands, and to play wherever they saw opportunity, sometimes getting trifling engagements in dancing-rooms, sometimes dependent on the goodwill of a chance audience in a beer-garden or small house of entertainment. He did not earn much, but was no longer entirely dependent on the very meanest exercise of his industry, and may be said to have obtained a footing on the lowest rung of fortune's ladder.

On June 9, 1830, a few days after completing his twenty-fourth year, Jakob committed himself to the second great adventure of his life. He married, choosing for his wife Johanna Henrika Christiana Nissen, who was forty-one years of age and in very humble circumstances. She was small and plain, and limped badly; was sickly in health, and somewhat complaining; of a very affectionate if rather over-sensitive disposition, and had a sweet expression in her light-blue eyes that testified to the goodness of her heart. She was an exquisite needlewoman, possessed many good housewifely virtues which she exercised as far as her very limited opportunities allowed, and is said to have been endowed with great refinement of feeling and superior natural parts. One of her husband's colleagues has described her as having faded, later on, into a "little withered mother who busied herself unobtrusively with her own affairs, and was not known outside her dwelling."

---

* Vol. II, Chap. XXII.

The strangely-matched couple began their life together on the smallest possible scale, and in February of the following year a daughter was born to them, who was christened Elisabeth Wilhelmine Louise. The young father's material resources seem to have remained much as they were, but before this time his dogged perseverance had added yet another instrument to the list of those he had already practised. He contrived to learn the double-bass, and as his friends increased, and he became more known, he began to get occasional engagements as double-bass substitute in the orchestras of small theatres. Meanwhile he did not neglect his other instruments, but performed on either as occasion presented itself.

On May 7, 1833, the angel of life again visited the poor little home, and Johanna Henrika Christiana presented her husband with a son, who was baptised on the 26th of the same month at St. Michael's Church, Hamburg. The child, being emphatically the "son of Johann," was called by the single name Johannes, after his father, mother, and paternal grandfather, and the grandfather was one of the sponsors.

The house in which Johannes Brahms was born was in Speck Lane, subsequently known as 60 Speckstrasse, and formed part of the Gänge-Viertel, the "Lane-quarter" of the old Hamburg. Want of space within the city walls had led to the construction of rows of houses along a number of lanes adjacent to one another, which had once been public thoroughfares through gardens. A neighbourhood of very dark and narrow streets was thus formed, for the houses were tall and gabled, and arranged to hold several families. They were generally built of brick, loam, and wood, and were thrown up with the object of packing as many human beings as possible into a given area. The Lane-quarter exists no longer, but many of the old houses remain, and some are well kept and picturesque to the eye of the passer-by. Not so 60 Speckstrasse. This house does not form part of the main street, but stands in a small dismal court behind, which is entered through a close passage, and was formerly called Schlüter's Court. It would be impossible for the most imaginative person, on arriving at this spot, to indulge in any of the picturesque fancies supposed to be appropriate to a poet's birthplace; the house and its surroundings testify only to the commonplace reality of a bare and repulsive poverty. A steep wooden staircase in the centre, leads right and left, directly from the court, to the various stories of the building. Each of its habitations is planned exactly as every other, excepting that those near the top are contracted by the sloping roof. Jakob and Johanna lived in the first-floor dwelling to the left on facing the house. On entering it, it is difficult to repress a shiver of bewilderment and dismay. The staircase door opens on to a diminutive space, half kitchen, half lobby, where some cooking may be done and a child's bed made up, and which has a second door leading to the living-room. This communicates with the sleeping-closet, which has its own window, but is so tiny it can scarcely be called a room. There is nothing else, neither corner nor cupboard. Where Jakob kept his instruments and how he managed to practise are mysteries which the ordinary mind cannot satisfactorily penetrate, but it is probable that his easy-going temperament helped him over these and other difficulties, and that he was fairly content with his lot. If Johanna took life a little more hardly, it is certain that husband and wife resembled each other in their affection for the children, and that the strong tie of love which bound the renowned composer of after-years to father and mother alike, had its earliest beginning in the fondness and pride which attended his cradle in the obscure abode in Schlüter's Court.

The family moved several times during the infancy of Johannes, and their various homes are partly to be traced in back numbers of the Hamburg address-book, which may be consulted in the library of the Johanneum. These early changes, however, have but little interest for the reader, and it will suffice to record that when the hero of our narrative was four or five years old, and the proud senior by two years of a little brother Friederich, known as Fritz, they moved into quarters less confined than those they had yet occupied at 38 Ulricus-strasse. Here the anxious wife and mother was able to add a trifle to Jakob's scanty earnings, by engaging on her own account in a tiny business for the sale of needles, cotton, tapes, etc., which had been carried on for many years previously at No. 91 of the same street by the "sisters Nissen," and by taking as boarder an acquaintance of her husband's, who, though not a musician, remained a life-long family friend. The intimacy descended to the next generation, and his son, Herr Carl Bade, has many a droll anecdote to relate of Jakob, whom he remembers with affectionate regard.

From such particulars as can be gathered, it is evident that the childhood of "Hannes" gave early promise of the striking characteristics of his maturity, and that some of the most powerful sentiments of his after-life are to be traced to influences acting on him from his birth. Indications of his possession of the musical faculty were apparent at a very tender age. He received his first actual instruction from his father, but his sensitive organisation, aided by the music of one sort and another that he was constantly hearing, seems almost to have anticipated this earliest teaching. In his clinging affection for his parents the child was father to the man, and one of his constant petitions was to be allowed to "help." It is easy to imagine the little tasks he learned to perform for the mother whom he worshipped, and the feeling of pride with which he watched his tall father on the exercise-days of the Jäger corps may have had something to do with his partiality for his beloved lead soldiers, the favourite toys which he kept locked in his writing-table long after he was grown up. He was sent, when quite a young child, to a little private school on the Dammthorwall, close to his parents' house, where the teaching was probably neither better nor worse than that usual in the very small day-schools of the period. Until he was nearly eight his musical education was carried on

at home, and did not include the study of the piano. It
seems to have been taken for granted that he would, in due
course, follow his father's calling, which was gradually
ripening into that of a reliable performer in the humbler
orchestras of the city. It is hardly surprising that Jakob,
who knew nothing about genius, and was not troubled by
notions about art for its own sake, should have looked
forward contentedly to the career of an orchestral player for
his boy. He himself, after more than twelve laborious years,
was only struggling into a position of acceptance by
musicians of this class. That Johannes should begin life by
taking his place amongst them as a fiddler or 'cellist, who
might work his way to some distinction, must necessarily
have appeared to him a sufficiently ambitious object, the
attainment of which would enable his son to support himself
and help the family. The orchestral players of the
Hamburg of that time carried on their work under peculiar
circumstances. They were bound together in a kind of
musical trade union, the Hamburger Musikverein, founded
in 1831, which protected them from competition, no member
being allowed to play in any band that included an out-
sider. They met constantly at their "Börse," or club,
through which most of their engagements were made. It
was open every morning for a couple of hours for the trans-
action of business, and there was a Lokal in the same building available for a chat over a glass of beer and a smoke.
The establishment was for some time presided over by a
man named Rose, whose son became well-known in Great
Britain as Carl Rosa, the proprietor of an English opera
company. Johann Jakob Brahms was one of the original
members of the Musikverein, and his copy of the rules, still
in existence, bears, underneath his signature, the date
May 1, 1831. The system of working by deputy was ex-
tensively practised in the arrangements of the union. If
a member engaged for a certain performance happened to
get a more lucrative offer for the same day and hour, he
would give notice to the "Börse" to furnish a substitute

for the first appointment. The substitute might repeat the
process in his turn, and it sometimes happened that a single
engagement passed through several hands in succession
before the date of its fulfilment. Under these conditions
music was very much a mere business, but, on the other
hand, orchestral players were expected to be fairly good
all-round musicians, capable of performing passably on
several instruments, and able to fill a gap at short notice.
Many of these men, who made the musical atmosphere with
which Johannes Brahms was familiar in his childhood, lived
in the Lane-quarter, partly because it was cheap, partly in
order to be near their "Börse," which was situated in the
Kohlhöfen. They were, as a rule, shrewd, hard-working,
honourable members of their profession, happy in their calling and in their mutual friendly intercourse, and striving
to bring up their children to improved circumstances.
Those among them who were not able to obtain better employment were glad to acquire experience, and to earn something, by playing in dancing-saloons and Lokals of various
degrees of repute, hoping for a rise of fortune in days to come.

Proofs of continual advancement in Jakob's career are to
be found in the fact that, from about the year 1837 onwards, his services were requisitioned from time to time as
substitute in the small band which played from six till
eleven, every evening throughout the year, in a room of the
Alster Pavilion, and especially in the circumstance that he
by and by became one of its regular members, succeeding
to the duties of double-bass player. The orchestra was
composed of two violins, viola, two flutes, and double-bass,
and performed "evening entertainment-music," consisting
of overtures, airs, operatic selections, and pot-pourris. The
public, which was a good one, was served with light re-
freshments outside, or crowded into the house to listen,
according to inclination and the season, and the musicians
were paid by contributions collected during intervals between the pieces. Count Woronzow from St. Petersburg,
who was present with his son in the audience one fine sum-

mer evening, was so delighted with the music, and so gratified at hearing the Russian national air played *con amore*
in his honour, that he not only put a gold piece on the
plate, but wanted to carry off the six performers to Russia,
guaranteeing that they would make their fortunes there,
and would not take a refusal till they had had a week or
two to consider the matter.

There lived at this time at No. 7, Steindamm, a young
pianist of Hamburg, Otto Friedrich Willibald Cossel, who
was well known to the set of men belonging to the musicians' union, and in great and just repute with them as a
teacher of his instrument. He was a pupil of the eminent
teacher and theorist, Marxsen of Altona, and had cherished
dreams of fame as a pianoforte virtuoso. Adverse circumstances, delicate health, and want of self-confidence, may
have been the causes of his failure to realise his aspirations;
but whether or not this be the case, he has left behind him
the reputation of having been a good player, an excellent
instructor, and a thoroughly high-minded man. He was
devoted to his art, and had a large number of pupils; but
they were chiefly recruited from the classes who could not
afford to pay much, and it was not in Cossel's nature to be
difficult on the question of remuneration. He was fain to
content himself with the consciousness of hard work well
done as a great part of his reward.

To Cossel came, one day in the winter of 1840-1, Jakob
Brahms with the little seven-year-old Hannes, a pale, delicate-looking child with fair complexion, blue eyes, and a
mane of flaxen hair falling to his shoulders. He was as
neat and trim as a new pin—a little "patenter Junge"—
and wore over his home-knitted socks pretty wooden shoes
such as are seen to this day in the shops of Hamburg, an
effective protection against the wet climate of the city. Too
pale and serious to be called pretty, there was a something
most attractive in his appearance, and when his face lighted
up on hearing the conclusion of his father's business Cossel's
heart was won.

"I wish my son to become your pupil, Herr Cossel," said Jakob, speaking in his native Low-German tongue. "He wants so much to learn the piano. When he can play as well as you do, it will be enough!"

The short interview brought about important results to Hannes, whilst for Cossel it insured the future enduring respect of the musical world. He soon perceived that in his new scholar he had no ordinary pupil, and his affection went out more and more to the docile, eager, easily-taught child. He got into the habit of keeping the little fellow after his lesson that he might practise on his piano, and be spared some of the fatigue entailed by constant walks between home, school, and the somewhat distantly-situated Steindamm. Hannes, on his part, grew passionately fond of his teacher, and the special relation in which he stood to him was soon recognised and accepted by Cossel's other pupils. The two were brought still closer together at the end of about a year, for Jakob and his wife, on the impending marriage of their boarder, moved again into smaller quarters close by—at No. 29, Dammthorwall—whilst Cossel took over their rooms in Ulricus-strasse. Well for Hannes that an admirable method of instruction enabled him to get through the necessary drudgery of acquiring a good position of the hand and free movement of the fingers at a very early age, and that he was prepared by wise guidance easily to encounter successive steps of his master's system, which included the practice of the best masters of études—Czerny, Cramer, Clementi—of the great classical masters, and of pieces of the bravura school in fashion at the time.

In the course of the year 1843 Cossel added to the many proofs he had already given of his affection for his pupil, an admirable instance of generosity and sacrifice of personal considerations. It became evident to him that, notwithstanding—or perhaps in consequence of—the rapid progress made by Hannes, influence was being brought to bear on Jakob to induce him to transfer the boy to the care of some other teacher, and he at once determined that in spite of

the keen pangs of disappointment any change would cause
him, his darling should, if possible, be placed under Marxsen. Various causes may have led him to this resolution—
anxiety to protect the boy from the chance of being thrown
too early on the world as a regular bread-winner, to the
detriment of the quiet course of his development; unselfish
desire that he should grow up with the prestige of association with a man of established musical authority; above all,
a profound sense of his own responsibility in regard to the
genius of which he found himself guardian, and of the duty
incumbent on him to submit its possibilities to the direction
of the widest experience and best skill attainable.

La Mara* has related, on Marxsen's authority, the steps
taken for the fulfilment of the plan, and their immediate
issue.   Cossel brought the ten-year-old Johannes to Altona,
with the request that his master would examine the boy,
and, if satisfied of his possession of the necessary gifts,
undertake his further musical instruction. Marxsen, however, did not prove ready to accept this charge. After
hearing Johannes play "very capitally" some studies from
Cramer's first book, he pronounced him in the best hands,
saying nothing could be more desirable for the present
than that he should remain, as heretofore, under Cossel's
guidance.

The friends of the family, however, continued to press
Jakob, pointing out that Cossel had been too retiring in his
own case, prophesying that the history of his career would
be repeated in that of Johannes if some change were not
made, and insisting that the teacher was too cautious and
pedantic in his methods with the boy, who now required
to be brought forward. The upshot of these things was
that, a few months after the interview with Marxsen, a
private subscription concert was arranged "for the benefit
of the further musical education" of Johannes, which took
place in the assembly-room of the Zum Alten Raben, a

---

* "Musikalische Studien Köpfe," vol. iii.

first-class refreshment-house, long since pulled down, that
stood in its own pleasure-garden near the Dammthor. The
programme included a Mozart quartet for pianoforte and
strings, Beethoven's quintet for pianoforte and wind, and
some pianoforte solos, amongst them a bravura piece by
Herz, the execution of which, by the youthful concert-giver,
seems to have caused immense sensation in the circle of
his admiring friends. Hannes, who was the only pianist
of the occasion, was assisted in the quintet by Jakob and
three of his friends, and in the quartet by Birgfeld and
Christian Otterer, two well-known musicians of Hamburg,
and Louis Goltermann of the same city, afterwards professor at Prague (not to be confounded with the 'cellist-
composer, C. E. Goltermann, native of Hanover). The
concert was a great success both from an artistic and a
financial point of view, and as its result Jakob himself
visited Marxsen to prefer, in his own name and that of
Cossel, a second request that the distinguished musician
would accept Johannes as a pupil. This time Marxsen consented, saying he would receive him once a week provided
that the lessons from Cossel were continued without interruption side by side with his own. The mandate was
carried into effect, and the arrangement worked smoothly
for a time without let or hindrance; but the successful concert had brought danger as well as advantage in its train.
An impresario, who had obtained admission on the occasion to the "Old Raven," conceived the idea of taking
Johannes on a tour and exhibiting him as a prodigy, and
presently made proposals to this effect to Jakob, who, not
unnaturally, was transported to the seventh heaven by the
dazzling prospects which the wily stranger presented to his
imagination. The first step to be taken, for which he prepared, probably, with some perturbation of mind, was to
break the news to Cossel.

"Well, Cossel," he said, finding the young musician at
home, "we are going to make a pile of money."

"What?" shouted Cossel.

"We are going to make a pile of money. A man has been who wants to travel with the boy."

Poor Cossel! all his worst fears seemed about to be realised; his heart leapt to his mouth.

"Then you are a word-breaker!" he thundered.

It was now Jakob's turn to look aghast, for Cossel, as described by all who knew him personally, was no stickler for ceremony, and could show his wrath right royally when he felt he had righteous cause for indignation. "You are a word-breaker!" he cried, and adopting a sudden idea, went on: "You said to me, 'You shall keep the boy till he knows as much as you do.' He can only learn that from Marxsen!"

A heated argument followed, which ended in a compromise. The affair was to be allowed to stand over for a time, and, in fact, several succeeding months passed as quietly as heretofore. But the impresario renewed his proposal, and the struggle recommenced. Cossel perceived the only means of securing a permanent victory for the benefit of Hannes, and he determined to use it, cost him what it might. It lay in his own complete self-renunciation. He went again to Altona, and besought Marxsen to take entire charge of the boy's musical career, only to be once more refused. Marxsen did not yet feel convinced that the great progress made by Johannes during the past year had been due to other qualities than those of assiduous industry and eager wish to learn. Cossel, however, was not to be beaten. He returned to the attack, actually declaring to his bewildered master that the boy made such rapid strides he felt he could teach him nothing more. The kind Marxsen at length gave way, and consented to take the musical education of Johannes into his own hands henceforth, and to teach him without remuneration, saying he did so the more willingly since the parents were not able to pay for the training they wished to secure for their child, and because he had become fond of the little pupil for his own sake.

"How could you let yourself be put off from such business?" said Aunt Detmering after the impresario had been finally dismissed. She had been partner with Johanna in the little shop of the "sisters Nissen," and had married into somewhat better circumstances than Jakob's wife. "I can't interfere in it," answered Johanna simply, for her boy's good was more precious to her than silver and gold, in spite of her hard, struggling existence. "Min soote Hannes!" she would say, throwing her arms round him, when he came up sometimes to give her a kiss.

Thus was the rich, budding faculty of Johannes guided to the safe shelter of Marxsen's fostering care, and it is not too much to say that Cossel, by his noble action, secured the future of the genius the significance of which he was the first to recognise. It would be idle to speculate about the unrealities of a non-existent might-have-been, and to contemplate a fancied picture of Brahms' career based upon circumstances and events other than those actual to his childhood. It is, however, certain that no mere natural musical endowment, however splendid, can attain to its perfect growth without having been put in the right way, and those who have entered into the heritage of Brahms' songs and symphonies, his choral works and chamber music, may well cherish Cossel's name in grateful remembrance. Although he will not again occupy a prominent place in our account of Brahms' life, his private relations with his pupil did not cease. His piano and his sympathy were still at the service of Hannes, who was grateful for one and the other, and who, remembering his early teacher and friend to the end of his life with admiring affection, strove, as opportunity served in later years, to obtain for him the more widely-known professional position to which his qualities so justly entitled him. Cossel died in 1865 at the age of fifty-two.

CHAPTER II.

1845-1848.

Edward Marxsen—Johannes' first instruction in theory—Herr
Adolph Giesemann—Winsen-an-der-Luhe—Lischen—Choral society of school-teachers—"ABC" Part-song by Johannes—The
Amtsvogt Blume—First public appearance—First visit to the
opera.

EDWARD MARXSEN was born on July 23, 1806, at Nienstädten, a village close to Altona, where his father combined the callings of schoolmaster and organist. His musical talent showed itself in early childhood, and was
cultivated by his father to such good purpose that, whilst
still a lad, he became competent to take the organist's duty
from time to time when a substitute was needed. He was
not, however, destined for the musical profession, and was
on the verge of manhood when he was at length allowed
to follow his unconquerable desire to apply himself with
all his energies to the serious study of art. At eighteen he
became the pupil of Johann Heinrich Clasing, a musician
well qualified to bring up his students in the traditions of
the classical school in which he had himself been trained.[*]
His warm interest was soon aroused by the enthusiasm and

---

[*] Clasing was a pupil of C. F. G. Schwenke, who succeeded C. P.
Emanuel Bach as cantor and music-director of St. Catharine's
Church, Hamburg. On the death of Emanuel Bach in 1788, a por-
tion of his library came into Schwenke's possession, including the
score, in Sebastian Bach's own handwriting, of the great B minor
Mass.

6

unremitting application of his new pupil. Marxsen allowed nothing to interfere with the regularity of his lessons, and walked the two miles separating Nienstädten from Hamburg and back again, on dark winter evenings, by the light of his hand-lantern, no matter how stormy the weather. He continued to live at home, studying, teaching, and helping more and more frequently with the organ, till he reached the age of twenty-four, when his father's death left him free from ties. He soon resolved to go to Vienna, with the especial purpose of perfecting his theoretical knowledge under Ignaz von Seyfried, a prolific composer now chiefly remembered as editor of the theoretical works of his master, the renowned Albrechtsberger. Seyfried received the new-comer cordially, and, probably finding Marxsen's musicianship to be but little inferior to his own, treated him, during his lengthened sojourn at Vienna, more as a friend than a pupil. He did not give him formal instruction, but admitted him to frequent musical intercourse, which was chiefly devoted to the discussion of artistic questions and to the free interchange of opinion, and which brought to the younger musician, amongst other benefits, the special gain of an exceptional insight into the principles underlying Beethoven's development of form. Seyfried's society was interesting and stimulating. He had had pianoforte lessons, as a child, from Mozart, and had been on terms of personal acquaintance with Haydn and with Beethoven, who was his hero. He was of a kind disposition, moreover, and the many opportunities he was able to offer for forming friendships, for hearing music, and for living in musical society, were placed unreservedly at the disposal of his protégé. Marxsen at the same time pursued his study of the pianoforte under Carl Maria von Bocklet, a pianist and musician of eminence, and a very successful teacher, who had enjoyed the favour of Beethoven and been the close intimate of Schubert. Bocklet was one of the earliest to appreciate the genius of the younger master, and, with his colleagues Schuppanzigh and Linke, gave the first performances, early in 1828, of Schubert's two pianoforte trios, written a few months previously.

Marxsen returned to Altona, after an absence of between two and three years, with the matured confidence of the travelled musician who has associated with the authorities of his art, his previous enthusiasm for the works of the great Vienna masters and for the then known instrumental works of the mighty Sebastian Bach fanned into ardent worship. That his mind was sufficiently powerful to rise entirely above the musical artificiality and bad taste of his time cannot be said. To us, who belong to a generation that has been educated on the purist principles first made widely acceptable by Mendelssohn's influence and since popularised by the genius of a few famous executants, with Clara Schumann, Rubinstein, and Joachim at their head, it is difficult to realise the revolution that has taken place in the general condition of musical art since the days when Marxsen, three years Mendelssohn's senior, was young. Many things were then accepted and admired in Vienna, in Berlin, in Leipzig, in London, which would now be regarded as impossible atrocities. Marxsen was capable of setting the Kreutzer Sonata for full orchestra, but this is hardly so surprising as that the Leipzig authorities should have produced the arrangement at one of the Gewandhaus concerts, or that Schumann should have mentioned it indulgently, on whatever grounds, in the *Neue Zeitschrift für Musik*.

Marxsen came for the first time before the public of Hamburg on November 19, 1833, at the age of twenty-seven, in a concert of his own compositions. Such a programme was a novelty in the northern city, and excited attention. The occasion was successful, and established the reputation of the concert-giver as a sound and earnestly striving musician, and from this time his position as a teacher and theorist continuously rose. He was a man of catholic tastes and liberal culture, and his influence over his pupils was not merely that of the instructor of a given subject, but was

touched with the power of the philosopher who has a wide
outlook on life.   The central aims of his theoretical teaching were to guide his pupils to a mastery of the principles
illustrated in the works of the great composers, and to encourage each student to develop his own creative individuality on the firm basis thus afforded. He produced a very
large number of works, which include examples of the most
complex as well as of the simpler forms of composition, and
many of them were brought to a hearing. That few show
the attempt to appeal to a higher tribunal than the musical
taste of the day may, perhaps, be a sign that Marxsen was
conscious of not being endowed with original creative power,
and did not try to go beyond his natural limitations. He
had a genial, encouraging manner which invited his pupils'
confidence, and his lively interest in all questions concerning literature, philosophy and art, gave constant impulse to
the minds of the really gifted amongst them, which was not
the least of the benefits they derived from association with
him.

We shall not be far wrong if we fix the age of Johannes,
at the time he became entirely Marxsen's pupil, as about
twelve; and from this date his time, always well employed,
must have been very fully occupied. He had to go to
Altona for his pianoforte lessons (the question of his learning composition had not yet arisen), to practise at Cossel's
or at the business house of some pianoforte firm—for there
were too many interruptions at home—and to go regularly
to school.   Not to the one on the Dammthorwall mentioned
above. He now attended F. C. Hoffmann's school in ABC-
strasse, an establishment several grades higher than that of
which he had formerly been a pupil, and one of good repute
in its degree.   Hoffmann was a conscientious as well as a
humane man, and won the liking and respect of his scholars.
He gave them sound elementary instruction, and even had
them taught French and English. Brahms retained some
knowledge of both languages, as the present writer can
testify from her personal acquaintance with him, begun

when he had entered middle age. He could read English
to some extent, though he could not speak it, and was able
to help himself out, when necessary, with a phrase or two
of French, though his accent was hopeless. He preserved
a pleasant remembrance of Hoffmann in after-life, recommended his school on one or two suitable occasions, and
sent him a present on the celebration of his jubilee in the
middle of the seventies.

Marxsen's interest and pleasure in Johannes' progress increased every week as he became more convinced of his
exceptional capacity. "One day I gave him a composition
of Weber's," he says,* "going carefully through it with
him. At the following lesson he played it to me so blame-
lessly and so exactly as I wished that I praised him. 'I
have also practised it in another way,' he said, and played
me the right-hand part with the left hand." (No doubt
Weber's *moto perpetuum*, published by Brahms, without
opus number, as a left-hand study.)

Part of Marxsen's discipline was to accustom Johannes
to transpose long pieces at sight, a practice he had probably
learnt from Seyfried, who relates as a *tour de force* of Albrechtsberger that on some public occasion, when he had
to play on a low-pitched organ, he transposed an entire
Mass from G to G sharp at sight, and without error.
Brahms, it may be parenthetically remarked, continued to
find diversion in this pastime, and would play fugues of
Bach and other works for his own edification in various
transposed keys when at the height of his mastership.

The boy had, almost from infancy, shown signs of the
tendency to creative activity. Widmann† speaks of a conversation held with Brahms within the last decade of his
life, during which the master, recalling early memories,
described the bliss experienced by him as a very young child
on making the discovery, unaided, that a melody could

* La Mara, "Studien Köpfe."
† "Brahms in Erinnerung."

be represented on paper by placing large round dots in higher or lower positions on lines. "I made a system for myself before I knew of the existence of such a thing." When a few years older, he was fond of writing the separate parts of concerted works one under the other—of copying them into score, in fact. Nor was he to be kept from trying his hand at original composition. Louise Japha, an eminent pianist of Hamburg, whose more intimate acquaintance the reader will make later on, speaks of having heard him play a sonata of his own when he was about eleven, at Schroeder's pianoforte house, where she one day found him practising. Cossel, responsible for his advance in playing, is said to have been anxious at his spending too much of his time in these childish attempts; but the instinct was unconquerable, and Marxsen no doubt discovered this when he had Johannes constantly with him. After a time he began to teach him theory. Referring to the commencement of the new study, he writes to La Mara:

"I was captivated by his keen and penetrating intellect, and though his first attempts produced nothing of consequence, I perceived in them a mind in which, as I was convinced, an exceptional and deeply original talent lay dormant. I therefore spared myself neither pains nor trouble to awaken and cultivate it, in order to prepare a future priest of art, who should proclaim in a new idiom through his works, its high, true, and lasting principles."

At what age precisely Johannes began to earn regular money by playing in the dancing-rooms and Lokals of Hamburg cannot now be ascertained. It is possible that he occasionally performed on the violin from early childhood, in cases of emergency, as substitute for his father or one of his father's colleagues, though the conjecture is not borne out by reliable record. There is no doubt, however, that loosely repeated anecdotes have given rise to considerable false impression on the point. The notion at one time prevalent, that Jakob made systematic use of his boy from a tender age, employing his gifts for the family benefit, was

warmly repudiated by those who had the best means of
knowing the circumstances. "With the best will," declared Christian Otterer, who, about twelve years Johannes'
senior, retained until at the age of eighty, a bright and un-
clouded remembrance of old days, "I cannot recollect that
Johannes played, as a young child, in Lokals. I was daily
with his father at the time, and must have known if it had
been the case. Jakob was a quiet and respectable man,
and kept Hannes closely to his studies, and as much as possible withdrawn from notice."

"It cannot be true," said Mrs. Cossel repeatedly, referring to such tales; "my husband never mentioned such a
thing to me when speaking of Johannes' childhood; and
even if it had been proposed, I am sure he would never have
allowed it." Two authentic sources of information, however, establish the fact that from the age of about thirteen
the boy regularly fulfilled engagements of the kind. The
earnings derived from them were eagerly contributed to the
general family fund.

A glimpse of him at this period is furnished by Christian
Miller,* then a young musical student, who has related that
he used to play for a small payment on Sunday afternoons
during the summer of 1846, at a restaurant in Bergedorf,
near Hamburg. Miller heard him there, and, fascinated by
his performance, begged to be allowed to play duets with
him. After this the two lads met frequently until Miller left
Hamburg to become a pupil of the Leipzig Conservatoire.
The companionship would seem to have been tolerated
rather than actively desired by Johannes, who rarely spoke
when out walking with Miller, but was accustomed to march
along, hat in hand, humming!

There was a band of six members which had, during the
late eighteen-thirties, delighted the fashionable loungers of
the Jungfernstieg, patrons of the Alster Pavilion. Its activity had been continuous up to the year 1842, when the

---

* Steiner's "Johannes Brahms." Neujahr'sblatt der Allg. Musik-
gesellschaft in Zürich, 1898.

disastrous fire which broke out in Hamburg during the night of May 4-5, and was not extinguished till the morning of the 8th, destroying the churches of St. Nicholas and St. Peter, St. Gertrude's Chapel, the Guildhall, the old Exchange, the Bank, and over 1,200 dwelling-houses and warehouses, had interrupted the pleasant labours of the musicians. The Alster Pavilion had miraculously been left untouched by the flames, whilst the Alster Halle, a similar establishment close by, had been razed to the ground; and the demolition of the row of shops and houses on the Jungfernstieg had changed the agreeable promenade into a scene of ruin. Little could be thought of in the city for a time save how to meet and repair the ravages inflicted by the calamity, which had stricken the grave citizens of Hamburg with dismay, and made an impression of mixed bewilderment and awe upon the sensitive soul of our little Hannes that was never completely effaced. Gradually, however, public edifices and private houses were rebuilt, Hamburg was restored and beautified, and long before the year 1847, at which our story has arrived, the little orchestra had again become used to assemble, though with a somewhat changed personnel, in the familiar room of the Pavilion, to discourse in lively strains before the ever-shifting guests of the establishment. Jakob retained his position as bass player, and, from his long association with the house, had come to be regarded as an important support to its artistic attractions.

Amongst the most faithful patrons of the Pavilion concerts of this period was a certain Herr Adolph Giesemann, owner of a paper-mill and a small farm in the not very distant country townlet of Winsen-an-der-Luhe. He was in the habit of paying frequent business visits to Hamburg, and, being very fond of music, a performer on the guitar, and the possessor of a good voice, liked nothing better than to spend a leisure hour on the Jungfernstieg listening to a movement of Haydn or Mozart. A familiar acquaintance had grown up between him and Brahms. Giesemann willingly listened to Jakob's eager talk about the achievements of Johannes and the promise of his younger brother Fritz. He had a little daughter of his own at home in Winsen, and hoped she might some day be able to take her part in the private musical doings there—at any rate, learn to play the piano well enough to accompany his guitar. One evening in spring Jakob approached him with a request. His Hannes had found constant employment during the past winter in playing the piano until well into the night in the dancing-rooms of various Hamburg Lokals, and the something under two shillings earned by each engagement had amounted to a valuable addition to the scanty family means. But the late hours had told sadly upon his health. Now the work had ceased for a time, and the little toiler could be spared from home. Would Giesemann give him a few weeks' holiday at Winsen? The boy's musical services would be at his command in return. He could accompany him, play to him, and give pianoforte lessons to the little Lischen, a year younger than himself.

Giesemann's kind heart was instantly touched. He had no need to think twice about his own reply, and could answer for that of his wife. Johannes was to be made ready to accompany him back to Winsen after his next visit to Hamburg, which would take place very soon.

And so, in the bright springing month of May, when the buds were bursting and the birds singing, and the gray skies of Hamburg beginning to show a little blue, our dear Hannes took his departure from his big, busy native city to taste for the first time the delights of a free country life, with a kind little sister as companion. He never for a moment felt like a visitor on his arrival, but forgot his constitutional shyness, becoming a child of the house to be petted and brought back to health by fresh air and good food and Frau Giesemann's motherly care. Lischen was at school all the morning, but this was quite a good thing. Hannes had his tasks to attend to also, and could not afford to lose time, for Jakob had made such arrangements as were at his limited command to ensure that his boy's general progress should not suffer by the holiday.

Fresh air, however, was all-important, so Johannes had come provided with a small dumb keyboard for the mechanical exercise of his fingers, and every day after breakfast, after he had got through such practice as had to be done in the house, Frau Giesemann used to turn him into the fields with a bag slung over his shoulder, containing his books and lunch, the clavier under his arm, the notebook, without which he never stirred anywhere, peeping from his pocket, and orders not to show himself again till dinnertime. He had already been enjoying himself out of doors long before this hour. He used to rise at four o'clock, and begin his day by bathing in the river. Joined not long afterwards by Lischen, the two would spend a couple of delightful hours rambling about, discovering birds' nests and picking flowers.

Johannes was quite a simple child in spite of his fourteen years and hard experience, and revelled in the happy days passed amidst sunshine, wild blossoms, and fragrant air. He was very pale and thin, and had little strength on his arrival, but soon gained flesh and colour, to which the glass of fresh milk put by for him every day no doubt contributed. The animals about the place—the cows and pigs, the big dog, the doe—gave him great delight, and he was charmed when the crane spread its wings and flew high overhead as he and Lischen approached it, clapping their hands. He liked to join in the games with which the children of Winsen amused themselves by the river-side on cool summer evenings, but could not be persuaded to take part in the boys' rough sport, and would only play with the girls. The lads, of course, despised him for this, telling him he was no better than a girl himself; but he did not seem to mind, and continued quietly to follow his inclination. One evening, however, soon after his arrival, before he had picked up much strength, as he was returning with several children from wading in the river, Lischen well on in front, one or two rough boys set on him, emptied his pockets, and robbed him of all his possessions, even of the precious pocket-book. He could not help crying at this, but Lischen, seeing him standing on the bank rubbing his knuckles into his eyes, soon found out what was the matter, and, dashing back into the water, forced the molesters to restore everything to her.

To the pocket-book Johannes confided his inspirations on every subject. Sometimes it was a melody, sometimes a line or two of verse, that occurred to him. Then, whether he were walking, or climbing trees, or practising, or doing his lessons, out came the book that the idea might be fixed on the spot.

It was not long before his musical talents awakened the admiration of the neighbourhood. There was a pleasantly situated Lokal at Hoopte, a village about two miles from Winsen, which contained a large apartment suitable for dancing and music. This and one or two adjoining rooms were annually taken by the Giesemann circle for the Sunday afternoons of the summer season, and after morning church and mid-day dinner as many of the subscribers as felt inclined would meet there to pass a few sociable hours. Johannes soon became the central figure of these occasions. It was found that he could play, not only the most inspiriting music for the dancers, but a variety of solos also, including some lovely waltzes to which it was delightful to listen quietly; and on being asked, one day, to conduct the men's choral society that was to contribute to the afternoon's programme, he showed himself so astonishingly competent for the rôle he consented to assume, and inspired such confidence and sympathy, as he stood before his forces in short jacket and large white turn-down collar, his fair girlish face, with its regular features and shock of long, light hair, adding to the impression made by his childlike manner, that he was unanimously elected conductor of the society for so long as he should remain at Winsen; a period which was, as now decided, to be prolonged until he should be recalled to the recommencement of his autumn duties.

The men's choral society of Winsen consisted of about twelve members, the majority of whom were school-teachers of the neighbouring villages. The teachers Backhaus of Winsen, Albers of Handorf, Schröder of Hoopte, belonged to it; other prominent members were the goldsmith Meyer and the big master-baker Rieckmann, who had a splendid bass voice. The practices were held on Saturdays from six to eight o'clock, generally in Rector Köhler's school-room, because it contained a piano, but when this was not available, in the billiard-room of the Deutsches Haus, Winsen's best Lokal. The singers used to stand round the billiard-table, and Johannes would take his place at the top. Lischen was privileged to attend all meetings of the society during the period that her friend officiated as its conductor.

The boy found a most valuable ally in teacher Schröder, who had great talent and love for music, had worked hard at thorough-bass and counterpoint, and had been a composer since his fourteenth year. When Johannes came upon a knotty point in his theoretical studies that required discussion, he would walk over to Hoopte and consult Schröder, who was always ready with sympathy and counsel. He had not returned late one evening from an expedition of the kind, and Giesemann, becoming uneasy, was about to start in search of his young guest, when up drove the carriage-superintendent from Pattenzen, a few miles away. "Here is your Johannes," he cried as the boy jumped from the gig; "he went out by the wrong gate this morning and missed his way. I found him asleep by the side of a ditch some distance out on the Lüneburger Heath, the clavier by his side and the notebook fallen from his pocket; lucky they had not all rolled in together!"

The theoretical exercises and the little compositions for voices on which Marxsen encouraged his pupil to try his hand were regularly carried to Altona, for, with Marxsen's concurrence and the advice of the schoolmaster Hoffmann,

it had been arranged that Johannes should go every week
by steamboat to Hamburg and remain there two nights,
which allowed him a clear day for his music-lessons and for
general private instruction.   Now and then Lischen was invited to accompany him, and to share sister Elise's tiny
chamber in the Brahms' little dwelling on the Dammthorwall.   The journeys were easily managed, for "Uncle"
Adolph Giesemann's brother, manager of the restaurant at
the Winsen railway-station, was also contractor for the refreshment department of the steamboat service to and from
Hamburg, and nothing could be simpler than for one or
both of the children to go and return as his friends.   Frau
Giesemann used to see that they started with a liberal supply of "belegtes Brödchen," a crusty roll cut through,
buttered, and put together again, with slices of cold meat,
sausage, cheese, or what not, between the two halves.
Their friend the restaurateur provided each of them, at the
proper time, with a large mug of thin coffee, and Lischen
and Hannes, sitting together in the bottom of the boat,
thoroughly enjoyed these picnic dinners.

Johannes always began the day after his arrival at Hamburg by exercising his fingers on the upright piano that
stood against the parlour wall, on the music-desk of which
a book invariably stood open, into which he poked his head
—for he was very near-sighted—reading as he worked.
Lischen saw little of him afterwards, for his time was occupied by his various lessons, but she did not mind this.   She
soon became very fond of his dear, kind old mother, and
liked to watch her at her duties, sometimes able to help her
by fetching water from the pump at the bottom of the steps
outside the house, a task which Johanna's lameness prevented her from performing herself.   Lischen much
admired the portrait of Frau Brahms that hung above the
piano, and thought, as she looked at the youthful figure
arrayed in a pink dress made Empire fashion, with flowing
skirt, short waist, and low neck, the hair dressed with little
curls in front and a high comb behind, that Hannes' mother

must have been very pretty in her youth. The parlour was
rather bare, containing little beyond the piano, table, chairs,
a few shelves filled with books, and one or two small prints;
but Lischen did not think this mattered, as everything was
so neat and clean. She felt sorry, however, that it was so
dark, and that its one small window had no other prospect
than a close, dreary courtyard—for Johanna still had her
little shop in front—and proposed to Hannes that they
should bring some scarlet-runners from Winsen, which could
be planted in the courtyard and trained up sticks. There
would soon be something bright in front of the parlour
window. Johannes greatly approved of the plan, which
worked well up to the planting of the beans and the placing
of some immensely high sticks in readiness for the training.
After this stage it disappointed expectations, as the plants
failed to do their part and firmly abstained from growing.

It would have been impossible for Johannes to pass with
entire enjoyment through the months of his visit to Winsen
if he had been without the means of gratifying a taste
hardly less strong in him than his passion for music. From
the very early age at which he was first able to read, he had
been devoted to books, and, whilst showing the child's
natural preference for the romantic and wonderful, had displayed strange discrimination in the choice of his favourite
tales. He had always contrived by some means or other
to provide himself with reading material, preferring books
for his little birthday and Christmas gifts, buying them
from time to time from pedlars' wheelbarrows with his collection of halfpennies, or begging the loan of a volume from
a friend. Brahms' exceptional knowledge of the Bible grew
from the time when, as a young child, he was accustomed
to eat his dinner with the book lying open beside his plate,
absorbed in the Old Testament stories which were then his
prime favourites, misty speculations forming in his brain
which laid the foundation of his future attitude towards
many of life's problems. He had not been long at Winsen
before he had exhausted the mental nourishment afforded

by Uncle Giesemann's collection of volumes. Fortunately,
another resource was at hand. There was a lending library
in the neighbourhood belonging to a certain Frau Löwenherz, a Jewess, who had a son called Aaron. With Aaron
the two children made friends, and of him, in the absence
of sufficient funds to pay the full price of a constant supply
of literature, they sought counsel. He proved an able adviser, and, whilst promising to obtain for them access to
the coveted books, showed that he was not wanting in the
capacity of turning opportunity to profit on his own account.
He promised that he would, on his private responsibility,
bring one volume at a time for the perusal of Hannes and
Lischen, to be put back when done with and replaced by
another; the price demanded and agreed to for this secret
service being one groschen (about a penny) for each supply.

By this expedient Hannes and Lischen—the latter having
probably been the active partner in striking the bargain,
for Johannes had few spare pennies—found themselves provided with as many books as they could desire. Their best
time for reading was when they sat together by the river-
bank, or fished in the pond during the afternoon. Forgetting their rods, they used to pore silently over the open
book supported between them, devouring one tale after
another of knights and tournaments, outlaws and bandits.
Aaron received very particular instruction as to the kind of
selections he was to make, and took pains to suit the taste
of his patrons. He appeared one afternoon with a volume
containing the history of "The Beautiful Magelone and the
Knight Peter with the Silver Keys." That was a red-letter
day in the history of the young subscribers to the lending
library which neither Hannes nor Lischen ever forgot. The
romance made an indelible impression on both of them.
As for bandits, what better could Johannes desire than a
work bearing the stimulating title of "The Robbers," which
Aaron offered another day, insisting with justifiable pride
on the success of his researches? The book was written
by one Schiller, and proved so satisfactory that Hannes

begged Aaron to be on the look-out for other volumes bearing this name on the title-page.

It might be expected that the young conductor of the Winsen Choral Society and the pupil of the distinguished musician of Altona would turn his studies to account by writing something for the use of his choir, and so it was. Johannes composed an " ABC " four-part song for his school-teachers, consisting of thirty-two bars in two-four time, preceded by three bars of introduction and followed by a kind of signature. The introduction and first three of the four eight-bar phrases had for their text the letters of the alphabet arranged, first in order, and then in syllables of two letters as in a first spelling lesson; the fourth phrase was set to a few words introduced at random. The composition closed with the words " Winsen, eighteen hundred seven and forty," sung in full chorus, *lento* and *fortissimo*, on the reiterated tonic chord. The little composition, tuneful and spirited, showing a feeling for independent part-writing, and conceived in a vein of boyish fun that was fully appreciated by the teachers, was soon succeeded by a second, " The Postilion's Morning Song," composed to the well-known words " Vivat! und in's Horn ich stosse." The young musician was also requested by a deputation from the school-children of Winsen to assist them in the performance of a serenade with which they were desirous of greeting their Rector Köhler on his birthday. He accordingly looked out one suitable to the occasion, arranged it in two parts, practised the boys and girls until they were perfect with it, and conducted the performance outside the Rector's house on the eve of the birthday celebration. He was very strict and serious when engaged in these professional duties, beat time with great verve, and insisted on careful observance of the *pianos* and *fortes*, as well as on the proper graduation of the *rallentandos*. The singing of the Ständchen was declared brilliantly successful by the quite considerable audience that assembled near the Rector's house to enjoy it.

Rumours of the increased musical acitivity of Winsen could not fail to reach the ears of the Amtsvogt, Herr Blume, an official of good social standing residing there, whose duties, as administrator of some of the rural districts of northern Hanover, brought him into touch with the life of such parts of the country as were included in his circuit. Herr Blume was not far short of seventy when Johannes paid his first visit to the Giesemanns, but his interest in music and love for Beethoven's art were as strong as ever, and Johannes, before leaving Winsen, was invited to his house, and pressed to use his piano for practice. The boy delighted the Amtsvogt by playing with him some four-hand pianoforte arrangements of Beethoven's works, and won the heart of Frau Blume, in spite of his shy, awkward manner, by his simple, childlike nature. If, as was hoped, he should be able to repeat his visit to Uncle Giesemann next year, he was to come often to the Blumes' house, and use the piano as long as he liked. Great regret was felt throughout the circle of Winsen friends at the news of the young musician's impending departure, but the arrival of autumn brought with it the necessity for the resumption of duties in Hamburg, and nothing remained save to hope for a renewal of the pleasures his long visit had brought to many beside himself.

Johannes returned to his home in such a satisfactory condition of health and spirits that he was able, with Marxsen's approval, to take a decided step forward in his career. He played in the Apollo Concert-room on November 20, at a benefit concert given by Birgfeld, already known to our readers as the violinist of the subscription concert at the "Old Raven," performing Thalberg's Fantasia on airs from "Norma." Marxsen's affection for his pupil and appreciation of his gifts are clearly to be read in the summary of concerts which appeared a week later in the *Freischütz*, a widely-read Hamburg paper to which he was one of the chief contributors:

"Birgfeld's concert is said to have been interesting and

7

enjoyable as regards both the vocal and instrumental portions of the programme. A very special impression was made by the performance of one of Thalberg's fantasias by a little virtuoso called J. Brahms, who not only showed great facility, precision, clearness, power, and certainty, but occasioned general surprise and obtained unanimous applause by the intelligence of his interpretation."

On the 27th of the same month, Johannes appeared in the small room of Tonhalle at a concert of the pianist, Frau Meyer-David, whom he assisted in the performance of a duet for two pianofortes, also by Thalberg, whose fame was at this time at its height. Marxsen's influence is again apparent in the special mention of Johannes in the *Freischütz* review, though it is evident, from the mis-spelling of the name, that he was not the writer of the notice :

" The duet performed by the concert-giver and the young pianist Bruns, who lately appeared for the first time in public with such marked success, gave satisfaction, and was played with laudable unity and facility."

With the exception of a mere record of the same performance in the *Hamburger Nachrichten*, no further mention of Johannes is to be found in the newspapers of the winter 1847-48. It was passed by the young musician in much the same routine of severe study by day and fatiguing labour by night as the previous one had witnessed. He was, however, spared in the spring for another visit to the Giesemanns' house, to which he returned as to a second home. The members of the choral society were delighted to welcome their conductor, who, in the course of the season, added to their répertoire by arranging two folk-songs for use at the practices. These must be accepted as the earliest recorded illustrations of the partiality for national songs and melodies which remained one of the great composer's most characteristic traits, and which culminated, less than three years before his death, in the publication, in seven books, of his well-known collection of German Volkslieder.

Johannes was frequently at the Blumes' this year, and

often played duets with the Amtsvogt. Lischen's pianoforte lessons were not resumed, as they had not been attended by any great result. It was difficult to confine her
to the house to practise on bright summer afternoons, when
she longed to be enjoying herself out of doors. She never
entirely forgot what Johannes had taught her on his first
visit, however, and continued to be very fond of music. It
was hoped that by and by it might be possible to have her
voice thoroughly trained. Johannes felt sure it would
develop into a fine one.

Meanwhile she succeeded in procuring for her companion
the greatest pleasure he had as yet experienced. He wanted
very much to hear an opera, and Lischen thought she would
like it, too, so one day, when they were going together to
Hamburg, she persuaded her father to stand treat for two
places in the gallery. It was to be a great night. Formes,
then of Vienna, had been secured for a few weeks by the
managers of the Stadt Theater (the opera-house of Hamburg), and was making a great sensation. Lischen and
Hannes were to hear him in "The Marriage of Figaro," the
title-rôle of which was one of his great parts. They started
early from the house on the Dammthorwall, supplied by
Frau Brahms with some buttered rolls, and waited for two
hours in the street before the door opened, which was part
of the pleasure. They got capital places, and enjoyed
sitting in the gallery before the performance, looking at
the house and seeing people come in. But when the music
began Johannes was almost beside himself with excitement,
and Lischen has never to this day forgotten his joy.
"Lischen, Lischen, listen to the music! there never was
anything like it!" Uncle Adolph was made so happy
when he heard all about the evening and perceived the delight he had given, that he said the visit to the opera must
be repeated, and accordingly the pair of friends went a
little later on, to hear Kreutzer's "Das Nachtlager von
Granada," which both of them enjoyed very, very much.

Johannes was not able to stay so long at Winsen this

year as last, and still greater sadness was felt as the day
drew near on which his visit would terminate, as it was the
last of the kind he would pay. It was his confirmation
year. He was past fifteen now, his general school education was finished, and he was to take his position in the
world as a musician who had his way to make and would
be expected to contribute regularly to the support of his
family and the education of his brother Fritz, destined for
a pianist and teacher. He copied out the four-part songs,
dedicated to the Winsen Choral Society, beautifully, as a
parting present to Lischen, putting headings to each in
splendid calligraphy, and adding her name with a special
inscription. Lischen treasured the manuscripts long after
she had become a wife and mother, in memory of a happy
episode of her youth.

There was a solemn farewell ceremony at the last meeting
of the choral society, which took place at the Deutsches
Haus. After the conclusion of the practice, the conductor
addressed his singers in a poem written by himself for the
occasion, which began with the line : "Lebt wohl, lebt wohl,
ihr Freunde schlicht und bieder" (Farewell, farewell, ye
friends, upright and simple). An instant's sorrowful silence
followed; then there was a tremendous stamping and clapping and shouting, and the big master-baker Rieckmann,
calling out, "Here, young one!" hoisted Johannes over his
shoulder pickaback, and marched several times round the
table, followed by Lischen and the other members of the
society, singing a last chorus.

It was a concluding scene of Johannes' childhood, which
had been unusually protracted, in spite of its drawbacks;
but, as everybody said, he was to come often again to
Winsen, and whenever he should be able to take a short
relaxation from the serious duties of life awaiting him, he
would know where to find a number of friends ready to
greet his arrival amongst them with heartiest welcome.

CHAPTER III.

1848-1853.

Johannes' first public concert—Years of struggle—Hamburg Lokals
—Louise Japha—Edward Reményi—Sonata in F sharp minor—
First concert-tour as Reményi's accompanist—Concerts at Win-
sen, Celle, Lüneburg, and Hildesheim—Musical parties in 1853
—Leipzig and Weimar—Robert Schumann—Joseph Joachim.

IT was on September 21, 1848, that Johannes made his fresh
start in life by giving a concert of his own, thus presenting
himself to his circle as a musician who was now to stand on
an independent footing. It took place in the familiar room
of the "Old Raven," "Herr Honnef's Hall," with the
assistance of Marxsen's friends, Madame and Fräulein
Cornet, and some instrumentalists of Hamburg. The price
of tickets was one mark (about a shilling), and the programme, as printed in the *Hamburger Nachrichten* of the
20th, was as follows:

FIRST PART.

1. Adagio and rondo from Rosenhain's Concerto in A
   major for Piano, performed by the concert-giver.
2. Duet from Mozart's "Figaro," sung by Mad. and
   Fräul. Cornet.
3. Variations for Violin, by Artôt, performed by Herr
   Risch.
4. "Das Schwabenmädchen," Lied, sung by Mad. Cornet.
5. Fantasia on Themes from Rossini's "Tell," for Piano,
   by Döhler, performed by the concert-giver.

SECOND PART.

6. Introduction and Variations for Clarinet, by Herzog, performed by Herr Glade.
7. Aria from Mozart's "Figaro," sung by Frl. Cornet.
8. Fantasia for Violoncello, composed and performed by Herr d'Arien.
9. (a) "Der Tanz"   } Lieder, sung by Mad.
   (b) "Der Fischer auf dem Meer " } Cornet.
10. (a) Fugue by Sebastian Bach.
    (b) Serenade for left hand only, by E. Marxsen.
    (c) Étude by Herz, performed by the concert-giver.

Unattractive as it now seems, this selection of pieces was no doubt made with a view to the taste of the day, and the inclusion of a single Bach fugue was probably a rather daring concession to that of the concert-giver and his teacher. The two vocal numbers from "Figaro" may be accepted as echoes of the boy's delight on the evening of his recent first visit to the opera. No record remains of the result of the concert, but its success may fairly be inferred from the fact that it was followed, in the spring of 1849, by a second, for which the price of the tickets was increased to two marks. This was announced twice in the *Nachrichten* as follows :

"The undersigned will have the honour of giving a musical soirée on April 14 in the concert-room of the Jenisch'schen Haus (Katharine Street, 17), for which he ventures herewith to issue his invitation. Several of the first resident artists have kindly promised their assistance to the programme, which will be published in this journal.

"J. BRAHMS, Pianist."

The programme was appended to the third and last advertisement of April 10 :

FIRST PART.

1. Grand Sonata in C major, Op. 53, by Beethoven. (The concert-giver.)
2. Romance from Donizetti's "Liebestrank." (Th. Wachtel.)

3. Schubert's "Ave Maria," performed on the Horn by Herr Börs.

4. "O geh' nicht fort," Lied, by E. Marxsen, sung by Frl. Cornet.

5. Fantasia for Piano on a favourite Waltz, composed and performed by the concert-giver.

SECOND PART.

6. Concerto for Violin, by Fr. Mollenhauer, performed by Herr Ed. Mollenhauer.

7. Songs. Me. Cornet.

8. Fantasia on Themes from "Don Juan," by Thalberg, performed by the concert-giver.

9. Duet, sung by Me. and Frl. Cornet.

10. Variations for Flute, by Fräsch, performed by Herr Koppelhöfer.

11. Air Italien, by C. Meyer, performed by the concert-giver.

The performance of Beethoven's "Waldstein" sonata, Op. 53, was regarded long after the close of the eighteen-forties, as a great technical feat, and, taken together with the execution of the "Don Juan" fantasia, would represent something near the height of the pianistic virtuosity of the time, whilst with the Fantasia on a favourite waltz the concert-giver made his first public entrée as a composer. This work must be identified with the variations on a favourite waltz mentioned by La Mara, as having been played at his concert by the young Brahms, of which one variation took the form of a "very good canon." Marxsen's notice of the concert in the *Freischütz* of April 17 was the only one that appeared :

"In the concert given by J. Brahms, the youthful virtuoso gave most satisfactory proofs of advancement in his artistic career. His performance of Beethoven's sonata showed that he is already able to devote himself successfully to the study of the classics, and redounded in every respect to his honour. The example of his own composition also indicated unusual talent."

Although the report adds that the room was so full as to oblige many listeners to be content with seats in the ante-room, it is probable that the young musician found concert-giving more vexatious and expensive than useful or profit-able. Though he appeared from time to time at the benefit-concerts of other artists, and repeated his own fantasia at one given on December 5 by Rudolph Lohfeldt, his third soirée in Hamburg, given under conditions of which he could not at this time have dared to dream, did not take place till after the lapse of another decade. The four or five years immediately succeeding his formal entry into life were, perhaps, the darkest of Brahms' career. Money had to be earned, and the young Bach-Mozart-Beethoven en-thusiast earned it by giving wretchedly-paid lessons to pupils who lacked both talent and wish to learn, and by his night drudgery amid the sordid surroundings of the Hamburg dancing-saloons.

It was an amelioration in his life and a step forward in his career, when he was engaged by the publisher, August Cranz, as one of several contributors to a series of popular arrangements of light music, published under the name "G. W. Marks." We have read in Widmann's pages of the spirit in which the great composer, a few years before his death, recalled these passages of his struggling youth :

"He could not, he said, wish that it had been less rough and austere. He had certainly earned his first money by arranging marches and dances for garden orchestras, or or-chestral music for the piano, but it gave him pleasure even now, when he came across one of these anonymously circu-lating pieces, to think that he had devoted faithful labour and all the knowledge at his command, to such hireling's work. He did not even regard as useless experience that he had often had to accompany wretched singers or to play dance music in Lokals, whilst he was longing for the quiet morning hours during which he should be able to write down his own thoughts. 'The prettiest songs came to me as I blacked my boots before daybreak.'"

And if the master could so speak and think of his early trials, must not we, who are, perhaps, the richer through them, treasure the remembrance of the nights of uncongenial toil through which he passed to become, even on the threshold of life, its conqueror and true possessor? The iron entered his soul, however, and the impression derived from his night work remained with him till death. He was accustomed to read steadily through the hours of his slavery. Placing a volume of history, poetry, or romance on the music-desk before him, his thoughts were away in a world of imagination, whilst his fingers were mechanically busy with the tinkling keys. He did not lift his eyes to the scene before him after his first entrance, though there were times when he felt it with shuddering dismay. It is, however, right to repeat that, as we have hinted in a previous chapter, this kind of industry was a more or less recognised means by which struggling musicians of the class to which Jakob Brahms belonged, were enabled to help their needy circumstances, and it would not be difficult to name more than one executant afterwards well known who fulfilled similar engagements in youth. The position of Johannes was not in itself exceptional, though the contemplation of it is now startling from its contrast with his tender nature, his sensitive genius, and the great place which he ultimately won.

An engagement of which Kalbeck speaks, to act as accompanist behind the scenes and on the stage of the Stadt Theater, may have been less irksome to the young musician than his other hack work, and it is possible to believe that the experience drawn from it may have been of some appreciable value to him in after-life, even though his artistic development did not result in dramatic composition. Evidence is not wanting, however, to show that he kept his thoughts steadily fixed upon the higher practical possibilities of his profession, and that, though his position continued very obscure, it did not remain at a standstill. His terms to pupils increased to about a shilling a lesson, and occasionally he was able to get more. Every now and then he obtained a small concert-engagement, or officiated at a

private party, and on one occasion he appeared with Otto
Goldschmidt, the then leading pianist of Hamburg, who
was about four years his senior, in a performance of Thalberg's duet for two pianofortes on airs from "Norma."

Conditions at home remained unfavourable for practice,
and Johannes now worked regularly at the establishment
of Messrs. Baumgarten and Heinz, where an instrument was
always at his service.   Here, one day, he met Fräulein
Louise Japha, who remembered the circumstance, already
recorded in these pages, of having heard him play five or
six years previously as a child of eleven.   A talk ensued, a
sympathetic note was struck, and a comradeship quickly
grew up between the two young musicians.   Louise, born
in 1826, and therefore some seven years the senior of
Johannes, was possessed of high musical endowment.   At
the time of which we write, she was the pupil of Fritz
Wahrendorf for pianoforte, and of William Grund for theory
and composition.   She achieved eminence later on, becoming
well known in Germany and a great favourite with the
public of Paris.   Her competent sympathy was a valuable
addition to young Brahms' pleasures in life, in the days
when he knew little of congenial artistic companionship.
They met constantly to play duets and compare notes as
to their compositions, for Louise was a song-writer of
ability.   Johannes used to discuss with her both his favourite authors and his manuscripts.   One day it was a long
exercise in double counterpoint that he brought to show
her, another day a pianoforte solo.   On a third occasion
he produced a pianoforte duet in several movements, which
he begged her to try with him, and, acknowledging its
authorship at the close of the performance, asked her
opinion of the work.   This proving generally favourable,
the composer, going more into detail, took exception to
one of his themes, which he feared was rather "ordinary,"
but when Louise was half inclined to agree with him, he
cried angrily: "Why did you not say so yourself? Why
was I obliged to ask you?"

He was always composing, and as time went on, was ably guided by Marxsen to the practice of the large musical forms, over which he soon acquired conspicuous mastery, showing extraordinary facility in applying to them the skill he had gradually attained in free contrapuntal writing, whilst allowing to his fancy the stimulus of the classical-romantic literature that appealed with special force to his imagination. "It came into my head after reading so-and-so," he would say. The whole of his small amount of spare cash was devoted to the purchase of second-hand volumes from the stalls to be found in the Jews' quarter of Hamburg, and what he bought he read. Sophocles and Cicero, Dante and Tasso, Klopstock and Lessing, Goethe and Schiller, Eichendorff, Chamisso, Pope, Young, and many other poets, were represented in the library collected by him between the ages of sixteen and twenty-one.* His favourite romances were those of Jean Paul and E. T. A. Hoffmann, whose influence over his mind is easily recognisable in the published compositions of his first period. No other work on which he might be engaged, however, prevented him from the composition of many songs. He threw one off after another. "I generally read a poem through very slowly," he said to Louise, "and then, as a rule, the melody is there."

Fräulein Japha was before her time in conceiving an enthusiasm for Schumann's art, and tried hard to win over Johannes to an appreciation of its beauties, but he was too entirely under the influence of Marxsen, who, in training him as a composer, rightly proceeded on strictly orthodox lines, to become a present convert. He, on his part, made efforts to induce Louise to change her teachers and put herself under his master. She had quite other views, however. Schumann and his wife paid a visit to Hamburg in 1850, appearing several times in public, and Louise resolved that if it could be made possible, she would enter on a fresh course of study of composition and the piano under the two

---

* Cf. Kalbeck, p. 186.

great artists respectively. She only waited for a convenient opportunity to carry out her plan. Johannes approached Schumann in another fashion, by sending a packet of manuscripts to his hotel and begging for his opinion. It is no wonder that the master, who was besieged on all sides during his fortnight's stay, found no time to look at them, and returned the parcel unopened.

It must not be supposed that the young Brahms was always so companionable as we have shown him when in the society of his chosen friends. He had his moods. Christian Miller's early experiences of his persistent taciturnity had not been exceptional. He spent a few evenings at the Japhas' house, but Louise's family, her sister Minna only excepted, by no means took a fancy to her favourite. One evening, when he was about eighteen, a gentleman of the Japha circle, who had been interested in hearing him play the scherzo now known as Op. 4, the earliest written of his published instrumental works, accompanied him on the way home, and made repeated but quite hopeless efforts after sociability. Not one word would Johannes say. Perhaps he felt subsequent secret prickings of conscience, for he made confession to Louise, though not in any apparently repentant spirit. "One is not always inclined to talk," he said; "often one would rather not, and then it is best to be silent. You understand that, don't you?" "No, you were very naughty," she told him, but forgave him nevertheless. She could overlook his occasional whims. She perceived his genius, admired his candid nature, and felt her heart warm to him when he talked to her of the old mother to whom he was devoted, and of Marxsen, whom he revered with all the enthusiastic loyalty of his true heart. Soon after his walk with the Japhas' friend he had a chance opportunity of playing his scherzo to Henry Litolff, who bestowed high praise on the composition.

Meanwhile the friends at Winsen faithfully remembered their young musician. Uncle Adolph and friend Schröder seldom missed going to see him when occasion brought either of them to Hamburg, and Lischen came over to be introduced to Madame Cornet and Marxsen. Johannes persevered in his desire that her voice should be trained for the musical profession, and wished her to obtain a good opinion on the subject. The verdict of the authorities proved, however, unfavourable to the project.

Of the general invitation to visit the Giesemanns Brahms gladly availed himself, staying sometimes for a few days, sometimes in the summer for a week or two, as his occupations allowed. He was never again able to undertake the choral society, but there was always a great deal of music at the Amtsvogt's house when he was at Winsen, as well as at the Giesemanns' and Schröders'. Town-musician Koch was a good violinist, and but too happy to have the chance of playing the duet sonatas of Haydn, Mozart, and Beethoven with such a colleague, and every now and again compositions were looked out in which Uncle Giesemann could take part with his guitar. Pretty Sophie Koch, the younger of the town-musician's two daughters, took great interest in these artistic doings, and it was rumoured, as time went on, that her fondness for music was not untinged by a personal element connected with the Giesemanns' popular guest. If this were so, Johannes himself was probably the last person to become observant of it. He was wholly absorbed in his profession, and several quite independent informants have concurred in describing him to the author as being, at this time of his life, something less than indifferent to the society of ladies, and especially of young ones. For his early playmate, Lischen, his affection continued unchanged, and with her he remained on the old terms of frank and cordial friendship.

It happened as a natural consequence of the political revolution which took place early in the year 1848 in Germany and Austria, that, during the year or two following its speedy termination, there was an influx into Hamburg and its neighbourhood of refugees on their way to America. Conspicuous among them were a number of Hungarians of

various sorts and degrees, who found such sympathetic
welcome in the rich, free merchant-city that they were in
no hurry to leave it. Some of them remained there for
many months on one pretext or another, and amongst these
was the violinist, Edward Reményi, a German-Hungarian
Jew whose real name was Hoffmann.

Reményi, born in 1830, had been during three years of
his boyhood a pupil of the Vienna Conservatoire, studying
under Joseph Böhm, now remembered as the teacher of
Joachim. He had real artistic endowment, and played the
works of the classical masters well, if somewhat extravagantly; but something more than talent was displayed in his
rendering of the airs and dances of his native country, which
he gave with a fire and abandon that excited his hearers to
wild enthusiasm. Eccentric and boastful, he knew how to
profit to the utmost by his successes in Hamburg, where he
created a furore. Johannes, engaged one evening to act as
accompanist at the house of a rich merchant, made his
personal acquaintance, and Reményi, quickly perceiving
the advantage he derived from having such a coadjutor,
made overtures of friendship in his swaggering, patronising
way, which were not repulsed by the young pianist. Brahms
had, in fact, been fascinated by Reményi's spirited rendering of his national Friskas and Czardas; he was willing
that the chance acquaintance should be improved into an
alliance, and, on his next visit to the Giesemanns' house,
was accompanied by his new friend.

The violinist had connections of his own in the neighbourhood. Begas, a Hungarian magnate, had settled down into
a large villa at Dehensen, on the Lüneburg Heath, that had
been placed at his disposal for as long a time as he should
find it possible to elude or cajole the police authorities, and
kept open house for his compatriots and their friends. To
his circle Brahms was introduced, and much visiting ensued
between Dehensen and Winsen, for one or two musicians
staying with Begas were pleased to come and make music
with Reményi and Johannes, and to partake of the Giese-

manns' hospitality.   It was a feather in Brahms' cap, in the
eyes of many of his friends, that he had been able to capture
for Winsen such a celebrity as Reményi, though they were
not all quite of one mind.   Lischen, for example, did not
care for him at all, but much preferred the tall, handsome
fiddler Janovitch, with his flashing black eyes and his velvet
jacket, who wrote a splendid characteristic waltz expressly
that he might dedicate it to her.   The jolly party broke up
suddenly at last, running off to take speedy ship for
America, for they had heard that the police were on their
heels.   Johannes, who happened to be at Winsen when this
crisis occurred, accompanied them as far as Hamburg,
where he remained to pursue his ordinary avocations.
Meanwhile the Friskas and Czardas continued to revolve in
his brain.

Time went on, the Hungarians were no longer vividly
regretted, and somewhere about the autumn of 1852, Brahms
was left more lonely than ever by the departure of Louise
Japha, who found opportunity to carry out her cherished
wish to stay at Düsseldorf, where the Schumanns had now
been settled for about two years.   Her sister Minna was to
accompany her, to carry on the cultivation of her own special
gift under Professor Sohn, of the Düsseldorf Academy of
Art.   The thought of losing his friend caused Johannes
great sorrow.   "Do not go," he entreated; "you are the
only person here that takes any interest in me!"   His
prospects do not seem to have been improving at this time,
and his best encouragement must have been derived from
his own sense of his artistic progress.   This was advancing
by enormous strides, the exact measure of which is furnished by the manuscript of the Sonata in F sharp minor
at one time in the possession of Hofcapellmeister Albert
Dietrich.   It bears the signature "Kreisler jun.," a pseudonym adopted by Brahms out of love for the capellmeister
Johannes Kreisler, hero of one of Hoffmann's tales, and the
date November, 1852.

This work, which, though published later on as Op. 2,

was written earlier than the companion sonata known as Op. 1, is, in many of its fundamental characteristics, immediately prophetic of the future master. In it the mastery of form and skill in contrapuntal writing, the facility in the art of thematic development, the strikingly contrasted imaginative qualities—here subtly poetic, there large and powerful—bring us face to face with the artist nature which united in itself high purpose, resolute will, sure capacity, sensitive romanticism, boundless daring. The fancy, however, has not yet crystallised; the young musician has still to pass out of the stage of mental ferment natural to his age before he will be able to mould his thoughts into the concentrated shape which alone can convince the world. The sonata, not perhaps destined ever to become widely familiar, must always remain a treasure to the sympathetic student of Brahms' art, not only by reason of the beauties in which it abounds, but also because it is absolutely representative of its composer as he was at nineteen. We may read his favourite authors in some of its movements without the need of an interpreter, and we know, from his own communication to Dietrich, that the melody of the second movement was inspired by the words of the German folk-song, "Mir ist leide, Das der Winter Beide, Wald und auch die Haide, hat gemachet kahl."

It would be difficult, and is fortunately unnecessary, to trace the exact steps of Reményi's career after his flight from Germany. For the purpose of our narrative the facts suffice that he reappeared in Hamburg at the close of 1852, giving a concert in the Hôtel de l'Europe, which does not seem to have created any great sensation, and that he found himself in the same city in the spring of 1853. Brahms, depressed by the hopeless monotony of his daily grind, was no doubt glad enough to see him, and, as his slack time was at hand, it was proposed, perhaps by Reményi, perhaps by Uncle Giesemann, possibly by Johannes himself, that the two musicians should give a concert to their friends in Winsen, who would, no doubt, hail the prospect of such an

BRAHMS AT THE AGE OF TWENTY.

event, and assist it to the utmost of their power. Communications were opened, and the proposal was not only entertained, but developed, as such ideas are apt to do. If at Winsen, why not also at Lüneburg and Celle? Amtsvogt Blume had influence in both towns, which he would be only too happy to exert. In the end, the project expanded into the plan of a concert-tour. Johannes and Reményi would give performances in the three localities named, and from Celle it would be no distance to go on to Hanover, where the twenty-one-year-old Joachim, already a European celebrity, had a post at Court. Reményi had known him for a short time when they had both been boys at the Vienna Conservatoire; they would go and see him. He was bound to welcome his compatriot and former fellow-pupil. Who could tell what might happen?

The two artists left Hamburg for Winsen on April 19. No doubt Brahms felt some heart-stirrings as he set out on this his first quest of adventure and probably not the least ardent of his anticipations was that of making the personal acquaintance of the celebrated violinist whose first appearance in Hamburg at the Philharmonic concert of March 11, 1848, with Beethoven's Concerto, remained vividly in his remembrance as one of the few great musical events of his own life. Before starting, he exacted a promise from his mother that she would write to him regularly once a week—not a mere greeting, but a real letter of several pages. It was a serious undertaking for Johanna, who was not practised in penmanship, but she gave her word to Hannes, and found means to keep it. The travellers took but little luggage with them. Such as Johannes carried was made the heavier by his packet of manuscripts, which contained his pianoforte sonata-movements and scherzo, a sonata for pianoforte and violin, a pianoforte trio, a string quartet, a number of songs, and possibly other works. One programme was to suffice for the concert *tournée*, and this the two artists had in their heads.

The exact date of the Winsen concert is forgotten, ap-

parently beyond chance of recall, but the event may be fixed
with certainty as having taken place in the last week of
April.   In the meanwhile both musicians were the guests of
the Giesemanns, and spent the greater part of their mornings practising together, beginning before breakfast.   They
gave a great deal of time to the Hungarian melodies, and
it would seem as though Johannes had been preparing a
pianoforte accompaniment; for they repeated the periods
over and over again, Reményi becoming very irritable
during the process.   The season was a warm one; they
worked energetically in their shirt-sleeves, and the violinist
more than once made his colleague shout by bringing the
violin bow suddenly down on his shoulder to emphasise the
capricious *tempo* he required.   One morning Johannes, very
angry, jumped up from the piano, and declared he would
no longer bear with Reményi; but the concert came off
nevertheless, and turned out a brilliant success.   It took
place in the large room of the Rusteberg club-house; the
entrance fee was about eightpence, and the profits to be
divided came to rather over nine pounds.   Beethoven's
C minor Sonata for pianoforte and violin headed the programme, and was followed by violin solos; Vieuxtemps'
Concerto in E major, Ernst's "Elégie," and several Hungarian melodies, all accompanied by Brahms, who, it must
be remembered, was but the junior partner in the enterprise.   Only one thing was to be regretted.   Schröder had
been ill, and could not come to Winsen for the concert.
He managed, however, to attend a repetition of the programme, which the two artists gave the next day in his
schoolroom at Hoopte, expressly in order that he might get
some amount of pleasure out of the great doings of the
neighbourhood.

The next concert took place on May 2 at Celle.   It had
been arranged with the assistance of Dr. Köhler, a well-
known inhabitant of the town, probably a relation of the
Rector of Winsen, and a friend of Amtsvogt Blume, who,
besides seeing through the business arrangements, had neg-

lected no opportunity of arousing general interest in the event. The single public announcement appeared in the *Celler'scher Anzeiger* of Saturday, April 30:

" Next Monday evening at seven o'clock the concert of the Herren Reményi and Brahms will take place in the Wierss'-schen room. The subscription price is 12 g.gr.* Tickets may also be obtained of Herr Wierss jun. at Herr Duncker's hotel, and on the evening at the room for 16 g.gr."

At Celle there was a sensation. The two artists, going, on the morning of May 2, to try their pieces in the concert-room, were dismayed to find that the only pianoforte of which it boasted was in such an advanced state of old age as to be unusable for their purpose. Classical concerts were rare events in Celle, and it had occurred to no one to doubt the excellence of the instrument; a piano was a piano. It was arranged that every effort should be made, during the few hours that remained, to procure a better one, and a better one was actually discovered and sent in just as the hour had arrived for the concert to begin. But a fresh difficulty arose. The second instrument proved to be nearly a semitone below pitch, and Reményi refused to make so considerable a change in the tuning of his violin. What was to be done? The practised and intrepid Johannes made short work of the difficulty. If Reményi would tune his fiddle slightly up, so as to bring it to a true semitone above the piano, he himself would transpose his part of the Beethoven sonata a semitone higher than written, and play it in C sharp minor instead of C minor. No sooner said than done. The young musician performed the feat without turning a hair, though his colleague allowed him no quarter, and the performance was applauded to the echo. Reményi behaved well on this occasion. Addressing the audience, he related the circumstances in which he and his companion had found themselves placed, and said that all approval belonged by right to Brahms, whose musicianship had saved the situation. History does not relate whether

---

* Two Guter Gröschen were of about the value of 2½d.

the young hero transposed his parts throughout the evening, or whether the old instrument was sufficiently serviceable for the accompaniments of the violin solos, and the question does not appear to have suggested itself until the present time, when it cannot be solved. Johannes himself seems to have thought but little of his achievement. Writing presently to let Marxsen know how he was getting on, he mentioned the incident, not as worthy of comment, but as one amongst others.

The day after these events Reményi and Brahms retraced their steps as far as Lüneburg, where they were welcomed by Herr Calculator Blume, son of the Amtsvogt. At his hospitable house they were presented to the musical circle of the town, so far as it included members of the sterner sex. At the earnest persuasion of Brahms, no ladies were invited to the party arranged by Frau Blume in the interests of the forthcoming concert. "It is so much nicer without them," he said, and was so serious about the matter that his hostess regretfully gave way to him. He played part of the C major Sonata, on the composition of which he had lately been engaged, on this private occasion, making but little impression with it. Perhaps the double consciousness, which cannot but have been secretly present with him, of his great artistic superiority to Reményi, and of the quite secondary place to which he found himself relegated whenever they appeared together, may have increased the awkward shyness which placed him at such a disadvantage by the side of his colleague. He was incapable of making any effort to assert himself in general society, and attracted little notice from ordinary strangers who had no particular reason for observing him closely. However, everyone behaved very kindly to him throughout the journey. He was certainly a good pianist, and accompanied Reményi delightfully.

The concert was advertised in the *Lüneburger Anzeiger* of May 7, the twentieth birthday anniversary of our Johannes:

"The undersigned propose to give a concert on Monday evening, the 9th inst., at 7.30, in Herr Balcke's Hall, and have the honour to invite the attendance of the music-loving public. Amongst other things, the concert-givers will perform Beethoven's Sonata for Pianoforte and Violin in C minor, Op. 30, and Vieuxtemps' grand Violin Concerto in E major.

"Tickets to be had," etc.   "EDWARD REMÉNYI.
                                      JOHANNES BRAHMS."

Again a great success was scored, and the next day a second concert "by general desire" was announced, with the same programme and special mention of the "Hungarian Melodies," for Wednesday, May 11. It brought the visit to Lüneburg to a brilliant conclusion, and the performances were again repeated on the 12th at a second concert in Celle, advertised in the Celle journal of the 11th.

With the account of these five soirées, exact record of the public concerts of the journey is exhausted. Neither advertisement nor local recollection of any other can be traced, though Heuberger speaks, on the authority of Brahms' personal recollection, of two given at Hildesheim.* The first was very sparsely attended, and the artists, after supping at a restaurant where they seem to have made merry with some companions, paraded the streets with a queue of followers until they arrived underneath the windows of a lady of position who had been their principal patron. Reményi greeted her with some violin solos, the assembled party followed suit with a chorus, and the ingenious advertisement proved so successful that a second concert-venture on the following evening drew a crowded audience. The circumstances thus related point to the conclusion that the first concert at Hildesheim was hastily arranged, and the explanation may be that some unexpected introduction caused the musicians to visit the town. This would fit in with the fact that there is no reference in any Hildesheim journal of the date to Brahms and Reményi, and with the

---

* Heuberger, "Musikalische Skizzen."

absence of all knowledge, on the part of several persons still living who have personal associations with the journey, of any other concerts than those in Winsen, Lüneburg, and Celle, and of one other of a different kind in Hanover, to which we shall return.

It is necessary for the understanding of what is to follow that we should here part company, for a time, with the travellers. Before introducing Johannes to the great musical world which he is to enter before long, we must glance at the party questions by which it was agitated in the early eighteen-fifties, and which had hitherto been unknown or unheeded by our young musician in the inexperience of his secluded life.

The musical world of Leipzig, the city raised by the leadership of Mendelssohn to be the recognised capital of classical art, had become split after the death of the master in November, 1847, into two factions, both without an active head. The Schumannites, whilst receiving no encouragement from the great composer whose art they championed, decried Mendelssohn as a pedant and a phrase-maker, who, having nothing particular to say, had covered his lack of meaning by facility of workmanship. The Mendelssohnians, on the other hand, declared Schumann to be wanting in mastery of form, and perceived in his works a tendency to subordinate the objective, to the subjective, side of musical art. The division soon spread beyond Leipzig throughout Germany, and, in the course of years, to England, with the result that Mendelssohn, once a popular idol, was rarely represented in a concert programme.

Meanwhile Franz Liszt, perhaps the greatest pianoforte executant of all times, and one of the most magnetic personalities of his own, had exchanged his brilliant career of virtuoso for the position of conductor of the orchestra of the Weimar court theatre, with the avowed noble purpose of bringing to a hearing such works of genius as had little chance of being performed elsewhere. He declared himself

the advocate of the "New-German" school, and, making
active propaganda for the creeds of Hector Berlioz and
Richard Wagner, succeeded in attracting to his standard
some of the most talented of the younger generation of
artists, amongst whom Joseph Joachim, Joachim Raff, and
the gifted and generous Hans von Bülow, were some of the
first converts.   There were, therefore, three different schools
of serious musical thought in the year 1853, each of which
boasted numerous and distinguished adherents.

The purists of Leipzig held sacred the memory of Mendelssohn, clung to the methods as well as the forms of
classical tradition, and declined to recognise as legitimate
art anything that savoured of progress.

The Schumannites believed it possible to give musical
expression to the world-spirit of the time by expanding
their methods within the old forms—i.e., by free use of
chromatic harmonies, varied cadences, mixed rhythms, and
so forth.

The Weimarites, rejoicing in the potent leadership of
Liszt, declared they would no longer be hampered either
by old methods or old forms, which they regarded as worn
out and perishing of inanition.

The party disputes as to the respective merits of Mendelssohn and Schumann, were as nothing beside the violent
controversies which raged for years around the theories
professed by the founders of the so-called "music of the
future."   For some time the battle was fought chiefly
between the "academics" of Leipzig and the "revolu-
tionists" of Weimar.   The classical-romantic art of
Schumann had points of contact with that of each of the
extremists.   Animated by new impulse and instinct with
modern thought, it was by no means coupled by the leaders
of the new party with that of Mendelssohn, but was accepted by them for some years with more than toleration,
and some of the master's works, such as the overtures "Gen-
oveva" and "Manfred," were performed at Weimar under
Liszt's direction.   Schumann himself, however, whilst

warmly appreciating the great qualities of Wagner's musicianship, was well aware that any relationship between his own works and that of the new school was merely superficial. He was second to none in his reverence for the forms of the great masters, upon which he based his compositions, and, though it may possibly be the case that the originality of his idiom did not attract the entire sympathy of Mendelssohn, he clung to the memory of this departed friend as that of a beloved comrade-in-arms.

Schumann, who had long since retired from his labours as editor of the *Neue Zeitschrift für Musik*, of which he was the founder, lived quietly at Düsseldorf, where he had, in 1850, succeeded Ferdinand Hiller as municipal conductor. The success achieved by him there, during the first season of his activity as director of the orchestral subscription concerts and the choral society, was only transient. His reserved nature, and the progress of the malady that threatened him, unfitted him for the position, and he was subject to the constant annoyance that resulted from differences with his committee. To this was added the serious disappointment of knowing that the periodical to which he had devoted untiring energy during some of the best years of his life, had become, under the editorship of Franz Brendel, the organ of the New-German party, from whose principles he felt increasing alienation. These vexations probably augmented his nervous condition, and his habitual silence and reserve increased. His chief pleasure was found in the absorbing work of composition, and in his generous sympathy with a group of young musicians who regarded themselves as his disciples. Perhaps feeling that the best part of his own career was already behind him, he lived in the constant hope that someone would appear of creative genius sufficiently decisive to indicate him as the worthy successor to the prophet's mantle of classical art.

Many of our readers are aware that Joseph Joachim was born on June 28, 1831, at Kittsee, a village near Presburg in Hungary; that at the age of twelve he had learnt all that

the distinguished violinist, Böhm, of the Vienna Conservatoire, master of many famous pupils, could teach him; and
that he lived at Leipzig, well known at the Conservatoire,
though not its pupil, for the next six years, happy during
the first four of them in the affection of Mendelssohn, to
whom he was passionately attached, and who lost no opportunity of furthering his protégé's genius and of laying the
foundation of his future career.

It was not until after Mendelssohn's death that either
of the party questions to which we have referred became
acute, and Joseph grew up an unquestioning believer in
the principles of musical tradition, which he reverenced
with something of religious fervour. The loss of Mendelssohn left him, at the age of sixteen, lonely and disconsolate, in spite of his being himself already a distinguished
personality and a universal favourite. The peculiar place in
his life which the master had occupied could not again be
filled, and for more than two years he was unable to regard
anyone as even the partial successor to his best affections.
It happened, however, that two events of the year 1850,
awakened in his heart something of the personal enthusiasm
which had made his early happiness. A few weeks spent
by the Schumanns at Leipzig in the month of March, convinced him of his sympathy with the composer and his art;
and a visit which he paid to Weimar in August, on the
occasion of the first performance of Wagner's "Lohengrin," stirred him so strongly that by the end of the year he
had resigned his position in Leipzig and taken up his residence in Weimar as concertmeister in Liszt's orchestra.*

Here he lived for two years, and it seemed for a time as
though he would become one of the most enthusiastic of the
band of young musicians, amongst whom were Bülow,
Raff, Cornelius, and the violoncellist, Cossmann, who proclaimed themselves disciples of the new school. His genius
and his already eminent position as an artist made him by

---

* The concertmeister is the leader—i.e., leading violin of the orchestra. The capellmeister is the conductor of the orchestra.

far the most important member of the group, and he was
treated by Liszt almost on equal terms, as a younger colleague. In the constant companionship of this fascinating
master, Joachim felt some renewal of the satisfaction in
life which he had experienced when with Mendelssohn at
Leipzig; but his early convictions and affections were too
deeply rooted to be effaced by newer impressions, and his
allegiance to the school of the future was not permanent.
Liszt's aspirations, as the composer of sounding orchestral
works which Joachim ought to have admired, but could
not, gradually caused the young concertmeister to feel his
position a false one, and he was glad to accept a post offered
him, at the close of 1852, as court concertmeister and assistant capellmeister at Hanover. By this step he regained
his independence without hurting the feelings of his Weimar
friends. His absence of warmth on the subject of the
Symphonic Poems had, indeed, been observed by Liszt, but
Joachim had naturally refrained from expressing himself
about them in detail, and Liszt could not guess that his
young companion had conceived a positive aversion to his
compositions. Joachim remained for some years yet on
terms of affectionate intimacy with Liszt, Bülow, and the
others, and was, indeed, so lonely and depressed during the
first few months of his residence in Hanover, that he was
impelled to express his state of mind by the composition
of an overture to "Hamlet." Sending the manuscript to
Liszt in the middle of March, he wrote:

"I have been very much alone. The contrast between the
atmosphere which is constantly resounding, through your
influence, with new tones, and an air which is completely
tone-still, is too barbarous. Wherever I have looked there
has been no one to share my aims—no one; instead of the
phalanx of like-minded friends at Weimar . . . I took up
'Hamlet' . . . I am certain that you, my ever-indulgent
master, will look through the score, and will advise me as
though I were sitting near you, dumb as ever, but listening
eagerly to your musical wisdom."*

_____

* Moser's "Life of Joachim."

The Festival of the Lower Rhine, held in the year 1853 at Düsseldorf (May 15-17), was a particularly brilliant function. The names of Robert and Clara Schumann, Ferdinand Hiller as chief conductor, Joseph Joachim, the English artist Clara Novello, and others of high distinction, roused lively expectations which were perhaps exceeded by the performances. Schumann's D minor Symphony, Pianoforte Concerto played by his wife, and Overture and final chorus on the "Rheinweinlied," all given under his own direction, were received with enthusiasm; and the first appearance on the Rhine of the young concertmeister from Hanover, with Beethoven's then little-known Violin Concerto, resulted in a triumph that defies description. "He opened a veritable world of enchantment." "He was the hero of the festival." "We will not attempt to describe his success; there was French frenzy, Italian fanaticism, in a German audience," say the critics of the day.

For our readers, the peculiar interest of the occasion lies in the fact that Joachim, increasingly attracted by Schumann's art and individuality, took advantage of his few days' stay in Düsseldorf to draw closer his relations with the master, and it may be said that his future attitude was finally determined at this time. He saw in Schumann the living representative of the music that he loved, and to him and his became bound henceforth by ties that death itself was but partially able to sever.

CHAPTER IV.

1853.

Brahms and Reményi visit Joachim in Hanover—Concert at Court—Visit to Liszt—Joachim and Brahms in Göttingen—Wasielewski, Reinecke, and Hiller—First meeting with Schumann—Albert Dietrich.

Leaving Düsseldorf on May 18, the day following the close of the festival, Joachim proceeded on a week's visit to Weimar, and, returning thence to spend a day or two at home in Hanover before settling for the summer at Göttingen, where he proposed to attend University lectures, was surprised by a call from Reményi and Brahms.* His first attention was naturally devoted to his old school-fellow, but by and by he turned to the stranger, and an account of the interview may be given in his own words:

"The dissimilar companions—the tender, idealistic Johannes and the self-satisfied, fantastic virtuoso—called on me. Never in the course of my artist's life have I been more completely overwhelmed with delighted surprise, than when the rather shy-mannered, blonde companion of my countryman played me his sonata movements, of quite undreamt-of originality and power, looking noble and inspired the while.

---

* The accounts of some authors place the visit in Göttingen. They must be regarded as, in this respect, mistaken. Joachim was positive, when consulted by the author on the point. "The whole scene lives clearly in my memory," he said; "it occurred in my rooms in Princes Street, Hanover."

His song, 'O, versenk dein Leid,' sounded to me like a revelation, and his playing, so tender, so imaginative, so free and so fiery, held me spell-bound. No wonder that I not only foresaw, but actually foretold, a speedy end to the concert-journey with Reményi. Brahms parted from him soon afterwards, and, encouraged before long by an enthusiastic recognition, marched proudly onwards in his own path of endeavour after the highest development."[*]

Reményi had not been mistaken in building hopes for the success of the concert-journey upon the chance of an interview with Joachim, who proved the medium through which both he and his companion were guided to the respective spheres for which each was peculiarly fitted. The great violinist was at this, his first interview with Brahms, so deeply penetrated by the certainty of his genius, so impressed by its daring, and so profoundly touched by the evident sincerity and childlike freshness of his nature, that he took the newcomer then and there to his heart, and made his cause his own. The conviction to which he had been stirred is reflected in a few lines written by him at the end of May or beginning of June, shortly after his arrival in Göttingen, whither he was immediately followed by the two concert-givers:

"MY DEAR JOHANNES,
"The piano has not arrived; it is afraid of the wet weather! Your sonata need not fear this, however. No doubt it struggles bravely like all your things against the waters of triviality! How would it be if we were to meet at Wehner's (a musician of Göttingen) from ten to twelve with violin, music, and (last but not least) friend Reményi, to bring the composition to life, i.e., to play it? . . . . "[†]

Joachim's enthusiasm did not exhaust itself in mere professions of goodwill. He was prompt to use his influence in high quarters on behalf of his new friend, and exerted it

---

[*] Festival address at Meiningen, October 7, 1899.
[†] Brahms-Joachim Briefwechsel, No. 1.

N.B.—The letter refers to the sonata for pianoforte and violin mentioned on p. 97 of this volume.

to such good purpose as to procure for the travellers an immediate engagement to appear before King George and the royal circle of Hanover:

"There is in Brahms' playing," he wrote to the Countess Bernstorff, a lady of great musical accomplishment attached to the Hanoverian court, "that concentrated fire, what I may call that fatalistic energy and precision of rhythm, which prophesy the artist and his compositions already contain much that is significant, such as I have not hitherto met with in a youth of his age."*

To Heinrich Ehrlich, court pianist at Hanover, who was present on the important occasion of Brahms' first performance before a royal audience, and has recorded that his debut was made with the E flat minor Scherzo. Joachim wrote:

"Brahms has a quite exceptional talent for composition and a nature that could have been developed in its integrity only in the strictest retirement—pure as the diamond, tender as snow."

On Brahms' departure for Hanover, he was warmly pressed by the generous young concertmeister to return to Göttingen if his relations with Reményi should come to the early termination which Joachim anticipated for them.

From Hanover, Reményi and Brahms travelled to Weimar, where Joachim had ensured them a welcome by writing to Liszt on their behalf. Of the first meeting between the world-famous musician, who lived in a style of ostentatious luxury in a house on the Altenburg belonging to the Princess Caroline von Sayn-Wittgenstein, and the obscure young composer from the Lane-quarter of Hamburg, we have, fortunately, the account of an eye-witness, William Mason, of New York, who was at the time resident in Weimar as a pupil of Liszt, and one of the ardent young champions of the new school.

"One evening early in June," says Mason,† "Liszt sent

---

* Ehrlich's "Dreissig Jahre Künstlerleben."
† "Memoirs of a Musical Life."

us word to come up the next morning to the Altenburg, as
he expected a visit from a young man who was said to have
great talent as a composer, and whose name was Johannes
Brahms. He was to come accompanied by Edward
Reményi.

" The next morning, on going to the Altenburg with
Klindworth, we found Brahms and Reményi already in the
reception-room with Raff and Pruckner. After greeting the
new-comers, of whom Reményi was known to us by reputation, I strolled over to a table on which were lying some
manuscripts of music. They were several of Brahms' unpublished compositions, and I began turning over the leaves
of the uppermost of the pile. It was the pianoforte solo,
Op. 4, Scherzo in E flat minor. . . . Finally Liszt came
down, and after some general conversation he turned to
Brahms, and said : ' We are interested to hear some of your
compositions whenever you are ready and feel inclined to
play them.'

" Brahms, however, who was in a highly nervous state,
declared that it was quite impossible for him to play, and
as the entreaties of Liszt and Reményi failed to induce him
to approach the piano, Liszt went over to the table, saying,
' Well, I shall have to play '; and taking the first piece at
hand from the heap of manuscripts, he performed the scherzo
at sight in such a marvellous way, carrying on, at the same
time, a running accompaniment of audible criticism of the
music, that Brahms was surprised and delighted. Raff
found reminiscences, in the opening bars, of Chopin's
Scherzo in B flat minor, whereupon Brahms answered that
he had neither seen nor heard any of this composer's works.
Liszt then played a part of Brahms' Sonata in C major,
Op. 1.

" A little later, someone asked Liszt to play his own sonata, a work which was quite recent at that time, and of
which he was very fond. Without hesitation he sat down
and began playing. As he progressed, he came to a very
expressive part, which he always imbued with extreme
pathos, and in which he looked for the especial interest and
sympathy of his listeners. Glancing at Brahms, he found
that the latter was dozing in his chair. Liszt continued
playing to the end of the sonata, and then rose and left the
room. I was in such a position that Brahms was hidden
from my view, but I was aware that something unusual had

taken place, and I think it was Reményi who told me what had occurred. It is very strange that among the various accounts of this first Liszt-Brahms interview—and there are several—there is not one which gives an accurate description of what took place on the occasion; indeed, they are all far out of the way. The events as here related are perfectly clear in my own mind; but not wishing to trust implicitly to my memory, I wrote to my friend Klindworth, the only living witness of the incident except myself, as I suppose, and requested him to give me an account of it as he remembered it. He corroborated my description in every particular, except that he made no specific reference to the drowsiness of Brahms, and except also that, according to my recollection, Brahms left Weimar on the afternoon of the day on which the meeting took place; Klindworth writes that it was on the morning of the next day—a discrepancy of very little moment.''

It is to be observed, in the first place, with reference to this interesting account, that Brahms' panic was probably caused by his finding that he was expected to play before not only Liszt himself, but a party of his pupils, the most unnerving kind of audience with which he could possibly have been confronted; and in the second, that Reményi, in saying his companion had fallen asleep, unquestionably merely intended to convey the meaning that he had not taken prudent advantage of his opportunity to ingratiate himself with the great man. The very different methods employed by the violinist for the advancement of his own ambition are illustrated by a letter written by him to Liszt soon after this first interview which throws an illuminating sidelight upon the scene and its immediate sequel. It is clear that Reményi at once took steps for the purpose of ingratiating himself with the leader of Weimar and his rising young musicians by acquainting himself with, at all events, the names of Liszt's compositions, and announcing himself a convert to the New-German music. He remained associated with the party for a considerable time, and Liszt recognised his gifts whilst ridiculing his extravagances. The letter referred to opens with a kind of preamble:

"This scribbler ventures to address the great man, after having heard the sonata, the scherzo, the rhapsodies, the Dante fantasia, etc. One must have courage to dare to write to such a man. Let us see, let us try, nevertheless. We shall see whether I have the talent to continue. Now to work!

"TISZTELT LISZT UR!

"Admirable compatriot!

"I am here on the Altenburg, the place where I have had the happiness (read effrontery) of being received by Liszt, and where I have the happiness of finding myself again!

"Conceive the immense joy you have given me by forwarding the letter addressed to me from Hungary. Every bad thing is of some use; when I reflect that this bit of a Hungarian letter has procured me the sublime lines of Liszt —Ah! yes, I have read this letter four or five times—no! devoured it, but not altogether; some fragments fortunately remain for me to point to proudly in the future (when I shall have become a great man??!!): do you see, gentlemen? I am a happy mortal. I possess the writing—no, *a personal letter from Liszt*. You may be assured that that is *everything* for me—it will be my talisman! If you by chance ask what I am doing, really I cannot tell you—of what interest can it be to you if I scrape on the violin or compose some new mazourek fantastiques? That is zero for you. . . .

"As for my political confession, it is already sent—Raff has edited it!

"Now, I think this letter is much too long. I shall finish it by telling you quite simply, but very sincerely, that the good God has you in His holy keeping, and that He ever directs your genius for the honour and glory of the human race in general, and particularly (but particularly) of your dear country.

"Adieu, great compatriot!

"I subscribe myself,

"E. REMÉNYI,

"Citizen of the Altenburg, ci-devant of Hungary.

"P.S.—Brahms has left for Göttingen."*

---

* From La Mara's "Briefe hervorragender Zeitgenossen an Franz Liszt."

And no wonder ! one feels inclined to exclaim, on reading the postscript, the first of three appended to the epistle. Johannes must have felt that his power of endurance was being strained to its utmost limit by daily association with such a comrade, and determined to break it, helped, very likely, to his resolution by the recollection of the very different personality of that other violinist, the young king of fiddlers, who had invited him to Göttingen. The story frequently related, that Brahms and Reményi, or one of them, stayed on for several weeks as Liszt's guests at the Altenburg, is contradicted by all contemporary testimony, negative as well as positive evidence. It is established by one of Joachim's few dated letters, that he wrote to Weimar on Brahms' behalf on June 15; and by a letter of Liszt's of June 29 to the Princess Caroline von Sayn-Wittgenstein that the Weimar master had, at the latter date, left the Altenburg for the summer. Moreover Liszt writes in a letter to Joachim of June 23 :

" . . . . Reményi and Brahms are staying in the rooms formerly occupied by Bülow. I am obliged to you for having introduced them to me and am glad to believe that they will become creditable artists."[*]

The morning at the Altenburg can, indeed, have left little behind it in the mind of our musician beyond a feeling of mortification, and Mason expressly states that the impression it produced on the young men present was that it had not been a success. It is likely that Klindworth was substantially correct as to the exact date of Brahms' departure from Weimar. Perhaps hoping to appear to better advantage in a *tête-à-tête* interview, he seems to have called a second time on Liszt, who presented him with a leather cigarette-case in which was placed an autograph inscription in remembrance of their meeting.[†]

---

[*] " Briefe von und an Joseph Joachim," edited by Johannes Joachim and Andreas Moser. Vol. I.

[†] According to a personal communication to the author by Frau Dr. Langhans-Japha, to whom Brahms showed the case.

Towards the close of June, then Joachim, at work one day in his rooms at Göttingen, had hardly time to call out, "Come in" in answer to a knock at the door, before the door opened and in walked Brahms. This was the beginning of the intimate acquaintance between the two youthful musicians, which ripened into the historic friendship that endured until the death of Brahms forty-four years later. What a discovery was each to the other! Alike in no respect, perhaps, save in earnest devotion to art, and a profound feeling of obligation in her service, the dissimilarity of their dispositions was such as to make them mutually interesting and to cement the growing bond between them. To Joachim the worship of art, adored goddess though she might be, could never be all in all; it could never appease the craving for human sympathy which, since Mendelssohn's death, he had at times felt to be almost intolerable. Johannes, haunted by a vision of the delight of intimate sympathy, was not convinced of its being either possible or indispensable, and knew that he could, if necessary, live his life without it. To Joachim, possessed of strong likings and antipathies, and firm to convictions involving a principle, it was not difficult, in a conflict of mere inclinations, to yield. In Johannes, with all his childlike sweetness of nature, there dwelt an ineradicable combative instinct. To Joachim life had been one continued triumph; he had never known even the taste of failure. A personality from childhood, he had conquered his world once and for all with scarcely an effort. Hannes had passed his days in obscurity, and had seen and known only struggle. And now, to Joachim, who had never had to plan for his own advancement, what a fresh joy it was to think and hope and suggest for the future of Johannes, and to Johannes, who had known little of the satisfaction of intelligent appreciation from colleagues of his own standing, what an astonishing experience was this enthusiastic and authoritative approval from such a comrade! The companions, engrossed in the first place by their compositions—

for Joachim was engaged upon two overtures, and Johannes busy with sonatas and songs—found plenty of time for other occupations. They studied and made music together, and walked and talked and dined together, and compared opinions and argued and agreed together. No doubt Johannes heard much about the Leipzig of Bach and Mendelssohn, and he found to his surprise that Joachim, the unparalleled interpreter of Bach and Beethoven, shared Louise Japha's opinion of Schumann's music. He certainly touched Joachim's heart by his loving talk of Hamburg, rich in proud traditions, and not without art memories of its own, associated with the great names of Klopstock and Lessing, of Telemann and Keiser, of Handel and Mattheson and Emanuel Bach. The fêted violinist, familiar since his ninth year with one or other centre of musical learning, brilliant pupil of the conservatoire of Vienna, beloved favourite of that of Leipzig, listened, moreover, with no little interest to all that Johannes chose to relate of his solitary studies with his Marxsen. The happy young Hamburger felt that he could tell Joseph anything. He spoke to him of his struggles, his kind friends at Winsen, his acquaintance with Louise Japha, the difficulties of his journey with Reményi. Joachim was so much interested in the Winsen episodes that he could not refrain from writing to Uncle Giesemann to tell him that his young musician would be a great man some day.

In one thing only Johannes would not bear his friend company. He declined to attend the university lectures of Ritter and Waiz, voting lectures a bore, and preferring to take his mental food, as usual, from books. He was very ready, however, to join the jovial fellowship that met at the Saxsen, the students' club-restaurant frequented by Joachim and his friends. He entered with great zest into all the fun of the social evenings, and on the night when he and Joachim were called upon, as the youngest of the party, to perform the "Fox-ride," he sat astraddle on his little chair, and galloped round the table with the court concertmeister from Hanover as though he were bent on keeping his terms with the most serious-minded student of them all. The happy holiday was crowned by a concert given by the two "students," which attracted an over-flowing audience and provided Brahms with welcome funds for the prosecution of his immediate plans. He wished to make a walking excursion along the Rhine before the sum-mer should have passed away, and left Göttingen about the middle of August, armed with several of his friend's visiting-cards with which to introduce himself to musical houses on his route. The acquaintance which Joachim desired to secure for him above all others was that of Schu-mann, but Johannes, probably sore from his recent experiences of an interview with a leader surrounded by his followers, was uncertain if he should stay at Düsseldorf. The separation between himself and Joachim was to be a short one only. They were to meet in October at Hanover, where Johannes was to pass the winter in his friend's society.

We have to picture our traveller as passing, during the next two or three weeks, from point to point along the beautiful Rhine valley in a frame of mind rendered almost ecstatic by the combined influences of his daily surround-ings, his recent experiences, and his well-grounded hopes for the future. We meet him again early in September in the house of J. W. von Wasielewski, who at this period filled a post as music-director at Bonn, and who has given an interesting account of Brahms' arrival in that city.

"Towards the end of the summer," he says,* "I was sur-prised by a visit from an attractive-looking, fair-haired youth, who delivered to me one of Joachim's visiting-cards, on the reverse side of which was his own humorously-written signature.† It was Johannes Brahms. Coming in the direc-tion from Mainz, he had travelled on foot through the Rhine valley, and presented himself to me staff in hand and knap-

---

* "Aus siebzig Jahren."
† "Joh. Kreisler, jun."

sack on his back. His fresh, natural, unconstrained manner impressed me sympathetically, so that I not only bade him welcome, but invited him to stay a day or two with me, to which he then and there consented. After the first hours of our intercourse, I naturally felt a desire to learn to know my guest from the musical side. He at once favoured me with a performance of one of his then unpublished early works, a pianoforte sonata, the quality of which immediately revealed to me his great talent for composition. I also heard him in other things. I particularly remember his characteristic execution of the Rakóczy March, which he was fond of playing and gave with great effect.''

Asked by Wasielewski whether he intended to visit Schumann, Johannes replied that he had come to no decision on the point, giving as the reason for his uncertainty, the failure of his effort to approach the master on his visit to Hamburg in 1850, and no persuasion of his new friend availed to bring him to a resolution. He did not quit the neighbourhood of Bonn immediately. Acting, no doubt, on Wasielewski's advice, he retraced his steps a little in order to present himself at a great house in the vicinity— that of Commerzienrath Deichmann, a gentleman widely known, not only from his wealth and hospitality, but also by the warm interest taken by himself and his family in matters connected with literature and art. Distinguished visitors of many varieties of social rank, from royal personages downwards, were entertained by Frau Deichmann at her residence at Mehlem, opposite Königswinter. Celebrities on a visit to the Rhine country were generally to be met in her drawing-rooms in the course of their stay, many of the artists resident in the neighbourhood belonged to her intimate circle, and young musicians of promise were received by her with especial kindness. Needless to say that the arrival of Brahms as Joachim's intimate was hailed by her with lively satisfaction, and the familiar friends of the house, amongst whom were Franz Wüllner, the 'cellist Reimers, Wasielewski himself, and other young musicians, hurried to Mehlem on receiving her hasty summons, prepared to extend to the

new-comer's performances as much approbation or criticism
as the event might justify.

"I found," said Wüllner, in a memorial speech delivered
after Brahms' death in the conservatoire of Cologne, "a
slender youth with long fair hair and a veritable St. John's
head, from whose eyes shone energy and spirit. He played
us the just-finished C major Sonata, the earlier completed
F sharp minor Sonata, the E flat minor Scherzo, and several
songs—amongst them the now familiar 'O versenk dein
Leid.' We young musicians were immediately delighted
and carried away by his compositions."

As might have been expected, Brahms was not allowed
to leave Mehlem immediately. He was persuaded to
remain on as the Deichmanns' guest, to improve his acquaintance with their friends, and to further explore the Rhine
and its beauties from their house, and it was during this
visit that he found the opportunity, eagerly desired by him
since his stay at Göttingen, to begin the real study of
Schumann's compositions, till now but little known to him.
What must have been his wonder and his joy as he found
himself brought face to face in many of their pages with
his favourite authors, Jean Paul and E. T. A. Hoffmann,
and perceived in them as in a mirror the dreamings of his
own soul! His surprise was probably but little less on
making the discovery that Schumann's tone-poems, with all
their fresh originality of method and their fascinating
romance, were no mere erratic imaginings, but were firmly
rooted in the great traditions of classical art. It is, perhaps,
impossible to realise in its strength the revulsion of feeling
that must have attended this first real spiritual meeting of
"Kreisler jun." with the composer of the "Kreisleriana";
but it is safe to say that it settled him in the determination
to pay the visit to Schumann which Joachim had planned
and that it had its share in producing the temper of mind
manifest in a letter written by Johannes in the third week

of September, whilst he was on a few days' excursion with
the boys of the Deichmann family, to the Amtsvogt Blume of
Winsen :

"DEAR HERR AMTSVOGT,

"Permit me to offer most heartfelt wishes for your
own and for Frau Blume's happiness on the joyful festival
which you celebrate this month.   The great esteem and love
which I have for you may excuse me for troubling you from
so great a distance, and perhaps at the wrong time, with
these lines; I only know that you celebrate your golden
wedding in the middle of this month.   May God long pre-
serve you in health, that I may often again, as hitherto,
spend many happy hours at your house.   In case you still
feel some interest in my fate, you may, perhaps, be pleased
to hear that I have passed a heavenly summer, such as I
have never before known.   After spending some gloriously
inspiring weeks with Joachim at Göttingen, I have now been
rambling about for five weeks according to heart's desire
on the divine Rhine.   I hope to be able to pass this winter
at Hanover in order to be near Joachim, who is equally noble
as man and artist.   Begging you to remember me most
warmly to your wife and daughter, I would also request you
to express my heartiest greeting to your son with his wife
and children, to dear Uncle Giesemann, and to all acquaintances.   With best greeting, Your JOH. BRAHMS.

"IN THE LAHNTHAL, *Sept.*, 1853."*

Johannes' thoughts were engaged at this time on the
Pianoforte Sonata in F minor, Op. 5, that was finally completed early in November.   Who that has really tasted of
the enchantment of that wonderful composition, great in
spite of its immaturity, can doubt, on reading these lines,
that the shining Rhine with its wooded heights, that Roland-
seck and Nonnenwerth and the Drachenfels, and the deep
blue sky and gorgeous starry nights, had their part, with
the romance and wonder and gratitude and delight dwelling

---

* This letter and another to Amtsvogt Blume, which follows in
Chapter VI, were first published in the *Lüneburger Anzeiger,*
March 29, 1901.

in his young heart, in the making of the work—not, perhaps,
in the sense of supplying the composer with a programme for
his inspiration; but as the sunbeam caught by the plant—as
mingling with his nature and becoming a portion of the
very elemental force that blossomed into the flower of his
imagination?

Yet another important halt was made by Brahms at
Cologne, where two more interesting names were added
to the long list of acquaintances already formed by him
during the short five months of his absence from home. He
delivered a letter from the university music-director of
Göttingen, Arnold Wehner, and a greeting from Wasielewski, to Carl Reinecke at the time professor of pianoforte and
counterpoint in the conservatoire of the Rhenish capital,
and Reinecke, after hearing some of his compositions, conducted him to Ferdinand Hiller's house, and subsequently
accompanied him to the railway-station at Deutz. Here
he took train for Düsseldorf,* full, no doubt, of fluttering
expectation at the thought that he was about to seek an
interview with the great master of his day; sole successor,
since the death of Mendelssohn, to the mighty giants in
whose traditions he had been steeped since early childhood
by Cossel and Marxsen. And as we accompany the young
musician in imagination on this last stage of his Rhine
journey, we may fittingly pay the tribute of passing remembrance to these two men. To their talents and attainments
and character he owed it that he was able to approach the
supreme hour of entrance upon the manhood of his artistic
life, shortly to dawn for him, with the certainty of equipment and devotion of purpose that had already stamped
upon his genius the unmistakable pledge of mastership.

Joachim had neglected no opportunity that had presented
itself since Brahms' departure from Göttingen for furthering
the interests of his new friend. A few days visit to the
Schumanns at the end of August had enabled him to enlarge

---

* " Gedenkblätter an berühmte Musiker," by Carl Reinecke.

to his heart's content to very sympathetic listeners on the
extraordinary gifts of the young musician with whom he
had formed so sudden an intimacy; and thus it came to pass
that whilst Johannes was still engrossed with the pleasures
of his Rhine journey, a welcome to the Schumanns' house
had been secured for him by the most potent influence that
could have been exerted there on his behalf. His first call
on the master recorded in Schumann's diary under date
September 30 in the words "Hr. Brahms from Hamburg,"
seems to have been merely preliminary, but in an entry of
the following day we read: "Visit from Brahms, a genius."
To October 1, therefore, must be referred the incidents related by Dr. Julius Schübring—whose account is supported
by the negative evidence of Schumann's memoranda of the
first week in October, taken together with certain details of
his later correspondence—of the first artistic interview
between the two composers. Schumann desired the young
Brahms to play something of his own composition. Scarcely
was the first movement of the C major Sonata concluded
when the master rose and left the room, and, returning with
his wife, desired to hear it again. And as Johannes had
played it three months previously to the amazement and
delight of Joseph Joachim, so he now played it to the amazement and delight of Robert and Clara Schumann; and when
he had finished one movement these two great artists bade
him play another, and at the end of that, another, and still
desired more, so that when, at length, the performance was
at an end their hearts had gone out to him in affection,
whilst in his the first link had already been forged of that
chain of love by which he soon became bound to the one and
the other till the end of both their lives.

Johannes lost no time in finding out his old friends Louise
and Minna Japha. What wonderful adventures he had to
relate to them, more than could be got through in one or
even two interviews! There was the tour with Reményi,
the performance at Court—how far away these things
seemed!—then the visit to Weimar, the student-life at Göt-

tingen, the journey along the Rhine. He had made the acquaintance of many young musicians, who had one and all welcomed his coming amongst them; he had been introduced to Hiller, become Joachim's closest friend, and now had, he thought, won Schumann's approval. "He patted me on the shoulder," Johannes told Louise, "and said, 'We understand each other.' What did he mean?" Schumann's meaning was made very obvious to Joachim, who received the following note from the master in answer to the introduction and messages of greeting he had sent him by Brahms: "This is he that should come."

To this verdict, delivered but a few days after Brahms' arrival in Düsseldorf, Schumann had been led by the hearing of a number of compositions great and small. The strength of the impression derived by the master from the performance of October 1 is well illustrated by the fact that Johannes was invited to play to him again the next afternoon; and, by the end of a week, Schumann had made acquaintance with as many of his young colleague's completed works as Brahms considered worthy of presentation to him. These included the pianoforte Sonata in F sharp minor, now known as Op. 2; the pianoforte scherzo, Op. 4; a sonata for violin and pianoforte, a trio-fantasia for strings, a string-quartet, and a number of songs; not to mention the arrangements of Hungarian melodies. Of the trio-fantasia Frau Schumann speaks particularly in a memorandum of October 4:

"Brahms played us a fantasia for pianoforte, violin and violoncello and his fine scherzo in E flat minor. Brahms' scherzo is another remarkable, youthfully mild piece, but full of imagination and glorious ideas. Here and there the sound of the instruments was not quite suited to their character, but these are but trifles in comparison with his rich imagination and mind."*

Louise Japha was present on this occasion and preserved a vivid recollection of it. "What shall I play?" asked

---

* Litzmann II, p. 282.

Johannes, crossing the room to her side when Schumann,
after the performance of the trio, again summoned him to
the piano. She suggested the scherzo: "Schumann has
heard your two sonatas; choose something short this time.
Play the scherzo, Schumann has not heard that." She
eventually got a scolding for her pains, however. Johannes,
nervous and excited, persuaded himself that his performance
of the piece was a failure. "Why did you give me that
advice?" he asked, returning to his faithful ally; "Liszt
did not care for the scherzo and now Schumann does not
like it."

We may now turn to the delightful account given by
Albert Dietrich,* one of Schumann's favourite disciples, who
lived at Düsseldorf in daily intercourse with the great composer, of his first acquaintance with the new-comer:

"Soon after Brahms' arrival in September, Schumann
came up to me before the commencement of one of the choral
society practices with mysterious air and pleased smile.
'Someone is come,' said he, 'of whom we shall one day
hear all sorts of wonderful things; his name is Johannes
Brahms.' And he presented to me the interesting and un-
usual-looking young musician, who, seeming hardly more
than a boy in his short gray summer coat, with his high
voice and long fair hair, made a most agreeable impression.
Especially fine were his energetic, characteristic mouth, and
the earnest, deep gaze in which his gifted nature was clearly
revealed."†

Here was another companion of the right sort for Brahms.
He and Albert met daily from this time forward during his
four weeks stay at Düsseldorf, breakfasting together at an
open-air restaurant in the Hofgarten, and sharing each
other's confidences and pleasures. Albert's recognition of
the powers of his new friend was no less thorough than

* "Erinnerungen an Johannes Brahms."

† Examination of the entries in Frau Schumann's diary (Litzmann) shows that the scene at the choral society must have taken
place either on September 30, the date of Brahms' arrival in Düsseldorf, or October 1.

Joachim's had been, and he sent enthusiastic reports of him
to Kirchner, Naumann, and other young musicians of the
Schumann set. Himself a *persona grata* in the various artistic circles of Düsseldorf, he was able to open to Johannes
a new and inexhaustible source of interest. He introduced
him to Schirmer, Lessing, Sohn, and other of the leading
painters, at whose houses the young musician heard much
talk about the sister arts which bore due fruit in a mind
whose first need was, in Joachim's words, "the harmonious
cultivation of its various powers and the loving assimilation
of all sorts of knowledge." A charming young society was
quite ready to welcome a new playfellow—and such a playfellow—into its midst, and Johannes was invited by Albert's
friends to many parties and excursions. He managed to
waive the objection to ladies' society which he had once
found insuperable, and discovered that a festivity from
which they were not rigorously excluded was not therefore
a necessarily tiresome affair! Music in general and his
music in particular, was much in demand at frequent evening
gatherings, and his hearers knew not whether they were
more delighted by his interpretations of the great masters
or of his own compositions.

"Everyone was filled with astonishment," says Dietrich,
"and the young people, especially, were dominated by the
impression of his characteristic, powerful, and, when necessary, extraordinarily tender playing. He used to receive
the enthusiastic praise accorded to his performances in a
modest, deprecatory manner.

"His constitution was thoroughly sound; the most strenuous mental exertion scarcely fatigued him, but then he could
go soundly to sleep at any hour of the day he pleased. With
companions of his own standing he was lively, sometimes
arrogant, dry, and full of pranks. When he came to see
me, he used to rush up the stairs, thump on the door with
both fists, and burst in without waiting for an answer. . . .
Brahms never spoke of the works with which he was busy,
or of his plans for future compositions, but he told me one
day that he often recalled folk-songs when at work, and
that then his melodies suggested themselves spontaneously."

At the Schumanns' house Brahms learned chess and table-turning. He was soon made free of the master's library, and borrowed from it many a book to lend to the Japhas, who had to submit to a term of quarantine during Minna's recovery from an attack of measles. Johannes refused, for his own part, to acquiesce in the decree, and paid long daily visits to the sisters as soon as they were able to receive him. He often sat at Louise's side reading with her from an open volume placed between them, as he had once been used to do with Lischen in the Winsen fields. One day he brought some volumes of Hoffmann, to re-read his favourite tales from Schumann's own copy. He carried the old memories and friends, and the simple home with its dear affections, faithfully in his heart throughout his excitements and successes, and throughout the weeks and months of his absence Johanna kept her promise to her boy. "Look," said Hannes one day, pulling a letter out of his pocket, and holding it open before Louise and Minna as he told them of the stipulation he had made, "I get one like this every week; my old mother keeps her promise. Some of it is copied from the newspapers; what is she to do when she has no more news? she cannot write a philosophical treatise, but she always sends me three whole pages."*

The passionate admiration quickly conceived by Brahms for the character and genius of Schumann, which was intensified by the recollection of his past misconception of the great composer's art, was returned in appropriate measure. Schumann became every day fonder of his young friend, and inclination united with conviction to strengthen the strong first impression he had received as to the extraordinary nature of his gifts. "Princeps" is written in one of Schumann's pocket-books against the name Johannes Brahms, added, in the master's handwriting, to a list of his favourite young musicians. It has sometimes been sug-

---

* At this period envelopes were not in universal use. The large "letter-paper" was folded and sealed, and addressed on the blank fourth page.

gested that the secret of the immediate fascination exercised over him by Brahms' compositions lay in his perception of their dissimilarity from his own. This, however, is only part of the truth. Though it be the case that Schumann's influence is not traceable either in the melody, harmony, or structure of Brahms' first published movements, it is equally the fact that the "delicate youth with dreamy expression, who, without a tinge of affectation, spoke naturally in poetic phrases; who signed his manuscripts 'Joh. Kreisler jun.'; who exactly answered Joachim's description, 'pure as the diamond, tender as snow'";[*] had elements in his many-sided nature of near kin to the characteristic spirit of Schumann's genius, which were by no means without influence on the individuality of his works, and especially the works of his first period. Schumann, astonished beyond measure by the mastery and originality of Brahms' technical attainment, was, in regard to his ideal qualities, certainly penetrated as much by the romance as by the independence, by the tenderness as by the power, by the subjective, as by the objective side, of his art, and the elder musician loved the younger as much because of the affinity as of the difference between them. Both contrasting sides of Brahms' nature are strikingly manifest in the very beautiful drawing of him which was executed for Schumann at this time by the painter de Laurens, a representation of which we are enabled by the kindness of Frau Professor Böie, to whom the original belonged, to place before the reader as one of our illustrations.

Schumann had not been forgetful of the overtures to closer intimacy made to him by Joachim in the spring of the year, and composed two concert-pieces for violin and orchestra about this time, during the writing of which the famous young violinist and his performances at the Düsseldorf festival were constantly present to his mind. In

---

[*] Ehrlich, "Dreissig Jahre Künstlerleben."

a letter to Hanover concerning these and other matters, written by him on October 8, the following passages occur : *

"I think if I were younger I could make some polymetres about the young eagle who has so suddenly and unexpectedly flown down from the Alps to Düsseldorf. Or one might compare him to a splendid stream which, like Niagara, is at its finest when precipitating itself from the heights as a roaring waterfall, met on the shore by the fluttering of butterflies and by nightingales' voices. . . .

"The young eagle seems to be content in the Lowlands; he has found an old guardian who is accustomed to watch such young flights, and who knows how to calm the wild wing-flapping without detriment to the soaring power."†

On the same day he wrote to Dr. Härtel, head of the great Leipzig publishing firm :

"A young man has just presented himself here who has most deeply impressed us with his wonderful music. He will, I am convinced, make the greatest sensation in the musical world. I will take an opportunity of writing more in detail about him."‡

Five days later, writing again on business to Joachim, who was to take part on the 27th, in the first Düsseldorf subscription concert of the season, he adds :

"I have begun to put together my thoughts about the young eagle. I should wish to help him on his first flight through the world, but fear I have grown too fond of him to be able to describe the light and dark colours of his wings quite clearly. When I have finished the paper, I should like to show it to his comrade [Joachim], who knows him even better than I do."

A postscript is subjoined : "I have finished the essay and enclose it. Please return it as soon as possible."

---

* "Robert Schumann's Briefe." Neue Folge. Edited by Gustav Jansen.

† The movements of the F minor Sonata were no doubt submitted to Schumann's criticism during the process of their composition.

‡ See, for this and other letters of Schumann, Dr. Jansen's collection referred to above.

REPRODUCTION OF BRAHMS' FIRST LETTER TO BREITKOPF & HÄRTEL, DATED THE 8TH NOVEMBER, 1853.

Zeilen entschuldigen, falls Ihnen der
Inhalt nicht willkommen ist

In erwartungsvoller Ergebenheit

Hannover d. 1ᵗ Nov 1853

Johs Brahms

Papenstieg N° 4, vor dem Friedrichst.)

A second letter to Dr. Härtel enters into some of the promised detail:

"You will see before long, in the *Neue Zeitschrift für Musik*, an article signed with my name on young Johannes Brahms from Hamburg, which will give you further information about him. I will then write to you more fully about the compositions he intends to publish. They are pianoforte pieces and sonatas, a sonata for violin and piano, a trio, a quartet, and a number of songs—all full of genius. He is also an exceptional pianist."

On the 14th of the month the Schumanns were pleasantly surprised by another visit from Joachim. The popular young concertmeister had been spending his time pleasantly enough during the progress of the events just related. After taking part in a festival at Carlsruhe, where he met his Weimar friends Liszt, Pruckner, Cornelius, Bülow, and the others, in full force, he had gone on to Basel with Liszt and some of the younger members of the party to be introduced to Wagner and pass a couple of days in his society, and was now returning to the duties of his post in Hanover. A day remained to be spent with his friends in Düsseldorf, part of which was, of course, devoted to the delights of music-making, and the short reunion was followed by a result of some permanent interest to the musical world. As Joachim was to come back to take part in the Düsseldorf subscription concert of the 27th, Schumann proposed to Dietrich and Brahms that a surprise should be prepared for his return in the shape of a sonata for pianoforte and violin to be written by the three of them jointly. Thereupon Albert undertook the first movement, Johannes the scherzo, and the master himself the intermezzo and finale. The work was duly completed within the ten days available for its composition; and its presentation, postponed until the more serious business of the concert should have been disposed of, took place on October 28 in the presence of the group of interested musicians and of Frau von Arnim (the Bettina Brentano of Goethe and Beethoven fame) and her daughter Gisela, a young lady much admired by Joachim. At an appointed moment Gisela, charmingly attired in rustic costume, stepped forward and handed a large basket of flowers to the hero of the occasion. Hidden beneath blossoms and foliage was the manuscript sonata of welcome, on the title-page of which Schumann had written:

"F. A. E.*

"In expectation of the arrival of their honoured and beloved friend,

"JOSEPH JOACHIM,

"This sonata was written by Robert Schumann, Johannes Brahms, Albert Dietrich."

The sonata was performed at an evening party at the Schumann's house, which followed the presentation, and Joachim was required to guess the authorship of the several movements, a problem he had no difficulty in solving correctly. The work remained in manuscript in his possession until the autumn of 1906, when he sanctioned the publication of the scherzo—the movement contributed by Brahms—by the German Brahms Society.†

The concert of the following day was the last given in Düsseldorf under the direction of Schumann, who was about to start with his wife on a concert tour in Holland. He was at this time seriously contemplating a permanent removal to Vienna, whence he had received overtures that were attractive to himself and Frau Schumann. Whether he would have made up his mind to the step cannot be determined. The decision was, as we know, taken out of his hands by one of the tragedies of fate.

---

* "Frei aber einsam" (free but lonely), Joachim's favourite device at this time.

† The complete sonata was published in 1938, and the first performance in England was broadcast on July 30 of that year.—R. H.

CHAPTER V.

1853.

SCHUMANN'S article appeared on October 28 in the *Neue Zeitschrift für Musik*. Brahms seems to have read it for the first time, however, in Hanover, whither, in pursuance of the plans formed in the summer with Joachim, he followed his friend on the evening of November 2. Its contents were so unexpected, and their influence on Brahms' career was so far-reaching, that, though it may already be familiar to many readers, it seems right to quote it *in extenso*.

" NEW PATHS.

" Years have passed—almost as many in number as those dedicated by me to the previous editorship of this journal, namely, ten—since I appeared on this scene so rich to me in remembrances. Often, in spite of arduous productive activity, I have felt tempted; many new and considerable talents have appeared, a fresh musical energy has seemed to announce itself through many of the earnest artists of the present time,* even though their works are, for the most part,

---

* " I have here in my mind Joseph Joachim, Ernst Naumann, Ludwig Norman, Woldemar Bargiel, Theodor Kirchner, Julius Schäffer, Albert Dietrich, not forgetting the earnest-minded E. F. Wilsing. As trusty heralds in the right path, Niels W. Gade, C. F. Mangold, Robert Franz, and St. Heller, should also be named here."

known to a limited circle only. I have thought, watching the path of these chosen ones with the greatest sympathy, that after such a preparation someone must and would suddenly appear, destined to give ideal presentment to the highest expression of the time, who would bring us his mastership, not in process of development, but would spring forth like Minerva fully armed from the head of Jove. And he is come, a young blood by whose cradle graces and heroes kept watch. He is called Johannes Brahms, came from Hamburg, where he has worked in obscure tranquillity, trained in the most difficult laws of art, by an excellent and enthusiastic teacher, and was lately introduced to me by an honoured, well-known master.* He bore all the outward signs that proclaim to us, 'This is one of the elect.' Sitting at the piano, he proceeded to reveal to us wondrous regions. We were drawn into circles of ever deeper enchantment. His playing, too, was full of genius, and transformed the piano into an orchestra of wailing and jubilant voices. There were sonatas, more veiled symphonies—songs, whose poetry one would understand without knowing the words, though all are pervaded by a deep song-melody—single pianoforte pieces, partly demoniacal, of the most graceful form—then sonatas for violin and piano—quartets for strings—and every one so different from the rest that each seemed to flow from a separate source. And then it was as though he, like a tumultuous stream, united all into a waterfall, bearing a peaceful rainbow over the rushing waves, met on the shore by butterflies' fluttering, and accompanied by nightingales' voices.

"If he will sink his magic staff in the region where the capacity of masses in chorus and orchestra can lend him its powers, still more wonderful glimpses into the mysteries of the spirit-world will be before us. May the highest genius strengthen him for this, of which there is the prospect, since another genius, that of modesty, also dwells within him. His companions greet him on his first course through the world, where, perhaps, wounds may await him, but laurels and palms also; we bid him welcome as a strong champion.

"There is in all times a secret union of kindred spirits. Bind closer the circle, ye who belong to it, that the truth of art may shine ever clearer, spreading joy and blessing through the world.   "R. S."

---

* Joachim.

Such was the proclamation by which Schumann, carried away by the impulsive generosity of his nature, designed to facilitate the entrance into the jealous musical world of the composer of twenty, whose gifts had not been tested by the publication of a single composition, whose name was hardly known to rumour.

"It is doubtful," says Mason, "if, up to that time, any article had made such a sensation through musical Germany. I remember how utterly the Liszt circle in Weimar were astounded at it. It was at first, no doubt, an obstacle in Brahms' way, but, as it resulted in stirring up great rivalry between two opposing parties, it eventually contributed much to his final success."

In sober truth, Brahms' worst enemy could scarcely have weighted him with a heavier mantle of immediate difficulty. It made his name an easy subject of ridicule to those who would in any case have been inclined to regard a new-comer with incredulity; it drew upon him the sceptical attention of others who might have been prepared to receive him with indifference or indulgence; it was calculated to awaken extravagant expectations in the minds of some whom it disposed to be his friends.

The musical world generally, adopted an attitude of hostile expectancy, and this was shared especially by the "Murls,"* as the young satellites of Liszt styled themselves. Their "Padisha," Liszt himself, could afford to be more or less indifferent, though he was not unobservant. "Avez-vous lu l'article de Schumann dans le dernier numéro de Brendel?" he says, writing on November 1 to Bülow, who replies on the 5th, alluding to supposed Brahms resemblances: "Mozart-Brahms ou Schumann-Brahms ne trouble point du tout la tranquillité de mon sommeil. Il y a une quinzaine d'années que Schumann a parlé en des termes tout-à-fait analogues du génie de W. Sterndale Bennett. Joachim, du reste, connaît Brahms, de même l'ingermanique Reményi."

---

* Anti-philistines.

What Brahms' own feelings were on reading the paper cannot be difficult of conjecture. Joy and bewilderment, gratitude and dismay, must have struggled within him for mastery. The steady sense of proportion which was one of his lifelong characteristics, the consciousness of the almost crushing weight of artistic responsibility thus thrust upon him at the outset of his career, must have conflicted severely with his natural loyalty and his delight at having won from Schumann such an overflowing measure of approval. To a man of weaker moral fibre, the temptation to overmuch exaltation or undue depression might have proved more than perilous. Brahms, however, was made of stuff that enabled him to face the situation, to accept it, and finally to triumph over it, and the means which he used are the only means that can enable even genius to win the kind of victory that he obtained. They were unswerving loyalty and single-hearted devotion to an exalted purpose.

The matter of the selection of works to be submitted for the approval of the publishers was much discussed both before and after the departure of Joachim and Johannes from Düsseldorf, with the result that Schumann wrote on November 3, to Dr. Härtel, and proposed for publication; as Op. 1, String Quartet; 2, Set of six Songs; 3, Pianoforte Scherzo; 4, Second set of six Songs; 5, Pianoforte Sonata in C major. He hoped, he said, to arrive at an understanding by which, whilst the young composer would derive an immediate pecuniary advantage, the publishers would not run too much risk, and he suggested that if the sale of the works should, after five years, have realized expectations, Brahms should then receive further proportionate remuneration. He proposed as first payments; ten Louis-d'ors (about £9 10s.) each, for the quartet and sonata, eight Louis-d'ors (about £7 12s.) for the scherzo, six (£5 14s.) for each of the two sets of songs—in all about £38. Should these proposals meet Dr. Härtel's views, he would put Brahms into direct communication with him in order that the works might be submitted for his consideration.

"He is an intimate of Joachim's in Hanover, where he proposes to spend the winter. Joachim has written an extremely fine overture to Hamlet, and an equally original and effective concerto for violin and orchestra, which I can recommend to you with the warmest sympathy."[*]

Schumann's kindness did not stop here. He sent a sympathetic note to Jakob Brahms at home in Hamburg, tidings of which, and of the rejoicing family circle, just established in a new dwelling at No. 7 Lilienstrasse, were forwarded by the father to the young musician at Hanover. Dr. Härtel did not delay in sending word that he would be glad to see the manuscripts, for on November 9, Schumann wrote him a letter of thanks for his favourable reply, and added:

"I will write to-day to Brahms, and beg him to go as soon as possible to Leipzig to introduce his compositions to you himself. His playing belongs essentially to his music. I do not remember to have heard such original tone effects before."

Dr. Härtel's note was forwarded to Hanover by Schumann in a letter to Joachim with the words: "Give the enclosed to Johannes. He must go to Leipzig; persuade him to do this, or they will get a wrong idea of his works; he must play them himself. This seems to me very important." After relating the arrangements pending with the publisher, he adds: "Once again, pray urge him to go to Leipzig for a week"; and concludes: "Now good-bye, dear friend. Write again before our Dutch journey, and tell Johannes, the lazy-bones, to do the same."

Johannes had, in fact, not written to Schumann since leaving Düsseldorf, and he still waited, letting nearly three weeks go by before thanking the master for his article in the *Neue Zeitschrift*. Perhaps this fact may be regarded as confirmation of the surmise that he had not read Schumann's prophetic announcement with feelings of unmixed satisfaction, but if it be so, he allowed no other

---

[*] "Robert Schumann's Briefe." Neue Folge. Edited by Gustav Jansen.

sign to appear of such a possibility. He very anxiously reconsidered his choice of works for publication, however, and before receiving Härtel's letter to Schumann, had forwarded to Leipzig a somewhat different selection from that decided on at Düsseldorf, withholding from it the string quartet. Having settled this matter as far as he could to his satisfaction, and brought himself to consent to Joachim's persuasions that he should go to Leipzig for a week, his attitude to Schumann remained one of unmixed gratitude and affection, as may be read in the following letter : *

"HONOURED MASTER,

"You have made me so immensely happy that I cannot attempt to thank you in words. God grant that my works may soon prove to you how much your affection and kindness have encouraged and stimulated me. The public praise you have bestowed on me will have fastened general expectation so exceptionally upon my performances that I do not know how I shall be able to do some measure of justice to it. Above all it obliges me to take the greatest care in the selection of what is to be published. I do not propose to include either of my trios, and think of choosing as Op. 1 and 2 the Sonatas in C and F sharp minor, as Op. 3 Songs, and as Op. 4 the Scherzo in E flat minor. You will think it natural that I should try with all my might to disgrace you as little as possible.

"I put off writing to you so long because I had sent the four things I have mentioned to Breitkopf and Härtel, and wished to wait for the answer, to be able to tell you the result of your recommendation. Your last letter to Joachim, however, informs us of this, and so I have only to write to you that I shall go, as you advise, within the next few days (probably to-morrow) to Leipzig.

"Further I wish to tell you that I have copied out my F minor Sonata, and made considerable alterations in the finale. I have also improved the violin sonata. I should like also to thank you a thousand times for the dear portrait

---

* The letters in this and the following chapters from Brahms to Schumann were first published by La Mara in the *Neue Freie Presse* of May 7, 1897.

of yourself that you have sent me, as well as for the letter
you have written to my father.   By it you have made a pair
of good people happy, and for life Your

" Brahms.

"Hanover, 16 Nov., 1853."

The reader may have noted that the work chosen by
Brahms with which to introduce himself, not only to
Joachim, but to the Deichmann circle, to Wasielewski, and
to Schumann himself, was the C major Sonata now known
as Op. 1; and the natural inference to be drawn, that he
considered it his best as it was his latest achievement, is
confirmed by his reply to Louise Japha when she asked him,
later on, why he had numbered his scherzo, a much earlier
work, as Op. 4.   "When one first shows one's self," he
said, "it is to the head and not the heels that one wishes to
draw attention."

That the composer was not mistaken, if we may thus take
his own estimate of his published works by implication, may
be safely affirmed.   Sharing the fundamental characteristics,
technical as well as temperamental, of the earlier written
work of the same form—unity of plan, wealth of resource,
impetuous vigour, dreamy romance, a breath that is repeatedly suggestive of the folk-lore in which the composer loved
to steep his imagination—the Sonata in C gives evidence
that the process of crystallization had already begun which
was to distinguish Brahms' development towards maturity,
which, indeed, did not stop at maturity, but may be traced
continuously down to the close of his career.   This process
is to be observed, as regards the work in question, in the
themes of the principal movements, which are not only more
pregnant in themselves, but are presented in more concentrated form than those of the Sonata in F sharp minor.
That the first theme of the opening movement bears traces
of the composer's study of Beethoven's Sonata in B flat,
Op. 106, is of no great consequence.   The question of
musical reminiscence is so frequently misunderstood that
it may be well to devote a few words to it on the threshold

of our narrative of Brahms' career as a composer, which
will take but little account of such occasional examples as.
may easily be found in his works—in the opening bars of
the scherzo of Op. 5, the second subject of the first allegro
of Op. 73, and so forth. No one would affirm that reminiscences are in themselves desirable, but they are almost
inevitable, and the important question is, not whether this
or that rhythmical figure, this or that passing melodic progression, may be found anticipated in some earlier work,
but whether it has been so used the second time as to have
become an integral part of a composition with a distinct
individuality of its own. The parentage of Brahms' sonata
Op. 1, as, indeed, of every work published by him, is.
loudly proclaimed by each one of its pages. The opinion
entertained by our composer, when in his maturity, of the
self-satisfied reminiscence-hunter, is well illustrated by his.
reply to a conceited acquaintance who was courageous.
enough, on an occasion late in the seventies, to draw his
attention to a transient resemblance in one of his great
works to a passage of Mendelssohn. "Some booby has.
already been telling me something of the kind" (So was
hab'ich schon von einem Rindvieh gehört), he answered.
"Such things are always discovered by the donkeys," he
said one day to a friend.

That the C major Sonata has been heard more frequently
than that numbered as Op. 2, and is still occasionally to be
found in a concert-programme, may be accepted both as
evidence and result of its advance upon the Sonata in F
sharp minor. The step from the C major to the F minor
Op. 5, is, however, more remarkable. In this work we find
not only that the "wild wing-flapping" of which Schumann wrote has been calmed by the faithful guardian with
strange increase of certainty and endurance to the soaring
power, but that the composer's advancing recognition of the
value of restraint has also strengthened the exceptional skill
in the treatment of form manifest in his earlier compositions.
In the quality of its ideas, the sonata is consistently roman-

tic. It has, indeed, but few rivals amongst works of musical art in its successful presentation of pure romanticism within the limits of classic form, and hence it possesses a peculiar interest, apart from that of its intrinsic beauty; as being illustrative no less of the young Brahms' participation in the spirit of his own time than of his reverence for the achievements of past generations.

In spite of its defects of immaturity and of the difficulties it presents both to listener and performer, the Sonata in F minor, which was a favourite with von Bülow, has grown very gradually into some measure of general acceptance, and it seems not impossible that it may some day be heard frequently in the concert room. Brahms played it in practically finished shape to Schumann and his wife when he called to take leave of them before his departure for Hanover on November 2. It is the only one of his extant works which was submitted to Schumann's criticism before final completion. In consequence of a mischance presently to be related, the violin sonata referred to in the letter quoted above and played at Göttingen by Brahms and Reményi, was never published.*

Amongst the young Schumannites who had been roused by Joachim's and Dietrich's accounts of Brahms to an extreme expectation, which had not been lessened by the appearance of Schumann's essay, was one Heinrich von Sahr, a musician from choice rather than necessity, who lived at Leipzig in the intimacy of the notabilities of its artistic circle. He had written in October to Dietrich:

---

* Schumann's memorandum of October 12: "Industrious. Music at home in the afternoon. F minor Sonata. Brahms played particularly well"—refers to his own Sonata in F minor.

This is made clear by Frau Clara's entry of the same date: "We had music at home in the afternoon. First I played Robert's F minor sonata, then Brahms' scherzo, then Robert's trio with Becker and Bockmühl"; which evidently means that Clara played her husband's two works and Brahms his own scherzo.

Compare Litzmann, pp. 280 and 283.

"Send me your real opinion of Brahms. I am dreadfully anxious to know him. . . . What is he like personally? Ah, write! do please write soon and tell me what you think of him. Is he still in Düsseldorf? What is his music like? What has he composed?"

Von Sahr was the first person in Leipzig to make Brahms' acquaintance. Carrying him off to his rooms the morning after his arrival, he insisted that Johannes should stay on as his guest, and constituted himself the guide of his new friend's immediate movements. He took him to call on his publisher, Dr. Härtel; on Julius Rietz, the conductor, and David, the celebrated concertmeister, of the Gewandhaus concerts; on Moscheles and Wenzel, Schumann's particular friends; Friedrich and Marie Wieck, Frau Schumann's father and sister; Julius Otto Grimm, a young musician whose room was on the same staircase as his own and who soon came to be numbered among Johannes' special friends; and introduced him, generally speaking, to the entire Leipzig circle. So rapid were the events of the next few days, that Johannes, who arrived in Leipzig on the evening of Thursday, November 17, was able to announce to Joachim the following Sunday that he had performed his C major Sonata and E flat minor Scherzo at Dr. Härtel's one day, played his violin sonata with David another; had been pressed to take part in a Gewandhaus chamber music concert, and invited by a second publisher, Senff, to send him any compositions he cared to dispose of.

"He is perfect," exclaims von Sahr in a letter to Albert Dietrich; "the days since he has been here are amongst the most delightful in my recollection. He answers so exactly to my idea of an artist. And as a man!—But enough, you know him better than I do. . . . Unfortunately, he can only stay till Friday. He has, however, promised, and I think he will keep his promise, to come again soon."

Important considerations had determined Johannes to return to Hanover for a few days at the end of his first week in Leipzig. He was anxious, in the first place, to make

himself quite certain, by means of a personal consultation
with Joseph, as to the propriety of certain dedications that
he desired to place on the title pages of his compositions.
He wished, also, to have his friend's opinion on the details
of some further desirable alterations in the F minor Sonata
which he proposed sending, together with a book of songs,
to Senff.   As it proved that the revision could not be completed immediately, it was agreed between the two young
musicians that the violin sonata should be despatched for
publication in the meantime.   This work was, however,
declined by Senff on the ground that it was against his rule
to publish compositions for violin and that he preferred to
wait for the sonata for pianoforte solo.

A letter written by Johannes early in December to inform
Schumann of his arrangements gives lively expression to
the satisfaction felt by him at the extraordinary turn in his
affairs.   The style of the address is in allusion to the brilliant success achieved by the master and his wife during their
concert journey in Holland.

" MYNHEER DOMINE,

"Forgive him, whom you have made so boundlessly
glad and happy, for the jesting address.   I have only the
best and most satisfactory news to relate.

"To your warm recommendation I owe my reception in
Leipzig, friendly beyond all expectation, and especially
beyond all desert.   Härtels declared themselves ready, with
great pleasure, to print my first attempts.   They are these:
Op. 1, Sonata in C major; Op. 2, Sonata in F sharp minor;
Op. 3, Songs; Op. 4, Scherzo in E flat minor.

"I delivered to Herr Senff for publication: Op. 5, Sonata
in A minor for Violin and Pianoforte; Op. 6, six Songs.

"May I venture to place Frau Schumann's name upon the
title-page of my second work?   I scarcely dare to do so,
and yet I should like so much to offer you a little token of
my respect and gratitude.

"I shall probably receive copies of my first things before
Christmas.   With what feelings shall I then see my parents
again after nearly a year's absence.   I cannot describe what
is in my heart when I think of it.

"May you never regret what you have done for me, may I become really worthy of you. Your

"JOH. BRAHMS."

The opening of December found the musical circles of Leipzig in a condition of unusual flutter and excitement. Berlioz had arrived from Paris; Liszt, supported by a body of his "Murls" from Weimar, on an occasion that was of considerable importance to the New-German party. Berlioz had, for the second time, been invited to conduct a selection of his works within the precincts of the classical Gewandhaus, and the second part of the subscription concert of December 1, was to be devoted to the following compositions: "The Flight into Egypt," "Harold in Italy," "The Young Shepherd of Brittany," the fairy Scherzo from "Romeo and Juliet," selections from "Faust," and the overture to the "Carnaval Romain." Brahms returned in time to be present with his friends on the occasion; which was made lively by the demonstrations and counter-demonstrations of two conflicting parties in the audience, but seems to have resulted as satisfactorily for the Weimarites as they could reasonably have expected. Brahms and his messiahship were discussed, and none too gently handled, at a supper-party at which Berlioz, Liszt, Gouvy, and others of their set, met after the concert, but the hostile attitude adopted towards the young musician was not enduring. The personal animus which Schumann's essay had aroused against him was generally disarmed, as he became known in Leipzig, by the attraction of his unassuming manner—the more speedily, perhaps, because it was felt that his modesty rested upon an underlying feeling of confidence in himself and his purpose. He at once showed his indifference to party jealousies, and ran some risk of offending his companions, by calling on Liszt, who, with Berlioz, Raff, Laub, Reményi, and others, was staying at the Hôtel de Bavière, and it will presently be shown that Liszt, who promptly returned the visit, reconsidered his

position to the young musician towards whom public attention had been so suddenly and strikingly directed.

Johannes presented himself on the Sunday (December 4)
following the Gewandhaus concert at two houses always
open to visitors on the first day of the week, into both of
which we are enabled to penetrate by means of detailed
accounts written immediately after the occurrences they
describe. One is contained in a volume by Helene von
Vesque;* the other in an "open letter" written by Arnold
Schloenbach to the editor Brendel, for publication in the
Neue Zeitschrift für Musik of December 9, 1853.

Hedwig, younger daughter of the wealthy house of
Salamon, was not only possessed of literary and artistic
talents, but of a magnetic personality which enabled her
to form many distinguished friendships. She was long
intimate with the families of Mendelssohn, Schumann,
Schleinitz, Hauptmann, and other leaders of musical Leipzig, knew Joachim as a boy, and was for some time looked
upon by her circle as the probable future wife of the Danish
composer, Niels Gade. At the time of which we write she
had nearly completed her thirty-second year, but her
marriage with the composer Franz von Holstein did not
take place until nearly two years later. The extracts from
her diaries and letters contained in Helene von Vesque's
book include several of interest to musical readers. Of
young Brahms she says:

"Yesterday Herr von Sahr brought me a young man who
held in his hand a letter from Joachim. He sat down opposite me, this young hero of the day, this young messiah of
Schumann's, fair, delicate-looking, who, at twenty, has
clearly-cut features free from all passion. Purity, innocence,
naturalness, power, and depth—this indicates his being.
One is so inclined to think him ridiculous and to judge him
harshly on account of Schumann's prophecy; but all is forgotten; one only loves and admires him. In the evening

---

* "Eine Glückliche. Hedwig von Holstein in ihren Briefen und
Tagebuchblättern."

he came to a small party at Elizabeth's [Hedwig's sister,
Frau von Seebach]. . . . He placed himself at a little table
near me, and spoke so brightly and continuously that his
friends at the other table could not be surprised enough, for
he is generally extremely quiet and dreamy. We had plenty
of points in common: Joachim, the Wehners, our mutual
favourite poets, Jean Paul and Eichendorf, and his, Hoffmann and Schiller. . . . He vehemently urged me to read
'Kabale und Liebe' and the 'Serapionsbrüder,' but above
all Hoffmann's musical novels, of which he spoke with real
enthusiasm. 'I spend all my money on books; books are
my greatest pleasure. I have read as much as I possibly
could since I was quite little, and have made my way without guidance from the worst to the best. I devoured innumerable romances of chivalry as a child until the "Robbers"
fell into my hands. I did not know that it had been written
by a great poet. I asked for something more by the same
Schiller, however, and so made gradual progress.' He
speaks in the same fresh way of music, and when I said to
him, 'You will not care so much about music when you have
a post as music-director or professor,' he answered smiling,
but quite decidedly: 'Yes; I shall not take a post.'

"And with all this independent strength, a thin boy's
voice that has not yet changed! and a child's countenance
that any girl might kiss without blushing. And the purity
and firmness of his whole being, which guarantee that the
spoiled world will not be able to overcome this man; for, as
he has been able to bear his elevation from obscurity to the
perilous position of an idol without losing any of his
modesty, or even his naïveté, so God who created such a
beautiful nature will continue to help him!"

Schloenbach's "open letter" is written in too inflated a
style to deserve a lengthy quotation, but one or two extracts
may be welcome as describing our composer's first semi-
public appearance in Leipzig. Franz Brendel's "at home"
on the particular Sunday in question was a more than usually brilliant function. "Composers, teachers, virtuosi,
lyric and dramatic poets, romancists, booksellers, critics
and journalists—even preachers—clever, artistic women,
charming girls," were gathered in the editor's reception-
rooms, and one artist after another performed for the edifi-

cation of the distinguished audience. A harp solo executed by Jeanette Paul, and rewarded by a double handshake from Berlioz; one on the pianoforte by Krause; a number of vocal contributions by the great tenor Götze—songs by Schumann and Wagner, and, in association with the accomplished amateur and Wagner enthusiast, Frau Lily Steche, the famous "Lohengrin" duet—formed the earlier part of the impromptu programme.

"The last performance of all was of special interest. Following maturity came immaturity, but immaturity of rare endowment and rich promise; immaturity already considerably defined, because possessed of individual power and true originality. We listened now to the young Brahms from Hamburg, referred to the other day in Schumann's article in your journal. The article had, as you know, awakened mistrust in numerous circles (perhaps in many cases only from fear). At all events it had created a very difficult situation for the young man, for its justification required the fulfilment of great demands; and when the slender, fair youth appeared, so deficient in presence, so shy, so modest, his voice still in transitional falsetto, few could have suspected the genius that had already created so rich a world in this young nature. Berlioz had, however, already discovered in his profile a striking likeness to Schiller, and conjectured his possession of a kindred virgin soul, and when the young genius unfolded his wings, when, with extraordinary facility, with inward and outward energy, he presented his scherzo, flashing, rushing, sparkling; when, afterwards, his andante swelled towards us in intimate, mournful tones, we all felt : Yes, here is a true genius, and Schumann was right; and when Berlioz, deeply moved, embraced the young man and pressed him to his heart, then, dear friend, I felt myself affected by such a sacred tremour of enthusiasm as I have seldom experienced. . . . If you should smile now and then whilst reading my letter, remember that it is the poet who has spoken, and that it was yourself who invited him to do so.

"LEIPZIG,"
    December 5, 1853.

It must not be forgotten, in connection with these effusive lines, that the party circumstances of the time and the excitement caused by Schumann's article made Brahms' appearance amongst the guests of Brendel, who had identified himself with the New-Germans, an event of importance, to be regretted by the younger and more excitable of the Leipzigers, and welcomed by the Weimarites. It no doubt contributed to the satisfaction expressed by Liszt, in a letter to Bülow, on his return to Weimar after a second appearance of Berlioz in Leipzig, and the sympathetic tone of this communication clearly shows that the motive of policy which dictated it was supported by a more personal feeling of approbation. He says on December 14:

"Je viens de passer quelques jours à Leipzig, où j'ai assisté aux deux concerts de Berlioz le 1ᵉʳ et le 11 de ce mois. Le resultat d'opinion à été en somme très favorable à Berlioz."

And two days later:

"Écrivez-moi de Hanovre, où vous ferez bien de passer une quinzaine de jours. Vous y trouverez Brahms auquel je m'intéresse sincèrement et qui s'est conduit avec tact et bon goût envers moi durant les quelques jours que je viens de passer à Leipzig en l'honneur de Berlioz. Aussi l'ai-je invité plusieurs fois à dîner et me plais à croire que ses 'Neue Bahnen' (New Paths) le rapprocheront davantage de Weimar par la suite. Vous serez content de la Sonate en Ut dont j'ai parcouru les épreuves à Leipzig et qu'il m'avait déjà montré ici. C'est précisément celui de ses ouvrages qui m'avait donné la meilleure idée de son talent de composition. Mille et mille tendres amitiés à Joachim, auquel j'ai fait demander sa partition de l'ouverture de Hamlet par Brahms et par Cossmann. Rappelez-lui que je désire beaucoup la faire exécuter à la prochaine représentation et la maintenir pour les représentations subséquentes."*

Brahms allowed himself to be persuaded, in spite of some inward trepidation, to make his first public appearance in Leipzig at one of the David Quartet Concerts, which took place regularly in the small hall of the Gewandhaus. The

---

* "Liszt's Briefe." Edited by La Mara.

programme of the occasion consisted of Mendelssohn's D
major Quartet, Brahms' C major Sonata and E flat minor
Scherzo, and Mozart's G minor Quintet. The reception of
the new works by the audience was not discouraging, in
spite of the absence from them of the qualities that go to
the making of an immediate popular success, and most of
the critics treated the composer sympathetically. Some of
them, not content with writing about his music, discussed
his appearance, and one described his "Raphael head."

"In the second Quartet concert, which took place on
December 17," says "Hoplit" [Dr. Richard Pohl, a writer
in the interests of the Weimar school, who was on the staff
of the *Neue Zeitschrift*], "Johannes Brahms presented himself to the public with his Sonata in C major and his Scherzo.
Schumann's article caused much division amongst the un-
initiated, but all doubt has been dispelled by Brahms' public
appearance, and we concur with all our heart, and with the
warmest satisfaction, in Schumann's opinion of the unassuming and richly-endowed young artist. There is something
forcible, something transporting, in the works which Brahms
performed the other evening. A ripeness rare in one so
young, a creative power springing spontaneously from a rich
artist-mind, are revealed in them. We find ourselves in the
presence of one of those highly-gifted natures, an artist by
the grace of God. Some roughnesses and angularities in the
outward, very independent form of Brahms' compositions
may be overlooked for the sake of the imposing beauty of
their artistic aim. His modulations are often of striking
effect; they are frequently surprising, but always fine and
artistically justifiable. Brahms' spirit is in affinity with the
genius of Schumann. He will, advancing steadfastly and
safely along his 'new paths,' some day become what
Schumann has predicted of him, an epoch-making figure in
the history of art.'

Stress was laid by the orthodox *Signale* on the originality
and freshness of the composer's invention, on the significance of his thematic material, and on his eminent gift for
presenting his ideas in varied and interesting forms. His
facility in unexpected modulations was noted, but, by this

critic, not always approved. With regard to the performance, "much appeared more difficult to the executant than to the creator, for the sonata is very hard to play, and Brahms is a better composer than virtuoso."

Brahms quitted Leipzig on the 20th in the company of Grimm, who had business to transact at Hanover. The intimacy that had sprung up between the two young men was to endure as a life-long friendship, and a treasured memorial of this period of its commencement is in the possession of Fräulein Marie Grimm—Brahms' manuscript of the set of songs, Op. 6, as arranged for publication with the inscription on the title-page: "To my dear Julius in remembrance of Kreisler, jun., 8 Dec., 1853."

Plans made by Johannes to spend a day or two in Hanover fell through, and towards evening on the day of his departure from Leipzig he was in his parents' arms.

It is not difficult to imagine something of the mother's feelings as she welcomed back the long-absent Hannes, who had always been as the apple of her eye, or to picture the simple preparations, the sweeping and scouring, the polishing and decorating, with which she and Elise anticipated his arrival; but who shall measure the father's joy on the return of his young conquering hero? The swiftly-progressing successes of Johannes' journey had been most literally Jakob's own personal triumphs, vindicating emphatically every one of the stages of his career; the obstinate disobedience of his boyhood, the pertinacious struggle of his youth, the reckless adventure of his marriage. What wonder that, as time went on, Johannes became to him as a sacred being in whose presence he felt awed and unable to speak or act naturally, but of whom, when alone with a sympathetic listener, he would talk unweariedly by the hour, tears of joy running down his cheeks.

As to Johannes himself, the feelings he had not been able to describe in his letter to Schumann were probably strong enough within his heart to touch the joy of the first home embraces with a gravity that did not immediately admit of speech. The first emotions over, however, an exuberant mirthfulness asserted itself in the bearing of the happy young fellow. He established at this time a custom from which he never afterwards departed. The first visit paid by him after his arrival was to Marxsen. One to the Cossels soon followed, and, on this occasion of his return from a first real absence, he went the round of several Lokals, where he had been accustomed to work regularly, and in his lightness of heart flourished on some of the instruments that had been the sign of his bondage, in very joy at his emancipation.

The radiance of this year's Christmastide in the little home where the young genius dwelt for a few days, the simple, unspoiled child of loving and beloved parents, might have been taken for granted. We possess an assurance of it, however, in some words written by Johannes, at the end of the year, to Schumann :

"HONOURED FRIEND,

"Herewith I venture to send you your first foster-children (which are indebted to you for their world citizenship), very much concerned as to whether they may rejoice in your unaltered indulgence and affection. To me, they look in their new form much too precise and timid, almost philistine indeed. I cannot accustom myself to seeing the innocent sons of Nature in such decorous clothing.

"I am looking forward immensely to seeing you in Hanover and being able to tell you that my parents and I owe the most blissful time of our lives to your and Joachim's too-great affection. I was overjoyed to see my parents and teacher again, and have passed a glorious time in their midst.

"I beg you to express the most cordial greetings to Frau Schumann and your children of

"Your

"JOHANNES BRAHMS.

"HAMBURG, in *December*, 1853."

As we have said in a previous chapter, the violin and pianoforte sonata that Johannes had thought of publishing

as Op. 5 was not given to the world. The manuscript was
mysteriously lost. How or by whose agency has never been
made clear. The known circumstances of the case lead to
the conclusion that it was borrowed by Liszt during his
Leipzig visit, and not returned. In a letter addressed six
months later to Klindworth, who was giving concerts with
Reményi in England, the Weimar master writes:

"Reményi does not answer me about the manuscript of
Brahms' violin sonata. Apparently he has taken it with
him, for I have, to my vexation, hunted three times through
the whole of my music without being able to find it. Do
not forget to write to me about it in your next letter, as
Brahms wants the sonata for publication."

There is a ring of vexation in these words which suggests
that Liszt felt responsible for the work. No trace of it was
discovered, however, until 1872, nineteen years after its disappearance, when, says Dietrich, "whilst I was staying in
Bonn to conduct my D minor Symphony, Wasielewski
showed me a very beautifully copied violin part, and asked
me if I knew the handwriting. I immediately recognised
it as that of Brahms' first period. We regretted very much
that the pianoforte part was not to be found. It will have
been the violin part of the lost sonata."

The works actually published, therefore, before and after
the New Year were—by Breitkopf and Härtel, the Sonatas
in C, Op. 1, and in F sharp minor, Op. 2, dedicated respectively to Joachim and Frau Schumann; the set of Songs,
Op. 3, dedicated to Bettina von Arnim, whose acquaintance
made by Brahms in Düsseldorf had been cultivated by him
during his visits to Hanover; and the Scherzo, Op. 4, dedicated to Wenzel; and by Bartholf Senff, the Sonata in F
minor, Op. 5, dedicated to the Countess Ida von Hohen-
thal, a lady to whom Brahms was presented by Grimm;
and the set of Songs dedicated to Louise and Minna Japha,
Op. 6. Schumann presented a copy of the songs, Op. 6,
to the Japhas immediately on their publication, on which he

wrote: "Den Fräulein Japha, zum Andenken an das Weihnachtsfest, 1853, als Vorbote des eigentlichen Gebers. R. Schumann."

In the two sets of songs, Op. 3 and 6, and in the third, Op. 7, dedicated to Dietrich and published but little later, may already be perceived the composer whose lyrics were destined to take their place in the heart of the great German people as a unique portion of a peculiar national treasure. Deeply original, absolutely sincere, of an imagination that is angelic in its purity, feminine in its tenderness, and virile in its reticent strength, Brahms' songs admit us to communion with a rarely ideal nature, and the intuitive power of perfect expression which marks some of his early lyrics anticipates the experience of his later years. The beautiful " O versenk dein Leid " will, no doubt, always be treasured as the most exquisite example, in its domain, of this early period of his fancy, but each of the three first song collections contains one or more tone-poems to which the music-lover returns with delight. Amongst them may be mentioned " Der Frühling " (Op. 6, No. 2) and " Treue Liebe " and "Heimkehr " (Op. 7, Nos. 1 and 6). The last-named little gem is the earliest written of the published songs; unfortunately, it has only one verse.

The energy of imagination dwelling within Brahms' songs is often the more striking from its concentration within the short form preferred by the composer in the majority of instances. In it, as time went on, he gave vivid expression to thoughts wistful or bright, playful or sombre, naïve or deeply pondered; and whilst his lyrics are especially characterised by the clear shaping of the song-melody, and the distinctness of the harmonic foundations upon which it rests, many of them derive an added distinction from a quiet significance in the accompaniment, which, whilst helping the musical representation of a poetic idea, never embarrasses the voice. In spite of their apparent simplicity, the accompaniments are, however, frequently difficult both to read and to perform.

It is to be said, generally, of Brahms' songs that they do
not betray the marked influence of either of the two great
lyrical composers who preceded him.   They have no affinity
with those of Schumann, and if many of them share the
fresh naturalness of Schubert's inspirations, this is rather
to be traced to a partiality for the folk-song, in which both
composers found an inexhaustible stimulus to their fancy.
On the other hand, in Brahms' songs we frequently meet
the musician who has penetrated so deeply into the art of
Bach that it has germinated afresh in his imagination, and
placed him in possession of an idiom capable of serving him
in the expression of his complex individuality.   Each song
bears the distinctive stamp of the composer's genius, though
hardly two resemble each other, and it would be difficult to
point to one that could be mistaken for the work of another
musician.

The young Kreisler was in the habit of presenting his
manuscripts, and especially those of his songs, to intimate
friends.   Most of these gifts bear his boyish, affectionate
inscriptions, some only the date and place of composition.
"Göttingen, July, 1853," is written at the end of an autograph copy of "Ich muss hinaus" presented at Düsseldorf
to the Japhas.   "Weit über das Feld" has a friendly inscription in his hand to the sisters.   His manuscripts—
probably the originals—of some of the songs from Op. 3,
notably "O versenk" and "In der Fremde," the latter
dated 1852, were given "To my dear Julius in kind remembrance" (J. O. Grimm).   Touching pictures arise in the
mind as one looks at these pages, some of them discoloured
by time, of the young idealist with his girlish face and long
fair hair sitting at his night toil, his soul whole and in his
possession, his thoughts straining towards the early morning hours, the only ones of the twenty-four which he was
certain of being able to devote to the loveliest inspirations
of his muse.   In the eager affection of the inscriptions is to
be read his bounding joy in his new freedom; in the devoted
remembrance with which his gifts have been treasured may

be perceived one of the qualities of his personality which he, perhaps, but little understood—the power of attracting the abiding love of loyal friends.

It is now time to sum up the real significance in the life of Brahms of the remarkable first concert-journey, the account of which has so long occupied our attention, and this may be done in a very few words. The journey was the transformation scene of his life. The obscure musician who, having been guarded from the dangers of prodigy fame, had started from Hamburg in April without prestige, without recommendations, without knowledge of the world, its manners or its artifices, had passed from the two or three provincial platforms on which he had appeared as Reményi's accompanist, to present himself as pianist and composer in the Leipzig Gewandhaus, and to return to his home in December the accepted associate of the great musicians of the day; recognised by Weimar, appreciated by Leipzig; encouraged by Berlioz and Liszt, claimed by Schumann and Joachim. Before he had well begun to climb the steep hill of reputation he had found himself transported to its summit. Starting hardly as an aspirant to fame, he had come back the proclaimed heir to a prophet's mantle. His life's horizon had been indefinitely widened, his whole existence changed. Back again amid the familiar scenes of Hamburg, the events of the past nine months must have seemed to him as the visions of an enchanted dream.

To the wise and faithful friend in Altona the occurrences which had startled the musical world had seemed in no wise astonishing.

" There was probably," wrote Marxsen later to La Mara, " but one man who was not surprised—myself. I knew what Brahms had accomplished, how comprehensive were his acquirements, what exalted talent had been bestowed on him, and how finely its blossom was unfolding. Schumann's recognition and admiration were, all the same, a great, great joy to me; they gave me the rare satisfaction of knowing that the teacher had perceived the right way to protect the individuality of the talent, and to form it gradually to self-dependence.''

These last words seem to indicate that here is a fitting opportunity for the brief consideration of a question which has not seldom been raised, and has received various answers, often biassed by prepossession. What was Marxsen's share in the art of Brahms? A Brahms would have learned what he did learn, if not from Marxsen then from someone else, has been the opinion of some people to whose judgment respect is due. Such influence as Marxsen had on Brahms' development was merely negative, is the reply of others; and it has been affirmed, on the authority of Herr Oberschulrath Wendt, that Brahms declared on one occasion that he had learned nothing from his master.*

Without stopping to discuss whether it has been just to the memory either of Brahms or of Marxsen to give the permanence and emphasis of print to whatever depreciatory words Brahms may have let fall in an unguarded moment to an intimate friend, it may safely be asserted that if our composer fortunately became aware, at an early age, of what had been the weak points of his master's teaching, he preserved, when at the height of his mastership, a clear recognition and grateful appreciation of the strong ones.

Marxsen has himself indicated, in the last sentence of the above quotation from his letter, the two main purposes of his teaching, both of which were attained by him in the case of Brahms with absolute success. To have '' protected the individuality '' of an endowment so powerfully original as that of our composer might, perhaps, be regarded as an easy achievement if taken alone; though even here it should be remembered that Marxsen made himself responsible, when the affectionate and impressionable Hannes was at a tender age, for his musical education, and must, therefore, have been instrumental in directing his creative energy to that study of the highest art by means of which it developed to such good purpose. To have trained his talent to the

---

* Kalbeck's '' Johannes Brahms,'' p. 34.

"self-dependence" it had attained by the time the young
composer was twenty, however, implies in the teacher a
distinctness of aim, a knowledge of method, an insight and
originality, an active and potent influence, which few will
fail to attribute to Marxsen who have a real acquaintance
with the large works of Brahms' earliest period, written at
the time that his formal pupilage was drawing or, in the
case of one work, had just drawn, to its close.

Limitation of space prevents the possibility of giving here
a detailed description of Marxsen's methods of instruction,
but, as some account of their excellencies and shortcomings
seems to be called for, it may be said that as a teacher of
free composition, and especially of the art of building up
the forms which may be studied in the works of Haydn,
Mozart, and Beethoven, he was great—the more so that
he did not educate his pupils merely by setting them to
imitate the outward shape of classical models. He began
by teaching them to form a texture, by training them
radically in the art of developing a theme. Taking a phrase
or a figure from one or other of the great masters, he would
desire the pupil to exhibit the same idea in every imaginable
variety of form, and would make him persevere in this
exercise until he had gained facility in perceiving the possibilities lying in a given subject, and ingenuity in presenting
them. Pursuing the same method with material of the
pupil's own invention, he aimed at bringing him to feel, as
by intuition, whether a musical subject was or was not
suitable for whatever immediate purpose might be in view.
The next step was that the idea should be pursued not
arbitrarily, but logically, to its conclusion—a conclusion
that was not, however, allowed to be a hard-and-fast termination. Marxsen's pupils were taught to aim at making
their movements resemble an organic growth, in which each
part owed its existence to something that had gone before.
"Unity clothed in variety" might have been his motto.

The strength and freedom of craftsmanship, the immense
resource imparted by such training, and the assistance lent

by its earlier stages to the later study of construction, hardly need pointing out, nor is it necessary to dwell upon particular instances of its efficacy in the case of Brahms. Every page of his instrumental music teems with illustrations of the fruitfulness of his youthful studies; their result lives in the very core of his technique, and to them may in great part be traced, not only his mastery of form, but the elasticity which from the first marks his essential adherence to the models of classical tradition.

The severe course of apprenticeship in the art of free contrapuntal writing to which Marxsen subjected his pupil, which furthered, and was itself helped, by his training, in thematic development, is abundantly evident in the movements of the three pianoforte sonatas, and the estimation of the precise value especially of the first two of these works is facilitated by some knowledge of the methods from which they resulted. That Brahms, when at the summit of his mastership, expressed his exact sense of his indebtedness to his teacher, to whom he constantly testified his gratitude and affection both by word and action, is in the knowledge of the present writer. Gradually in the course of his career he had, he said, made the acquaintance of nearly all the foremost musicians of Germany, and he believed that in the teaching of the logical development of a theme, and in the teaching of form, especially what is called "sonata form," Marxsen, even if he could be equalled could not be excelled.

Eminent as he was, however, as an instructor in the art of free imitative composition, in that of pure part-writing Marxsen was no trustworthy guide. That he had gone through a course of training in strict counterpoint, canon and fugue—the surest foundation for the attainment of facility in part-writing—in his early days under Clasing, and that he carried his pupils through the same branches of study, goes without saying, but he had retained neither the exact knowledge, nor the interest, necessary to enable him to impart to his pupils purity and ease in the strict

style of writing, or to train them to the effective application
of the contrapuntal skill they might have acquired, in
composition in pure parts for voices or instruments.

It would be a nice question to determine, however, whether
the very fact of Marxsen's deficiencies did not result in a
balance of gain to Brahms.   While his powers of imagination obtained from what his master did do, encouragement
and strength and facility in concentrating themselves into
shape, they were exempt by the absence of that which he did
not do from the danger of being dwarfed or intimidated.
Marxsen helped Johannes to the putting forth of his strength
in confidence and joy, and if the young musician ever felt
it irksome to have to go back to the confining and polishing
processes, he knew that the conquests won by him during
the time of his pupilage ensured him final victory in the
fresh course of serious study to which he soon voluntarily
submitted himself.

Marxsen's indifference to the study of part-writing is
strangely illustrated by the absence of his name from the
list of subscribers to the great Leipzig edition of Bach's
works; an absence which can hardly be accounted for, in
view of his enthusiasm for the instrumental works of the
mighty master, otherwise than by the supposition that his
vehement intolerance of religious creeds had impaired his
interest in the branch of musical art which originated and
reached its highest development in the service of the
churches.   The majority of the works made generally known
by the publications of the Bach Society were written for
use in the two churches for the musical portion of whose
services Bach was for many years responsible.   This
hypothesis is equally plausible in its application to the
church composers and learned contrapuntists of the early
Italian and German schools.

An interesting article on Marxsen is to be found in a
little book called " Künstler Charakteristiken aus dem
Concert-Saal," by his friend, Professor Josef Sittard, and
in an address given by this author at a Brahms memorial

concert in Hamburg immediately after the master's death, the following sympathetic allusion was made to the beloved teacher :

" Brahms had the rare good fortune of being trained under a teacher whose like does not fall to the lot of many young musicians. Pledged to no special artistic creed, sworn to no particular tendency or party, Marxsen had interest to bestow upon every important development of musical art. He never gave instruction on an inflexible scheme, but allowed himself to be guided by the separate requirements of each case. He was careful not to interfere with the individuality of young talent, not to meddle with the distinctive peculiarities of his pupil's creative ability; he only guided them within artistic confines. Brahms regarded his teacher with touching gratitude, and when at the height of his creative power still continued to send his compositions, before their publication, for Marxsen's critical inspection. Nothing is more indicative of the intimate relation between the two men than the letters (from Brahms to Marxsen) that I was permitted to see years ago."

Unfortunately for the musical world, only one or two scraps of this correspondence remain. On the death of Marxsen in 1887, Brahms' letters to his teacher were returned to him at his request, and were destroyed.

CHAPTER VI.

1854-1855.

Brahms at Hanover—Hans von Bülow—Robert and Clara Schumann in Hanover—Schumann's illness—Brahms in Düsseldorf—Variations on Schumann's theme in F sharp minor—B major Trio—First public performance in New York—First attempt at symphony.

WITH the opening of the year 1854, Brahms may be said to have entered upon the first chapter of his new life. The transition stage of his career had been defined with unusual sharpness of outline. The eventful journey had been as a bridge by which he had passed from youth to manhood. Behind it were the dark years of lonely effort with issue still untried, the gathering up of strength and treasure but dimly recognised by the worker, labouring under a thick haze of obscurity; in front lay, straight and clear, the pathway of endeavour towards a fixed goal, cheered by companionship and illumined by the consciousness of a measure of success already won. Having tranquillised his mind and shaken off the effects of months of excitement by nearly a fortnight's intercourse with his family and friends at Hamburg, Johannes was impatient to get quietly to work again, all the more since new and forcible motives—the sense of his responsibility to Schumann, and the desire to become as far as possible worthy of his encomiums—added their influence to the energy of his nature, and helped to spur him on to the resolve to outdo even his utmost.

Bringing his stay in Hamburg to a close with the opening
of the New Year, he left on January 3 or 4 for Hanover,
where he found a new introduction awaiting his arrival.
Hans von Bülow, who had passed Christmas in Joachim's
"dear society," writes on the 6th to his mother:

"I have become tolerably well acquainted with Robert
Schumann's young prophet Brahms. He arrived two days
ago, and is always with us. A very lovable, frank nature,
and a talent that really has something God-given about it."*

Bülow took an early opportunity of carrying out Liszt's
desire, hinted at in the letter of December 16. He played
the first movement of the C major Sonata on March 1 at
Frau Peroni-Glasbrenner's concert in Hamburg, and was
thus the first artist—always excepting the composer himself
—to perform a work of Brahms in public. That his atti-
ture towards our composer did not, during the succeeding
twenty years, correspond with this promising beginning, as
will be seen hereafter, may be chiefly attributed to the disappointment with which the disciples of the New-German
school gradually realised that their artistic aims were at
variance with the mature convictions of Joachim, whom
they reckoned for a while as one of themselves, and of
Brahms, whose allegiance they had hoped to secure.

Johannes, established in a lodging of his own at Hanover,
began the routine of work, diversified by intimate association with a few chosen friends, which he preferred to the
end of his life, and was soon absorbed in the composition
of his B major Pianoforte Trio. The intimacy between
Joachim and himself was now widened to a triple alliance
by the addition of Grimm, now living in Hanover, and
lively discussions were carried on in Joachim's rooms late
into the night by the three friends. The young violinist
had not been a smoker up to this time, but his companions
used to envelop him and themselves in such thick clouds of
tobacco, that one night, unable any longer to endure his

---

* Bülow's "Briefe und Schriften." Edited by Marie von Bülow.

sufferings passively, he suddenly declared his surrender, and began to puff away with the others, to Brahms' and Grimm's great delight.

Schumann had accepted an invitation from Hille, the founder and conductor of the "New Singakademie" at Hanover, to be present at a performance of his "Paradise and the Peri" on January 28, and, to the joy of the young musicians, wrote to Joachim to suggest that his visit, which was to be made in the company of his wife, should be the occasion of several public appearances. He continues:

"Now where is Johannes? Is he with you? If so, greet him. Is he flying high—or only amongst flowers? Is he setting drums and trumpets to work yet? He must call to mind the beginnings of the Beethoven symphonies; he must try to do something of the same kind. The beginning is the main point; when one has begun, the end seems to come of itself. . . .

"I hope also to see, or better still to hear, something new of yours soon. You, too, should remember the above-named symphony beginnings, but not before Henry and Demetrius.*

"I always get into a good humour when I write to you. You are a kind of physician for me.

"Adieu.

"Your R. SCHU."

Some idea of the happy week passed by the three friends in the constant society of their "master" may be gathered from Moser's charming description in his Life of Joachim. Schumann could not see enough of his beloved young favourites, Joachim and Brahms, and readily extended his cordiality to their companion Grimm. The third subscription concert was a veritable Schumann festival. Joachim conducted the master's fourth symphony, "evidently with great delight and love," says the *Hanover Courier*, as well as Beethoven's Pianoforte Concerto in E flat, played by Frau Schumann, and performed Schumann's lately-written Violin Fantasia dedicated to him and first played at Düs-

---

* Two overtures on which Joachim was working.

seldorf. There were plenty of opportunities for private meetings in Joachim's rooms, in the railway restaurant, and elsewhere, that were unshadowed by any presentiment of an impending catastrophe; for Schumann was unusually bright and communicative, and took pleasure in amusing his young friends with anecdotes of his own early experiences. The hours thus passed were tenderly remembered in after-years by those who had been gladdened by the setting radiance of a light soon to be extinguished.

"What a high festival we have had through the Schumanns' visit," writes Brahms, a few days after their departure, to Dietrich in Düsseldorf. "Everything has seemed alive since. Greet the great ones from me many times."*

A week after their return Schumann wrote:

"*February* 6, 1854.

"DEAR JOACHIM,

"We have been at home eight days, and have not yet sent a word to you and your companions. I have, however, frequently written to you with invisible ink. . . . We have often thought of the past days; may others like them come quickly! The kind royal family, the excellent orchestra, and the two young dæmons moving amid the scenes—we shall not soon forget it.

"The cigars are very much to my liking. It seems they were a handshake from Brahms, and, as usual, a very substantial and agreeable one.

"Write to me soon—in words and in tones!

"R. SCHU."

It is sad to realise that in less than a fortnight after sending this letter, so free from signs of depression, so bright and healthy in tone, Schumann had written down his last musical thought, the now well-known Theme in E flat; and that before the close of the month he was overtaken by the crisis of his terrible malady. Alarming symptoms declared

---

* This and all other extracts from Dietrich are taken from his well-known "Recollections of Brahms."

themselves in the night of February 10-11. The master was distressed by illusions of hearing, one note seeming to sound in his ear from the impression of which he was unable to free himself and which only gave place a day or two later to the sensation of entire movements played as though by a full orchestra. Early in the night of February 17-18 he rose to write down the theme in E flat which had, he said, been sung to him by angels, and during the following week his condition changed rapidly for the worse. He continued to occupy himself at his writing table during intervals of comparative relief from suffering, and was engaged on the 27th with the composition of variations on his theme when a moment's chance occurred that enabled him to escape the watchfulness of his devoted wife. Seizing it, he managed to leave his house unobserved, and, a few moments afterwards, had thrown himself into the Rhine. He was rescued by some sailors belonging to a nearby steamboat, and conveyed to his home in a carriage. But his state continued so distressing that Frau Schumann, herself needing care at the time, was not allowed by the doctors to see him, and he was taken on March 4, in accordance with his own desire, to the private establishment of Dr. Richarz at Endenich, near Bonn.

It would be difficult to describe in exaggerated terms the consternation with which a great part of the musical world, and especially the friends of Schumann's immediate circle, became aware of these overwhelming occurrences. Sorrow for the great master, love for the indulgent friend, alarmed sympathy for the stricken wife, kept the younger of his disciples in a state of restless agitation, which seems to have found its principal relief in the writing of letters of excited inquiry to Dietrich, the only one of their number on the scene of the catastrophe.

" Never in my life has anything so moved and deeply shaken me," wrote Theodor Kirchner, " as the dreadful occurrence with our honoured, beloved Schumann. . . . We should all be terribly lonely without him, and as regards myself, all pleasure in my own endeavours would be gone."

"Pray send me an exact description of the whole catastrophe *as quickly as possible*," so ran Naumann's letter, "especially if there is any hope of Schumann's complete restoration, how his unhappy wife has borne this cruel stroke of fate, and how you are yourself. I repeat my request for *immediate* news."

To the friends in Hanover, who had so lately seen Schumann in apparent enjoyment of unwonted health both of body and mind, the tidings, of which they first became informed through a paragraph in the *Cologne Gazette*, seemed too sudden and tragic to be credible.

"DEAR DIETRICH—" Joachim dashed off—

"If you have any feeling of friendship for Brahms and me, relieve our anxiety, and write word instantly whether Schumann is really as ill as the paper says, and let us know at once of any change in his condition. It is too grievous to be in uncertainty about the life of someone to whom we are bound with our best powers. I can scarcely wait for the hour that will bring me tidings of him. I am quite beside myself with dread.

"Write soon.

"Your J. JOACHIM."

It was impossible, however, to wait for an answer, and no letter could have appeased the desire of the affectionate young musicians to be on the spot; so Brahms, having no fixed duties to detain him, started immediately for Düsseldorf, and Joachim hoped to follow, if only for a couple of days. On March 3 Johannes sent his report:

"DEAREST JOSEPH,

"Do come on Saturday; it comforts Frau Schumann to see certain dear faces.

"Schumann's condition seems to be improved. The physicians have hope, but no one is allowed to see him.

"I have already been with Frau Schumann. She wept very much, but was very glad to see me and to be able to expect you.

"We expect you on Sunday morning, and Grimm on Wednesday.

"Your

"JOHANNES."*

"To my great relief," wrote Dietrich a fortnight later to Naumann, "Brahms came at once after hearing the dreadful news. Grimm is also here. Joachim was here for two days, and is coming again in a few weeks."

At the end of the letter he adds:

"Brahms has written a quite wonderful trio, and is a man to be taken in every respect as a pattern. With all his depth, he is healthy, fresh, and lively, entirely untouched by modern morbidness."

It now became the cherished duty of the young men to do what in them lay to support and comfort the sorely-tried wife in her desolation. Nothing, perhaps, could have helped and soothed her so much as the feeling that the tie which primarily bound them to her was that of their devotion to her husband, the knowledge that they mourned with her in a common grief, and that their sympathy was touched by their personal sense of what she had lost. Never, indeed, was more loyal sympathy offered for the consolation of sorrow, and it had its reward. After the first terrible days had been lived through, a calm and self-possession returned to the illustrious lady, which heightened, if possible, the young artists' admiration of her. The news from Endenich improved towards the end of the month, and on April 1 even became reassuring. The patient was now passing his time walking, or quietly sleeping, undisturbed by fits of anxiety or delusions of hearing; was gentle towards his attendant, had conversed a little with him, and had even made a joke appropriate to the day. Frau Schumann summoned up courage to look with hope to the future, and allowed herself to be persuaded to resume some of her ordinary avocations. The short remainder of the musical

---

* From the original letter, presented by Dr. Joachim to the author.

season was, indeed, passed in necessary retirement; but the
great pianist found solace in quietly studying her husband's
compositions anew with Dietrich, Brahms, Grimm, and
others of the circle, playing his great orchestral and choral
works with them on the pianoforte, and listening in turn to
their performances. Dietrich writes in March:

"Yesterday and the day before she went through the
whole of Schumann's 'Faust' music with us. We are with
her every day, and it is impossible for me to think of leaving
at present."

On June 11 Frau Schumann's seventh child was born.
His name, chosen in memory of Mendelssohn, was registered
as Felix, and Brahms was to stand sponsor, but it was decided that the christening ceremony should be delayed for
the present. Perhaps before long the father would be able
to take part in it with his loved ones. A touching memorial
of the efforts made by the young Brahms to divert the mind
of the longing wife from its burden of sorrow exists in his
Variations for Pianoforte, Op. 9, on a Theme of Robert
Schumann, which were written during Frau Schumann's
convalescence; each new variation being brought to her as
it was completed. Schumann's theme ("Album-blatt,"
Op. 99, No. 1), which refers to its composer's early work,

Op. 5 (Variations on a Theme by Clara Wieck), had been
chosen by Frau Clara as the subject of variations written by
herself for Robert's forty-third birthday, and an entry in
her diary records her appreciation of the affection which now
inspired Johannes with the idea of using it again.

"He tried to bring solace to my heart. He composed
variations on the beautiful, intimate theme, which made such
a deep impression upon me a year ago when I composed
variations for my beloved Robert, and touched me deeply
by his tender thoughtfulness."

Grimm, who remained at Düsseldorf during these months in close companionship with Johannes, christened his friend's work " Trost-Einsamkeit," and remembered it as such ever afterwards. It tells plainly enough the story of the young composer's thoughts. It is full of references to Schumann and his wife—notably in the ninth variation, which contains note for note reminiscences of Schumann's Album-Blatt, Op. 99, No. 2, and in the tenth, in which the first four bar of Clara Wieck's original theme

are introduced by diminution into the middle voice:

The work is astounding in its evidence of the mastery already achieved by the young composer over the technique of variation form, in which he uses the complicated resources of contrapuntal science with absolute playfulness. For one illustration of this the reader may again be referred to the tenth variation, in which the original bass of Schumann's theme is used as the melody of the upper part and its in- version as the bass part, whilst the original melody (quoted on p. 166) is imitated by diminution in the middle part.

We must resist the temptation to linger over the many
interesting details of this noble work, as the aim of our
pages is not a technical one; but we may note in passing
that, of the sixteen variations which it contains, five are
written in keys varying from that of the theme, a circumstance which again brings it into a certain association with
Schumann.* Brahms, in his five other independent sets of
variations for pianoforte, nearly follows the practice of the
earlier masters, who confined themselves to the major and
minor modes of one key.

Johannes had meanwhile, according to custom, sent the
completed manuscript of his trio to Marxsen, and had
speedily received it back again with his master's critical remarks. These he acknowledged on June 28 in a letter from
which the following brief extracts are taken, sending Marxsen, at the same time, the new variations and a collection of
short pieces written at odds and ends of time, which he proposed to call "Leaves from the Journal of a Musician,
published by the Young Kreisler."

"Let me thank you very much for having vouchsafed such
a long letter, such a detailed examination to my trio. I will
write about the proposed little alterations when I send you
the printed copy. I have allowed the trio to lie in order to
accustom myself to them."

Asking Marxsen if he considers the pianoforte pieces
worth publishing, he adds as to the proposed title: "What
do you think of it? Doesn't it please you? I must confess
I should be sorry to strike it out."† It must be presumed
that Marxsen's opinion was unfavourable, for the short
pieces did not see the light. We shall, however, meet with
one or two of them in a few concert-programmes before long,
and one will be found to have a particular interest for
English readers.

The B major Trio, published in 1854 by Breitkopf and

---

* *Cf.* Schumann's great variations: the "Etudes Symphoniques."
† Sittard's "Künstler-Charakteristiken."

Härtel as Op. 8, which remained for many years but little
known, has, with its beautiful youthful qualities, long since
become dear to those who have yielded their hearts to the
spell of Brahms' music.   The composer's fertile fancy has
betrayed him, in the first allegro, into some episodical
writing which somewhat clouds the distinctness of outline,
and impedes the listener in his appreciation of the distinguished beauties of the movement, and there are places in
the finale where a certain disappointment succeeds to the
conviction inspired by the impetuous opening subject; but
in wealth of material, in the rare beauty of its principal
themes, and in noble sincerity of expression, the trio occu-
pies a distinguished place even amongst the examples of
Brahms' maturity.   The scherzo with its trio are already
masterly both in conception and treatment, and in the
adagio we have promise of the deeply impressive slow
movements which were moulded in ever-increasing perfection of structure by the composer's ripening genius.   That
Brahms retained an affection for this child of his young
imagination is shown by his having published a revised
edition of the work so late in his career as the year 1891.
We must confess our preference for the original version,
which is consistently representative of the composer as he
was when he wrote it.   The later one, though in some respects more suitable for concert performance, does not appear
to us to have solved the difficulty of successfully applying
to a work of art the process of grafting, upon the fresh,
lovable immaturity of twenty-one, the practised but less
mobile experience of fifty-seven.

The trio was performed for the first time in public, to
the lasting musical distinction of America, on November 27,
1855, at William Mason's concert of chamber music in Dods-
worth's Hall, New York, by the concert-giver, Theodor
Thomas, and Carl Bergmann, to whom, therefore, belongs
the honour of having inaugurated the public performances
of Brahms' great series of works of this class.   It was
played, for the second time, at Breslau on December 18 of

the same year.   Many years elapsed before it was heard in
England.

As soon as she was able to travel, Frau Schumann resolved to seek rest and change of scene by visiting her
mother in Berlin, whither Joachim also proceeded from Hanover on a visit to some of his own particular friends.
Dietrich had quitted Düsseldorf some months previously to
follow prospects of success in Leipzig; Grimm and Brahms
remained behind to take charge of any urgent tidings from
Endenich; and to Johannes was especially entrusted the congenial task of putting Schumann's books and music in order.
This was soon accomplished to his satisfaction as he writes
to Dietrich :

"And now I sit there the whole day and study.   I have
seldom felt so happy as now, rummaging in this library."

On July 19, the very day of Frau Schumann's departure,
the happy news arrived that a marked improvement had
taken place in her husband's health.   He had spoken of
feeling better, expressed a desire to visit his friend Wasielewski at Bonn; above all, had picked flowers and evidently
wished them to be sent to his wife, whom he had not mentioned during his illness.   News and flowers were instantly
despatched to Berlin and were received with almost overwhelming feelings of hope and longing.

"I cannot describe my agitation," Frau Schumann writes
to Dietrich, after informing him of the tidings, "but I never
knew how difficult it is to bear a great joy! . . . . It often
seems to me as though I must lose my reason.   It is too
much, all that I have gone through already and that is yet
before me !"

Her agitation of mind made it impossible for her to stay
out the intended visit, and leaving her little daughter Julie,
who had accompanied her, behind under the grandmother's
care, she returned to her home four days after leaving it.

"Ah! How rejoiced I was when I entered the dear room
again," she writes, "and saw his writing-table, books, and

other possessions. I felt as though I had been long absent, and as though I now atoned for a wrong done to him, the dear one, who was thinking of me again and imagined me to be here whilst I was in Berlin."[*]

The later movements of the party are chronicled in a letter written by Johannes to the Amstvogt Blume, of Winsen :

"ULM, *August* 16, 1854.

"HONOURED SIR,

"You certainly think that your dear letter did not give me the least pleasure, as I have left it so long un-answered? Ah, the time lately has been so full of excite-ment that I was obliged to put it off from day to day. Frau Schumann went with a friend on the 10th of this month to Ostend for the benefit of her health. I, after much per-suasion, resolved to make a journey through Swabia during her absence. I did not know how greatly I was attached to the Schumanns, how I lived in them; everything seemed barren and empty to me, every day I wished to turn back, and was obliged to travel by rail in order to get quickly to a distance and forget about turning back. It was of no use; I have come as far as Ulm, partly on foot, partly by rail; I am going to return quickly, and would rather wait for Frau Schumann in Düsseldorf than wander about in the dark. When one has found such divine people as Robert and Clara Schumann, one should stick to them and not leave them, but raise and inspire one's self by them. The dear Schumann continues to improve, as you have read in my letter to my parents. There has been a great deal of gossip about his condition. I consider the best description of him is to be found in some of the works of E. T. A. Hoffmann (Rath Krespel, Serapion, and especially the splendid Kreisler, etc.). He has only stripped off his body too soon.—If you would give me pleasure, let me find a letter from you in Ddf.—is that quite too bold? I will write to you again, and more rationally, from there. I am writing this letter in the waiting-room of the railway-station, which accounts for its having become, probably, very confused.—A thousand

---

[*] Litzmann II, 322.

hearty greetings to dear Uncle Giesemann, I will write to
him also from Ddf.; heartiest greetings also to Frau Blume
and your daughter.   Remember with affection

"Your JOHANNES BRAHMS."*

Stopping at Bonn on his return journey to inquire after
the patient at Endenich, Brahms obtained permission to
look at Schumann, himself unseen, and from his position
behind an open window was able, after he had sufficiently
controlled his first agitation, to assure himself that the
master looked well and wore the kind, tranquil mien natural
to him; and on his arrival at Düsseldorf, whom should he
find there but Grimm, who, having missed the object of a
journey on which he, too, had set out, had likewise been to
Endenich, seen Schumann, and gained an impression of his
appearance and manner similar to that which had reassured
Johannes! †

Grimm left Düsseldorf in October, for Hanover, and remained there till the following year, when he settled in
Göttingen as a pianoforte teacher and the conductor of a
choral society.   Johannes also went north on a visit to his
parents, but for a few weeks only.   The Schumanns' house
had become a second home to him, and his place in the affections of its master and mistress that of a beloved elder son.
Almost every particular that had marked the course of his
year's acquaintance with them had been of a kind to stir his
true, loving, high-strung nature to its depths.   Schumann's
noble character, his quick affection for the young stranger
and unconditional acceptance of his art, the ideal relation
which united the great composer with his wife, the distinguished qualities of the gifted woman who found her
greatest happiness in consecrating her genius to the service
of her romantic love, the terrible blow which had separated
the two lives so closely linked, the sadness of the present,

---

* See footnote on p. 120.

† Compare Grimm's letter to Brahms, written also on August 16,
Brahms' "Briefwechsel," IV, No. 2.

the uncertainty of the future—each and all of these things had aroused in the heart of Johannes a tumult of feeling, a poignancy of affection, that allowed him no rest when he was out of immediate touch with the two people who were its object. He could study to his heart's content in Schumann's library, where books and music were unreservedly at his disposal; could be of use to Frau Schumann, who truly valued his sympathy and returned his affection; he was in constant communication with Joachim, and could have as much pleasant society as he cared for. In short, he felt that for the present his place was at Düsseldorf, and at Düsseldorf he remained.

It was in the spring of 1854 that he made the acquaintance of Julius Allgeyer, who, four years his senior, was at the time a student of copper-plate engraving in Düsseldorf under Josef Keller.

"Brahms," says Allgeyer in a letter of this date, "has Schiller's striking profile; his compositions sound different from everything else known to me. He has the bad manners of a frolicsome child and the understanding of a man."

There was much in the circumstances and characters of the two young men to foster an intimacy between them. Allgeyer's youth had, like that of Johannes, been passed in struggle, and he resembled Brahms in his restless hunger after general culture, which he endeavoured to satisfy by constant and varied reading. The composition of Brahms' Ballades for pianoforte, Op. 10, which belongs to this time, has a direct association with Allgeyer, to whom the young musician was indebted for his acquaintance with Herder's "Stimmen der Völker," the volume containing a translation of the Scotch ballad "Edward" that inspired the first of the pieces in question. Brahms' memory for such details is well illustrated by his dedication to Allgeyer of the Lieder und Romanzen, for two voices, with pianoforte accompaniment, Op. 75, published in 1878, the first number of which is a setting of "Edward." Another avowed instance of his partiality for Herder's collection is to be found in a still later work, No. 1 of the three Intermezzi for pianoforte, Op. 117, and it may be surmised that the book contains the secret key to the composer's thoughts during the writing of more than one other of the short pieces for pianoforte designated by the general name of "Intermezzo" or "Capriccio."

Brahms and Allgeyer remained intimate, though with intervals of some estrangement—if this be not too strong a term to express a temporary cessation of intercourse without alleged cause—until Brahms' death; and Allgeyer, who was introduced by Johannes to Frau Schumann, came to be regarded by her as belonging to the circle of her valued friends.*

Schumann's desire that his young protégé should apply his powerful ideal gifts and his skill in the handling of form to the composition of an orchestral work had not been disregarded by Brahms. He had tried his hand at an overture early in the year, and had worked through the spring and summer at a symphony, making his first attempts at instrumentation with the help of Grimm. It could not be otherwise than that the rapid succession of extraordinary events and vivid emotions which had agitated his spirit should prove a strong stimulus to his imagination; and it is not surprising to find that they moved him to the composition of a series of movements, two of which remain amongst the most powerful produced by him, one having been accepted by thousands of mourners all the world over as the most fitting musical expression known to them in the presence of profound grief. The symphony, as such, was never completed, but the work became known in the composer's intimate circle as a sonata for two pianofortes, of which the first two movements are now familiar to the world as the first and second of the Pianoforte Concerto in D minor, and the third is immortalised in the "Behold all Flesh,"

---

* Professor Carl Neumann's introduction to the second edition (1904) of Allgeyer's "Life of Anselm Feuerbach."

the wonderful march movement in three-four time of the German Requiem. Brahms frequently played the sonata at this period with Frau Schumann, or with Grimm, who did not hesitate to urge upon his friend his opinion as to the inadequacy of the form for the expression of the great ideas of the work.

The two sets of Variations composed respectively by Frau Clara and Johannes on Schumann's theme were published simultaneously, by Brahms' desire, in the autumn, with his Songs, Op. 7, dedicated to Dietrich, and the B major Trio; the variations by Johannes appearing as his Op. 9. The song "Mondnacht" also appeared this year, without opus number, in a book of "Album-Blätter" published at Göttingen.

The improvement in Schumann's condition went on so steadily that on September 13, the thirty-fifth anniversary of his wife's birthday, he was permitted to receive a letter from her. His answer, sent the next day, contains no allusion to Brahms, but brings Schumann's tenderness in his home relationships so vividly before the mind that a short extract from it will, we think, be welcomed by the reader.

"ENDENICH, *Sept.* 14, 1854.

"How I rejoiced, beloved Clara, to see your handwriting. High thanks for having written to me on such a day, and that you and the dear children still remember me. Greet and kiss the little ones! Oh, if I could see you and speak to you again, but the way is too far. So much I should like to know; how your life is going on; where you are living and if you still play as gloriously as formerly; if Marie and Elise continue to make progress, if they still sing also—if you still have the Klems pianoforte [a present from Schumann to his wife], where my collection of scores is (the printed ones) and what has become of the manuscripts (such as the Requiem, the Sänger's Fluch); where our album is, containing autographs of Goethe, Jean Paul, Mozart, Beethoven, Weber, and many letters addressed to you and me."

On the 18th he writes:

"What joyful news you have again sent me . . . that

Brahms, to whom you will give my kind and admiring greetings, has come to live in Düsseldorf; what friendship! If you would like to know whose is my favourite name, you will no doubt guess his, the unforgettable one! . . . If you write to Joachim, greet him. What have Brahms and Joachim been composing? Is the overture to Hamlet published? Has he finished anything else? You write that you are giving your lessons in the pianoforte-room. Who are the present pupils? Who the best? Are you not doing too much, dear Clara?"

He goes on to recall the happiness of the journeys made in his wife's company, begs that their double portrait may be sent him, would like some money, in order to be able to give to the poor people whom he meets in his walks, wants a list of his children's birthdays.

A week later, September 26, he says:

"What you write about . . . has given me the greatest pleasure. So also about Brahms and Joachim and their compositions. I am surprised that Brahms is working at counterpoint which does not seem like him. I should like to make acquaintance with Joachim's three pieces for pianoforte and viola. I can remember de Laurens' portrait of Brahms, but not the one of me. Thank you for the children's birthday dates. Who are to be sponsors for the little one, and in what church is he to be baptised? . . ."

In October he acknowledges the arrival of Brahms' variations, sent him by his wife:

"DEAREST CLARA,

"What pleasure you have again given me! Your letter and Julie's, Brahms' variations on the theme which you have varied, the three volumes of Arnim Brentano's Wunderhorn. . . . I remember Herr Grimm very well, we used to be together with Brahms and Joachim at the railway-station [in Hanover]; greet him and above all Fräulein Leser. I shall write to Brahms myself . . ."

That this renewal of intercourse with her husband cheered and encouraged Frau Schumann for the performance of her arduous public duties during the autumn season will be

TRIO.

2.
Allegro con moto.
Violino.
Violoncello.
Allegro con moto
Pianoforte
espressivo, legato
espressivo
legato
dolce
marc.
NB
NB
legato
poco più forte
ped. sempre
legato
poco più forte

readily believed. Under the necessity of a heavily increased weight of responsibility to her young children, she
had bound herself to the fulfilment of a long list of concert
engagements, which scarcely allowed her an interval of
rest. Happily, the reports from Endenich continued favourable. Joachim, writing to Liszt on November 16, says:

"What a happiness it is that Schumann's condition is
distinctly improved. I had a letter from him from Endenich
lately. He relates some of our common experiences quite
clearly, expressing himself in a kind, gentle way as though
he had just awakened from a dream. Everything seems
new to him, and he would like to participate in what is
going on, asks about compositions, about friends; one may
certainly hope for the best."

On November 27, having had time to study Brahms'
variations, Schumann writes, in the course of a letter to his
wife:

"The variations by Johannes delighted me at first sight
and do so still more on deeper acquaintance. I shall myself
write also to Brahms; does his portrait by de Laurens still
hang in my study? He is the most attractive and gifted
young fellow. I recall with delight the splendid impression
he made that first time with his C major Sonata, and afterwards with the F sharp minor Sonata and the Scherzo in
E flat minor. Oh, if I could only hear him again! I
should like his ballades also."

To Brahms, enclosed in the above:

"Could I but come to you myself, to see you again and
to hear your splendid variations or [to hear them] from my
Clara of whose wonderful interpretation Joachim has written
to me. How incomparably the whole is rounded off, how
one recognises you in the rich brightness of the imagination
and again in the profound art, united as I have not yet
known them. The theme emerging here and there, but very
secretly, then so vehement and tender. The theme then
quite vanishing, and at the end, after the fourteenth [variation], so ingeniously written in canon in the second; how
splendid is the fifteenth in G flat major, and the last. And
I have to thank you, dear Johannes, for all your kindness

13

and goodness to my Clara; she always writes to me about it. She sent me yesterday to my pleasure, as you perhaps know, volumes of my compositions and Jean Paul's Flegeljahre. Now I hope soon to see your handwriting, however great a treasure it is to me, in another form also. The winter is fairly mild. You know the Bonn neighbourhood. I enjoy Beethoven's statue and the beautiful view of the Siebengebirge. We saw each other last in Hanover. Only write soon to

"Your affectionate and appreciative

"R. SCHUMANN."

Brahms' answer speaks for itself:

"HAMBURG, *December* 2, 1854.

"MOST BELOVED FRIEND,

"How can I describe to you my pleasure at your dear letter! You have already so often made me happy when you have remembered me so affectionately in the letters to your wife, and now I have a letter belonging entirely to myself. It is the first I have had from you; I value it beyond measure. Unfortunately I received it in Hamburg, where I had come to visit my parents; I would much rather have received it from the hand of your wife.

"I expect to return to Düsseldorf in a few days; I long to be there.

"The overmuch praise which you bestow on my variations fills me with happiness. I have been studying your works industriously since the spring; how much I should like to hear your praise of them also! I have passed this year since spring-time at Düsseldorf; I shall never forget it, I have learned all the time to love you and your glorious wife more and more.

"I have never yet looked forward so cheerfully and confidently, never believed so firmly in a splendid future as now. How I wish it were near, and nearer still the happy time when you will be quite restored to us.

"I cannot then leave you any more; I shall try to earn more and more of your dear friendship.

"Good-bye, and think of me with affection.

"Your warmly venerating JOHANNES BRAHMS.

"My parents and your friends here think of you with the greatest veneration and love. The parents, Herr Marxsen, Otten, and Avé, particularly beg me to give you their most cordial greetings."*

On the 15th of the month Schumann wrote again to Johannes:

"ENDENICH, *December,* 1854.

"DEAR FRIEND,

"If I could but come to you at Christmas! Meanwhile I have received your portrait from my dear wife, your familiar portrait, and I know the place in my room quite well, quite well—under the mirror. I am still refreshing myself with your variations; I should like to hear several of them from you and my Clara; I am not completely master of them; especially the second, the fourth not up to time and the fifth not; but the eighth (and the slower ones) and the ninth—A reminiscence of which Clara wrote to me is probably on p. 14; what is it from? a song?†—and the twelfth—— Oh, if I could only hear you!"

The andante and scherzo from Brahms' F minor Sonata, Op. 5, were included by Frau Schumann in several of her concert programmes of the season, and the B major Trio was introduced by her in private circles to the music lovers of Breslau and Berlin. The sonata-movements, though received with indifference by the general public, were, on the whole, encouragingly noticed by the press. The *Vossische Zeitung* of Berlin dismissed them as wanting in clearness and simplicity, but the *National Zeitung* of the same city perceived in them evidence of an "hervorragenden Produktions-Vermögen," and a Frankfurt critic wrote:

"Frau Schumann deserves the highest acknowledgment for introducing Brahms' compositions to the public with her master-hand, and thus preparing the way for their acceptance."

The interest awakened by the performance of the B major Trio before some of the leading musicians of Breslau, led to

---

* See footnote on p. 136.

† The introduction by diminution of Clara Wieck's theme mentioned on page 167.

the inclusion of the work in the programme of the concert given by Messrs. Mächtig and Seyfrise later in the year, which has been already noted.*

During ten days of her northern tour, Frau Schumann made her headquarters in Hamburg, and Johannes, arranging his visit home in correspondence with her movements, was made happy by seeing the cordiality of the relations established between his great artist-friend and the members of his family circle: "Homely but respectable people," records Frau Schumann's diary, "where I honestly feel so well in this unpretending simplicity."

The last public event of the journey was a soirée given by Frau Clara and Joachim on December 21 in Leipzig. On the 23rd, after a quiet day in Hanover, the traveller returned to Düsseldorf, accompanied by Brahms and Joachim, to spend Christmas in the midst of her children.

Moved by his own restless solicitude concerning Schumann's state, as well as by the affectionate desire to relieve the anxiety that had racked Frau Clara's mind during more than two months of unceasing activity, Joachim went off to Bonn on the morning of the 24th to get news at first hand of the invalid. To his joy he was admitted to the first interview with a personal friend that had been allowed to the master since his residence at Endenich. The impression he derived was to some extent reassuring and there was comfort for the little party in the mere fact that one of their number had seen and conversed with Schumann. A touching picture of the gathering in Düsseldorf of those who stood first in the affections of the great composer is given in Brahms' next letter to him:

"MOST HONOURED FRIEND,

"I should like to write a great deal about the Christmas evening, which was made so happy to us by Joachim's news; how he told us about you the whole evening and your wife wept so quietly. We were filled with joyful hope that we may soon be able to see you again.

---

* See *ante*, p. 169.

"You always turn the days which would otherwise be days of mourning for us, into high festivals. On her birthday your wife was allowed to write to you the first letter. At Christmas a friend first talked with you, the only one to whom we should not grudge this happiness, but only desire for ourselves to be allowed to succeed him soon.

"On the first day of the festival your wife gave her presents. She will now be writing to tell you about it; how well Marie played your A minor Sonata with Joachim, and Elise the Kinderscenen, and how she delighted me with Jean Paul's complete works. I had not hoped to be able to call them my own for many years. Joachim got the scores of your symphonies, which your wife had already given me.

"I returned here the evening before Christmas; how long the separation from your wife seemed to me! I had so accustomed myself to her inspiring society, I had lived near her so delightfully all the summer and learned to admire and love her so much, that everything seemed flat to me, and I could only long to see her again. What nice things I have brought back with me from Hamburg, however! The score of Gluck's Alcestis (the Italian edition, 1776) from Herr Avé, your first dear letter to me and several from your beloved wife. I must thank you most warmly for a pleasant word in your last letter, for the affectionate 'thou'; your kind wife also makes me happy now by using the nice, intimate word; it is the highest proof to me of her favour; I will try always to deserve it more.

"I had a great deal to write to you, dearest friend, but it would probably only be a repetition of what your wife is writing, therefore I conclude with the warmest handshake and greeting. Your

"JOHANNES.

"DÜSSELDORF, 30 *December*, 1854."

Frau Schumann, having before her the fatigues of a concert-journey in Holland, allowed herself a brief rest during the first half of January, and was cheered by the most encouraging letters from her husband. He wrote on the 6th:

" . . . I wish also to thank you most particularly, my Clara, for the artist letters and Johannes for the sonata and

ballades.* I know them now. The sonata—I remember
to have heard it once from him—so profoundly grasped;
living, deep, and warm throughout, and so closely woven
together. And the ballades—the first wonderful, quite new;
only I do not understand the *doppio movimento* either in
this or the second, is it not too fast?† The close beautiful
—original! The second how different, how diversified, how
suggestive to the imagination; magical tones are in it.
The bass F sharp at the end seems to lead to the third
ballade. What shall we call this? Demoniacal—quite
splendid, and becoming more and more mysterious after
the *pp* in the trio. And the return and close! Has this
ballade made a similar impression on you, my Clara? In
the fourth ballade how beautifully the strange melody
vacillates at the close between minor and major, and remains
mournfully in the major. Now on to overtures and symphonies! Do you not like this, my Clara, better than
organ? A symphony or opera, which arouses enthusiasm
and makes a great sensation, brings everything else more
quickly forward. He must. Now greet Johannes warmly
and the children, and you, my dearest heart, remember your,
as of old, loving

" ROBERT."

Brahms was permitted to follow Joachim, and on January
11 paid the master a visit of several hours' duration, in the
course of which he played both to and with him. At its
close Schumann walked back to Bonn with his dear young
friend, and could not make up his mind to part with him.
Johannes tore himself away just in time to catch his train,
and wrote a few days afterwards:

" DEAR HONOURED FRIEND,

      " I must thank you myself for the great pleasure you
give me by the dedication of your splendid concertstück.‡
How I rejoice to see my name thus printed! Especially,

---

* In manuscript: Ballades for Pianoforte, Op. 10.

† The *doppio movimento* marked in the manuscript of the first
ballade was changed before publication to *allegro ma non troppo*, no
doubt in deference to Schumann's suggestion.

‡ Concert-allegro with Introduction for Pianoforte and Orchestra,
Op. 134.

too, that I, like Joachim, have a concerto of my own.*
We have often talked of the two works and which we like
best—we have not been able to decide.

"I think with joy of the short hours that I was allowed
to spend with you, they were so delightful—but passed so
quickly. I cannot tell your wife enough about them; it
makes me doubly glad that you received me with such
friendship and kindness, and that you still think of the
hour with so much affection.

"We shall be able to see you thus more and more frequently and pleasantly till we possess you again.

"I have taken the catalogue (chronological), as you
wished, to your copyist (Fuchs).

"I expect you would like the original of Jenny Lind's
letter. It is probably the handwriting that you want. I
need not write out the contents for you.

"We are sending Bargiel's new work, it will give you
great pleasure, as it does us; Op. 8 is a great advance upon
Op. 9. Both are dedicated to your wife; that is what I
should like to do always. I should like to take turns with
the names Joachim and Clara Schumann till I had courage
to add your name. That, probably, will not soon come
to me.

"Now good-bye, dear man, and think sometimes with
affection of your

"JOHANNES.

"DÜSSELDORF, in January, 1855."

"Do you remember that you encouraged me last winter
to write an overture to "Romeo"? For the rest, I have
been trying my hand at a symphony during the past summer, have even instrumented the first movement and
composed the second and third."

During the entire winter, the devotion to Frau Schumann,
through which Joachim and Brahms were alike eager to
express their veneration for the beloved master in his awful
trial, was shared between them in the most practical way.
Joachim remained her frequent artistic companion after her
return from Holland, and the success achieved by the two

---

* Fantasia for Violin and Orchestra, Op. 131, dedicated to
Joachim.

great musicians on the many occasions of their giving concerts together, during this and the following season, was
extraordinary and unvarying.   Johannes remained at
Düsseldorf to attend to Schumann's little requirements, and
to send cheery news of all that was going on at home to the
anxious wife and mother.   In February he writes to
Endenich :

"DEAR HONOURED FRIEND,

"Herewith I send you the things you wished for; a
necktie and the *Signale*.   I must be responsible for the first;
as your wife is in Berlin, I had to decide.   I only hope you
will like it, and that it is not too high?

"I also send you the *Signale*; some of the numbers are
missing, we have not been careful enough about them.
From this time forward you shall have them regularly.

"I can now already give you the most positive assurance
that Herr Arnold has had your proof of the 'Gesänge der
Frühe.'   There must be some other reason for his having
delayed the publication so long.

"I wonder if the long walk with me did you good?   I
expect so.   With what pleasure I think of the delightful
day; I have seldom been so perfectly happy!   Your dear
wife was very much calmed and pacified by my blissful
letter.

"I am entrusted with many greetings to you from all
your friends here.   I will particularly mention those from
your children and Fräulein Bertha.*

"May all go well with you, and may you often think with
affection of your

"JOHANNES."

"DÜSSELDORF, *in February*, 1855."

Another letter follows early in March :

---

* Fräulein Bertha Bölling, a young lady who was resident for
some years in the Schumanns' house as domestic help to Frau Schumann, to whom she was greatly attached, and in whose confidence she
stood high.   During the first few days of Schumann's illness, before
his removal to Endenich, she was allowed by the doctors to go in and
out of the sick-room, and her presence had a tranquillising effect on
the patient.

"HONOURED MASTER,

"You will have wondered very much that I wrote of an F sharp minor Sonata which was to be sent you with the other things, and none was there. I quite forgot to put it up this morning. I send it you now with the songs and choruses from 'Maria Stuart.' I think you will like to have them; you have often mentioned them.

"Your wife just writes to me, quite delighted with your letter. She is going to send you some beautiful music-paper. I was certainly quick, but not so particular. Only women do everything quickly and well at the same time.

"With warmest greetings, Your

"JOHANNES BRAHMS.

"DÜSSELDORF, *March*, 1855."

Of the F sharp minor Sonata, Op. 2, Schumann answers:

"Your second sonata, my dear, has brought me much nearer to you. It was quite new to me; I live in your music, so that I can half play it at sight, one movement after the other. I am thankful for this. The beginning, the *pp*, the whole movement—there has never been one like it. Andante and the variations and the scherzo following them, quite different from those in the others; and the finale, the sostenuto, the music at the beginning of the second part, the animato and the close—in short, a laurel-wreath for the from-elsewhere-coming Johannes. And the songs, the first one; I seemed to know the second; but the third—it has (at the beginning) a melody in which there are many good girls, and the splendid close. The fourth quite original. In the fifth such beautiful music—like the poem. The sixth quite different from the others. The rushing, rustling, melody-harmony pleases me."

To Joachim, Schumann writes on March 10:

"Your letter has put me into quite a happy mood. The great gaps in your artistic cultivation, and the so-called violinist's eye and the address; nothing could have amused me more. Then I recalled the Hamlet overture, Henry overture, Lindenrauschen, Abend-glocken, Ballade—books for viola and pianoforte—the remarkable pieces which you played with Clara one evening at the hotel in Hanover;*

---

* Joachim's compositions.

and as I went on thinking I began this letter . . . Johannes
has sent me last year's *Signale*, to my great pleasure, for
everything that has happened since February 20 was new to
me.   There has never been such a musical winter [1853-54]
as that and the following; such travelling and flying from
town to town, Frau Schroeder-Devrient, Jenny Lind, Clara,
Wilhelmine Claus . . ."

Thus the months passed on.   Towards the close of the
musical season Johannes listened to Beethoven's "Missa
Solemnis" in Frau Schumann's company at a concert in
Cologne, hearing it for the first time; and three weeks later
travelled with her to Hamburg in response to an invitation
to both artists from Capellmeister Otten, a well known
musician of the city, on the occasion of the performance of
Schumann's "Manfred" at Otten's subscription concert of
April 21.   A day was passed at Hanover on the return
journey, and on May 7, Brahms' twenty-second birthday
anniversary, Joachim joined his friends at Düsseldorf in
fulfilment of a promise to make his headquarters near them
this season during the period of his "free time"—free from
the fixed duties of his post in Hanover—which, according
to his contract, extended till the month of October.

Brahms' birthday presents included the manuscript of a
romance for the pianoforte composed for him by Frau
Schumann, and from the master the score of his overture to
"The Bride of Messina," both with affectionate inscriptions.   The following letter of thanks was the last written
by him to Endenich:

   "BELOVED, HONOURED FRIEND,

      "I must send you most heartfelt thanks for having
remembered me so affectionately on May 7.   How surprised
and delighted I was by the beautiful present and the loving
words in the book!

   "The day was altogether such a delightful one as one
does not often experience.   Your dear wife understands how
to give happiness.   You, however, know this better than
anyone.

   "A portrait of my mother and sister surprised me.   In

the afternoon Joachim came, we hope for a very long time.

"I heard the overture to 'The Bride of Messina' the other day in Hamburg, as you know. How much the deeply-earnest work took hold of me, and after 'Manfred'! I was wishing all the time that you were there to hear and see what joy you give by your splendid works.

"I have been longing for some time past to hear especially 'Manfred' or 'Faust.' I hope we shall hear the last, greatest, together some time.

"Only your long silence, which made us uneasy, could have kept me from sending you my thanks sooner; accept now the heartiest thanks for your dear remembrance on May 7, 1855.

"In hearty love and veneration,

"Your JOHANNES."

CHAPTER VII

1855-1856

EXTRAORDINARY interest was lent to this year's Festival of the Lower Rhine, again held at Düsseldorf (May 27-29), by the appearance at each of its three concerts of Madame Jenny Lind-Goldschmidt. According to traditional custom, and, indeed, by the *raison d'être* of these great Whitsuntide gatherings, the programmes of the first two days each included a large work for chorus and orchestra, and on this special occasion the combined singing societies of about a dozen towns furnished over 650 voices, perfected by many weeks' previous practice, for the performance of Haydn's "Creation" and Schumann's "Paradise and the Peri." That the selection of Schumann's beautiful work was due, in the first place, to a desire expressed by Madame Lind-Goldschmidt is, under the circumstances of the time, a specially interesting detail. The direction of the concerts was in the experienced hands of Ferdinand Hiller, and Concertmeister David of Leipzig had been invited to lead the splendid body of strings.

It hardly needs telling that Madame Goldschmidt's performance of the soprano solos in the two works mentioned created the usual extraordinary impression. The name "Jenny Lind" is almost synonymous with triumph.

"The most perfect purity and certainty of intonation,"
says Otto Jahn, "the most strictly correct interpretation, the
distinctness and clearness of accent, the extraordinary virtuosity in everything that belongs to vocal technique—all
this would suggest a great singer, and that she unquestionably is; but her peculiar characteristic lies in something
beyond such qualities. Her phenomenal power is to be
traced to the genius which, without disturbing the composer's intention, makes everything she sings literally her
own—the mystery of artistic reproduction in its highest perfection, which is as inexplicable as production itself, and
cannot be described by ordinary expressions."[*]

At the third and so-called "artists' concert," chiefly devoted to solos, Madame Lind was heard in trios from
Mozart's "Nozze" and Bellini's "Beatrice di Tenda,"
and in Mendelssohn's song "Die Sterne schaun in stiller
Nacht." The stormy applause, recalls, orchestra flourishes,
flowers, and poems, in which the enthusiasm of her audience
found expression were duly chronicled by the critics of the
day. The instrumental solos of this final programme were
in the hands of Otto Goldschmidt and Concertmeister David,
who performed respectively Beethoven's G major Pianoforte
Concerto and a violin concerto by Julius Rietz, conductor of
the Leipzig Gewandhaus.

The festival is remembered as one of the most brilliant on
record. The immense audience brought together by the
magic of one name was as remarkable for its character as its
numbers.

"To give a list of the celebrities is impossible," continues
Jahn. "Who could count them? To mention a few of
the foremost: critics were there, from Chorley of London to
Hanslick of Vienna; pianists, from Stephen Heller of Paris
to Stein of Reval; composers, from Gouvy to Verhulst; conductors, from Franz Lachner to Franz Liszt. The music-
directors were almost more numerous than the privy coun-
cillors in Berlin."

---

[*] "Gesämmelte Aufsätze über Musik."

" In Jacobi's garden," says Hanslick, " a spot hallowed to
me by its association with Goethe, I met Brahms and
Joachim one morning. Brahms resembled a young ideal
hero of Jean Paul, with his forget-me-not eyes and his long
fair hair."

This was Brahms' first meeting with the man who was
to be one of his most intimate friends and appreciative critics
during more than thirty years of his later career.

At a matinée given by Frau Schumann in honour of a
few of the famous musicians assembled at Düsseldorf,
Johannes again renewed his acquaintance with Liszt, in
whom equal ennui seems to have been produced by the
works of Haydn and of Schumann to which he had listened
on the two first concert days, and it may be accepted as
certain that the meeting did not further a rapprochement
between the leader of Weimar and Schumann's ardent
young friend. Our musician was introduced the same
afternoon to Madame Lind-Goldschmidt, meeting her on
speaking terms for the only time in his life. No especial
feeling of personal interest was awakened between the two
artists. Johannes' large capacity for the sentiment of par·
ticular enthusiasm was already absorbed by his devotion to
Frau Schumann, and it is not surprising, on the other
hand, that his lack of training in social conventionalities,
which allowed him on this and other occasions to per-
petuate some innocuous but decidedly pointless jokes,
should have somewhat offended the taste of the fastidious
lady who had had the élite of Europe and America at her
feet. Madame Goldschmidt's first personal impression was
strengthened by an occurrence shortly to be related, nor
did she ever develop any great sympathy for Brahms'
music. Special circumstances, however, placed her, in later
years, in a certain association with it which has an interest
of its own, and particularly to the music-lovers of England.
On the occasions of the fine performances of the composer's
Schicksalslied (April 29, 1878), and of his German Requiem (March 16, 1880, and April 6, 1881), given in St.

James's Hall, London, by the Bach Choir under the direction of its then conductor, Otto Goldschmidt, the great singer, long since retired from public life, was to be found amongst her husband's forces as leader of the sopranos; and the inspiration has not yet been forgotten which was lent to the choir by the co-operation of one, peculiarly fitted by her exalted temperament to appreciate, at all events, the penetrating earnestness of the master's art.

In spite of the melancholy circumstances that kept them in Düsseldorf—and anxiety about Schumann was again increasing—the early summer of this year was a happy one for Brahms and Joachim, who passed many hours of the day in each other's society. Johannes lodged in a flat above Frau Schumann's dwelling; Joachim lived close by. The mornings were devoted by each to his particular avocations, but these frequently brought them together, and they always made part of Frau Schumann's family party at her mid-day dinner during the few weeks she was able to remain at home. The afternoons and evenings were often spent in long walks and excursions. Joachim had forgotten his loneliness, and Johannes' affection for his dearest Joseph had become one of the mainsprings of his life.

"Johannes and I make a great deal of music together," writes Joachim. "We have played through all Haydn's lively sonatas amongst other things. The other day we played Bach's E major Sonata."[*]

The second fortnight of June was spent by Frau Schumann at Detmold, capital of the small principality of Lippe-Detmold, which, during the fifties and sixties, possessed a very flourishing and enterprising musical life. The reigning Prince, Leopold III, had inherited from his mother, a Princess of Schwarzburg-Sondershausen, a fine taste for music that was shared by his brothers and sisters, and soon after his accession he established a private orchestra, consisting of thirty-three, soon augmented to forty-

---

* "Briefe von u. an Joseph Joachim."

five members, under the conductorship of the violinist Kiel,
a pupil of Spohr. A certain number of court concerts were
given every year, the programmes consisting of a symphony, two overtures, and several solos, selected from the
works of the best classical and modern composers. The
Prince was not without interest in the New-German school,
and compositions by Wagner and Berlioz were given from
time to time. Now and then there was a performance of
the whole or part of some large choral work.

Prince Leopold's mother, the Dowager Princess, resided
with her daughters, the Princesses Luise, Friederike, and
Pauline, in the old castle not far from the palace, and it
had been settled that the talented Princess Friederike
should enjoy the advantage of lessons from Frau Schumann
during the short interval at the disposal of the artist. The
arrangement proved a great success, and not only with
regard to the lessons. Frau Schumann delighted a circle
of sympathetic listeners by playing at several court soirées,
was enthusiastically received at a public concert, and, on
the eve of her departure, played one of Beethoven's pianoforte concertos at an orchestral court concert, which was
made further memorable by the presence of Joachim and
his performance of the same master's concerto for violin.

Soon after the return of the two artists, the little party
at Düsseldorf dispersed for a time. Joachim started for a
tour in the Tyrol, and Frau Schumann, accompanied by
Fräulein Bertha and Johannes, went to Ems, where she
had announced a concert for July 15, for which Madame
Lind-Goldschmidt had, during the week of the Düsseldorf
festival, proffered her services. The date decided upon
was somewhat in advance of the one originally selected,
and Goldschmidt had been called to Sweden meanwhile on
affairs of importance. He interrupted his engagements,
however, and travelled to Ems, in order to put his services
at Frau Schumann's disposal by superintending the general
business of the concert and acting as his wife's accompanist; and it was in this connection that a certain appear-

ance of nonchalance in Brahms' proceedings caused a feeling of irritation in Madame Goldschmidt and himself.

The concert was to take place in a room of the Kurhaus, and, owing to the procrastination of some of the authorities, the arrangements to be made on the spot, including those for receiving and seating the large number of ticket-holders, could not be begun until within an hour or two of the time appointed for the commencement of the music. The result was hurry and confusion indescribable, and many last things had to be done even during the assembling of the audience. The brunt of the difficulties was borne by Goldschmidt, who successfully overcame them, but who was annoyed that Brahms, arriving with Frau Schumann and Fräulein Bertha a couple of days before the date of the concert, left again the next afternoon instead of remaining to make himself useful, and was seen no more in Ems. Starting for Braubach, he wandered about alone until the winding up of the concert business, which resulted in a clear profit of 1,340 thalers, left Frau Schumann at leisure again. There is no question that on this occasion it was his invincible dislike to a fashionable crowd which overcame his judgment, but it is not to be wondered at that his real or apparent indifference was commented on by those to whom it seemed inexplicable. Rejoining Frau Schumann and her companion on their departure from Ems on the morning of the 16th, Johannes passed ten happy days walking along the Rhine from Coblenz to Mainz and visiting Frankfurt and Heidelberg in their society. "They were happy days. I should never have thought I could have been so happy travelling with two ladies," he wrote from Heidelberg to Grimm. By the end of the month the three holiday makers were back in Düsseldorf.

The dreaded business of moving to a new house, with its inevitable uprooting of home associations consecrated alike by experiences of joy and sorrow, awaited Frau Schumann on her return, and was accomplished with a courage that enabled her to go north early in August to rest for some weeks at the seaside. Brahms, who definitely took up his abode in the new dwelling—the first-floor flat (étage) of 135 Poststrasse—remained in Düsseldorf to work hard at his pianoforte playing. Accustomed though he might be to declare that his spirits always rose with the spending of his last shilling, yet the precariousness of his outward circumstances had, in truth, weighed heavily upon his mind during the past year. No sure earnings could be derived from publishing; pupils were not to be easily obtained; and he had resolved to follow the advice of his two best friends and try his luck again as a concert player. He looked forward with dread to the ordeal and shrank from the partings it would involve, but kept to his plan; and in the course of September his intention of making a concert journey was announced in the *Signale*. Meanwhile, the return of Frau Schumann from Düsternbrook, near Kiel, and that of Joachim from the Tyrol, secured him a few more weeks of happiness.

"We passed Sunday (August) 26 very pleasantly," writes Frau Clara; "Joachim had much to tell us about his journey and Johannes and I rejoiced that we were all together again."

Joachim held private quartet evenings in his rooms twice a week throughout September, and the party assembled sometimes at Frau Schumann's house, where Johannes had now and again the opportunity of taking part in the performance of some work for pianoforte and strings. His reappearance in public took place, not in Leipzig as had been intended, but in Danzig, where he gave concerts with Frau Clara and Joachim on November 14 and 16, a change of plan that had at least the desired result of benefiting his pocket. A picture of him on his arrival in the town, given by Anton Door,* forms an amusing and perhaps instructive sequel to the foregoing account of the occurrences at Ems:

---

* *Die Musik*, first May number, 1903.

" I had hardly been a week in Danzig, when I saw great bills in the streets announcing the coming concert of Clara Schumann, Joseph Joachim, and Johannes Brahms. I at once called on Joachim, who received me with cordiality, and we chatted, as old acquaintances, of home and our experiences.

" During the whole time we were together, a slender young man with long, fair hair paced continually to and fro in the background smoking cigarettes, without troubling himself in the least about my presence, or even showing by an inclination of the head that he observed me; in a word, I was as empty air for him. This was my first meeting with Johannes Brahms."

Door became, nevertheless, in later years, a cordial friend and admirer of the composer.

Complete equality amongst the three performers was observed in the arrangement of the programmes. Each played solos, and both pianists performed with the violinist at either concert. Brahms' contributions included Bach's Chromatic Fantasia, which remained one of the *pièces de résistance* of his répertoire throughout his pianistic career, and two manuscript pieces, Saraband and Gavotte, from amongst the " Album-Leaves " which he had contemplated publishing in 1854.

Unfortunately his constitutional nervousness, combined with the discouraging effect of a bad pianoforte, to mar his artistic success.

The critical moment had now arrived when Johannes was obliged to bid farewell to his friends and go his own way. He played for the first time in his life with orchestra—and with success—at the Bremen subscription concert of November 20, contributing to the programme Beethoven's G major Concerto and Schumann's great Fantasia, Op. 17; and on the 24th, the date which he had anticipated with ever-increasing anxiety as it drew nearer, made his first appearance in Hamburg since the wonderful turn that had taken place in his fortunes in 1853, at one of G. D. Otten's annual series of orchestral subscription concerts.

No doubt he was additionally weighted by nervousness —that *bête noire* of executive artists to which, from the rarity of his public appearances, Brahms was peculiarly a prey—by feeling, not only that he was on his trial before his fellow-citizens, but that there were, in the audience, loving friends prepared to triumph on his behalf. He had chosen for performance Beethoven's E flat Concerto and unaccompanied solos by Schumann and Schubert, but although he was apparently satisfied with his reception and reported to his friends that he had "played with great animation," he achieved, if contemporary press accounts are to be trusted, little more than a *succès d'estime*.

"The pianoforte part of the concerto," said the critic of the *Hamburger Nachrichten*, "was played by Brahms with the modesty of a young artist, and was kept throughout in subordination to the whole musical effect of the symphonic concerto. In our opinion, he carried his reserve too far. He might, without detriment to the spirit of the work, have displayed rather more virtuosity. That he possesses it was shown by his playing of a canon by Schumann, and a march by Schubert for four hands, arranged by Brahms for two hands."

It will not have escaped the reader's attention that Brahms introduced no new important composition of his own on either of the occasions now chronicled, and that no mention has been made of any fresh publication from his pen since the autumn of 1854. The reason is not far to seek. Neither the extraordinary praise bestowed on his works by Schumann, Joachim, and their circle, nor the reserve with which they had been received by many musicians whose good faith could not be doubted, nor the acrimonious attacks of a portion, and especially the Rhenish portion, of the musical press, could influence to any appreciable extent the tribunal to which he had thus early in his career accustomed himself to submit his works in the last instance—his own searching self-criticism. He had, as has been seen, carried out Schumann's wish, and had tried his

hand on a symphony. The discovery that he had not sufficiently mastered some of the fundamental technical qualifications necessary for the successful fulfilment of such an
attempt no doubt prevented his carrying it to a conclusion.
It will be remembered, also, that he had withheld the string
quartet recommended to Dr. Härtel for publication by
Schumann in 1853. By the middle of 1855, he had sufficiently gauged both his strength and his weakness to have
made the resolve to apply himself to a fresh course of severe
study—study which should widen and strengthen and re-
fine his capacity in every direction, but which should have
as its special aim the attainment of greater facility and
purity in part-writing in the strict style. From this time,
for a period of five or six years, he worked on without view
to immediate publication, but only with a set determination
to become worthy of Schumann's high hopes. He insisted
before long that Joseph should join him in his studies;
and an exchange of exercises at fixed intervals, agreed upon
between the two young musicians, was kept up for some
years. Joachim was inevitably much less regular than
Brahms in sending his papers, and Johannes by and by
instituted a system of fines, to be paid and spent in books
in case of unpunctuality on either side. The chief burden
of the new rule certainly fell upon the famous young concertmeister, whose great and increasing popularity brought
innumerable concert-journeys in its train. The difference
in the character of the two men is pleasantly illustrated by
this episode, which shows Johannes insisting on having his
own way, and Joachim, from whom no excuse was accepted,
good-naturedly yielding, and wishing to do more than he
could possibly fulfil. Many interesting memorials of
Brahms' studies are in existence in the form of music-books,
printed or in manuscript, of which he possessed himself at
this period. Amongst them is an original edition of the
first part of Emanuel Bach's collection of his father's setting of German chorales (1765), on the cover of which is
Brahms' autograph and the date 1855, and at the end of

the book is an alphabetical index in Brahms' writing.* There is also a very beautifully copied manuscript (not by Brahms) of Sebastian Bach's "Kunst der Fuge," containing one or two trifling pencil corrections in our musician's unmistakable hand. ' On the fly-leaf is written "Joh. Brahms, Nov. 1855, Hamburg," also in pencil, in large and bold penmanship, probably in one of the styles taught at Hoffmann's school.* There are, too, a volume containing compositions by Orlando di Lasso;† and manuscript copies of, amongst other works, Palestrina's "Missa Papæ Marcelli," with Brahms' autograph and the date 1856; of Rovetta's "Salve Regina"; and, in Frau Schumann's hand, of a "Gloria" of Palestrina.‡ Still more valuable are the manuscripts of several original Mass movements by Brahms in four and six parts, presented later on by the composer to his friend Grimm,§ and these recall Dietrich's mention of an entire Mass written in canon for voices. This list shows clearly enough the nature of the young composer's aims. He was determined to become thoroughly acquainted with the historical development of his art, to know the why and wherefore, as well as the how and when, of what he had studied in the works of succeeding masters. The fascination exercised over his mind by the clear, pure style of the great early writers, whose learning is often used with such consummate ease as to be unsuspected by the untrained hearer, is evident enough in many of the choral works published by him later on. He exercised himself in the acquisition of their technique until it had become an instrument in his hand for the production of works which, like everything else that he gave to the world, bear the impress of his own individuality.

In the issue of the *Neue Zeitschrift für Musik* of December 14 a long article on Brahms appeared, the closing one

---

* Both in the possession of Mr. Evlyn Howard-Jones.
† In the possession of Professor Julius Spengel.
‡ In the library of the Gesellschaft der Musikfreunde, Vienna.
§ In the possession of Fräulein Marie Grimm.

of a series of three begun in July. Until this date, since
the very sympathetic notice written by "Hoplit" after the
young musician's début at the Leipzig Gewandhaus, not a
word had been printed in this paper about his compositions
save the bare announcements of publication, in spite of the
fact that nine opus numbers had been given to the world in
the interval, five of them being important instrumental
works, and three consisting severally of six songs. "Hoplit" had now come forward to take upon himself entire
blame for the omission, which, he declared, must not be
attributed to any indifference of the editor. Brendel had
not only sent him each work as it appeared, but had urged
him to write, asking repeatedly, "Why nothing about
Brahms?" His own great interest in the young composer,
his desire to find himself in complete accord with Schumann's opinion, his incapability of entirely agreeing with
it, had, he said, always led him to defer his criticism; and,
indeed, the reluctant and hesitating tone of the articles
leads to the conviction that they were written in complete
good faith.

"That Brahms found many opponents on his first appearance was an unusual distinction; it showed that he possessed a very significant artistic individuality. When, however, enthusiastic friends saw in him the prophet of a new
time, and especially when they proclaimed the completely
developed, ripe artist, we can only regard it as an amiable
excess of enthusiasm."

"Brahms," says the second and most interesting article,
"has sometimes been described as the most talented and
pronounced of the Schumannites. So far as this is true,
we regret it . . . . Schumann cannot be carried further.
. . . . His very important individuality quite unquestionably
possesses a high value, but only in its originality. Brahms
is, however, no imitator of Schumann. He displays, in the
whole bent of his nature and creative activity, an inner
affinity with him which is more than mere sympathy, and
has about it nothing forced or borrowed; but he possesses
an element not in Schumann which makes us believe that, if
it is only given to him to attain full development, he will

find his own paths. The more he succeeds in freeing himself from the characteristic Schumann nature, the more may be looked for from his future . . . .

"Brahms is not free from Schumann's danger; he, also, has the subtle habit of mind, the tendency to the indefinite and misty, which characterise the romanticists. He shares Schumann's strong faith, moreover, in impulses of genius and inspirations of the moment, to be followed without discrimination or resistance. He sometimes introduces passages which have neither presupposition nor consequence, but which are not therefore heaven-bestowed. His work is inconsistent and defective in style. He should have been regarded as an artist not yet mature. When all is said, however, it was an unusually striking phenomenon that such a young composer should exhibit in his first works a freedom in the handling of form, a diversity of harmonic and rhythmic development, and an abundance of ideas, such as are to be found in the works only of those who are called to become one day masters. And yet who will deny that much 'lies in the air' to-day which had formerly to be won by hard fighting, or to be developed entirely from within?"

Dr. Pohl's doubt evidently overcomes him again in the last sentence, and it would be quite unjust to refer his hesitation to the influence of party spirit, or to say that he had no ground for his feeling of uncertainty as to the destiny of our composer's genius. It is difficult now to realise the position of the critic who, in 1855, wished to write without bias of the Brahms of twenty-two; but the good faith of these *Neue Zeitschrift* articles is curiously confirmed by a few forcible words written in 1893 by an intimate friend of the Brahms of past sixty.

"Brahms' first works," says Hanslick,* "had interested me in a high degree—interested, however, rather than satisfied me. A young Hercules at the parting of the ways. Will he turn to the left, to the most extreme romanticism, or to the right, to the path of our classics?"

That Brahms himself had become aware of the problem that faced him is conclusively shown by the future course

---

* "Aus meinem Leben."

of his development; and, with the exception of the Ballades for pianoforte, Op. 10, dedicated to Grimm, mentioned by Schumann in his letter of January, 1855, and produced by Breitkopf and Härtel early in 1856, no work of his composition succeeded the publications of 1854 until after a period of six years.

Johannes again passed Christmas with Frau Schumann, and on January 10 played Beethoven's G major Concerto and unaccompanied solos by Schumann at the Leipzig Gewandhaus concert. The impression generally created by his performance is summed up by a few words in the *Signale* which suggest that he again rather overdid his artistic self-restraint :

"Many artists could certainly have displayed more technical brilliancy, but few have the capacity for bringing out so convincingly the intentions of the composer, or following as Brahms does the flight of Beethoven's genius and disclosing its full splendour."

The critic adds that the young artist, who thinks more of the work he happens to be interpreting than of self-display, has already won many friends in the art world by his compositions.

Paying a flying visit to Hanover on his way back to Hamburg, which is, just now, to be considered as his settled home, Johannes for the first time heard Rubinstein, who had come to play at one of the subscription concerts conducted by Joachim, and who shortly afterwards wrote to Liszt :

" . . . As regards Brahms, I hardly know how to describe the impression he made on me. He is not graceful enough for the drawing-room, not fiery enough for the concert-room, not simple enough for the country, and not general enough for the town. I have but little faith in this kind of nature."

It may be remarked here that Rubinstein never acquired a liking for Brahms' art, and that, to the end of his life, he expressed the opinion that the series of great masters had

ceased with Schumann. Rubinstein obtained a powerful
following, not only as pianist, but as composer, at Leipzig,
and in later years his works were pitted against those of
Brahms by the large and influential set of musicians and
amateurs of the typical Gewandhaus circle. The generosity
of Rubinstein's nature is too well established to leave room
for any suspicion of his having been moved by paltry
feelings of professional jealousy, and his repeated asseveri-
ations that he could find no music in Brahms' works must
be accepted as genuine expressions of his sentiments.

Many celebrations took place, during the opening month
of 1856, of the centenary of Mozart's birth (January 27,
1756), and Johannes, making his second appearance at
Otten's concerts on the 26th, contributed the D minor Concerto to a programme selected from the great master's
works. Whilst practising for the occasion at the house of
Messrs. Baumgarten and Heins, he made the acquaintance
of the critic and journalist E. Krause, between whom and
himself a permanent friendship was established. Krause
became one of the earliest and ablest supporters of his art.

But two concerts of the season remain to be mentioned—
one at Kiel, given by Brahms in association with the composer Grädener, of Hamburg, and the violinist John Böie,
when his solos were Beethoven's E flat Sonata, Op. 27,
No. 1, and C minor Variations; the other at Altona, where
he played Bach's Organ Toccata in F major, Beethoven's
"Eroïca" Variations, and, with Böie and Breyther, Schumann's trio movements "Märchen Erzählungen," and
Beethoven's Sonata for pianoforte and violin, Op. 96. He
passed February and March quietly with his parents,
making as much money as he could by teaching. Mention
may be made of a pupil in whom he was interested at this
time—Fräulein Friedchen Wagner, a cousin of Otten's,
and herself a pianoforte-teacher. Brahms' acquaintance
with her has an association, to which we shall presently
refer, with some of the works published by him in the early
sixties.

To this period is to be referred the composition of a
pianoforte Quartet in C sharp minor, which was shown to
Joachim soon after Brahms' return to Düsseldorf in April.
The work is identified by Joachim's discussion of the manuscript and quotation of one of its themes, in a letter of the
same month, as an early version of the pianoforte Quartet
in C minor published in 1895 as Op. 60.

Frau Schumann, who travelled without break, save for a
short interval in December, during the season 1855-56,
spent more than two months of the early part of the year
in Vienna, where Schumann's works were as yet but little
known to the general public. Appearing as the inspired
missionary of her husband's art, she succeeded in arousing
interest in his compositions, whilst her personal achievements as an executant excited extraordinary enthusiasm.
She gave six recitals, and introduced into two of her programmes respectively Brahms' Saraband and Gavotte and
the andante and scherzo from his C minor Sonata. The
critic of the *Wiener Zeitung* of that date, Carl Debrois van
Bruyck, speaks of them as "pieces of special beauty, which
confirm the impression of the young composer's exceptional
talent" already formed by him from the study of other
works, especially of a set of variations [Op. 9] and a book
of songs. The successful début of Brahms' name in a concert-programme and a prominent journal of the city to
which he was to belong during the second half of his life
is an interesting point in his history.

It will be convenient to refer at once to a detailed review
of our composer's early works contributed to his journal by
van Bruyck on September 25, 1857. At this date, as the
reader is aware, Brahms' publications had not increased
beyond the ten numbers already mentioned, and consisted
of the three sonatas, scherzo, variations, and ballades for
pianoforte, the B major Trio, and the first three books of
songs. The similarity of the remarks of the Vienna critic
with those contained in "Hoplit's" *Neue Zeitschrift* articles,
already referred to, is the more striking since van Bruyck

did not concern himself with the party conflicts of Germany. He was, however, a very great lover of Schumann's art, and if he had any bias in regard to that of Brahms, it inclined in favour of Schumann's young prophet.

He regards the variations as decidedly pre-eminent amongst the ten works. They convince him that Brahms has

"a genuine and entirely original talent, a finely-endowed artist nature. . . . Some of them are quite magic and ethereal, although the finest of all recalls Schumann, perhaps intentionally; and in others, especially the last, the young composer's tendency to the vague and mystical is rather unpleasantly and dangerously apparent. Next to the variations I should place the songs, which contain tones of penetrating depth and sweetness. . . . Brahms certainly stands within the sacred circle, and has already acquired a very definite power of achievement, though it may not at present be sufficient for his purpose; and it is the duty of serious, unbiassed criticism to protect him against the derision which the more highly gifted men have never escaped, especially when their endowment has been peculiarly individual. As we have said, Brahms' natural power seems to be lofty beyond all question, and the danger and doubt as regards his development lies, we think, in his partly instinctive, partly conscious striving after over-refinement; in his excessive bent to the dæmoniacal, the fantastic. Should he succeed in restraining this inclination, we may await with confidence many riper, more perfect fruits whether in the nearer or farther future."

The derision from which van Bruyck desired to protect Johannes emanated chiefly or entirely at this period from the Rhenish press. As it consisted chiefly of the vulgar commonplaces of the journalist—familiar at all times and in all countries—who has neither knowledge of his subject nor instinct to avoid displaying his ignorance, no example will be given of it in these pages.

Whilst Frau Schumann was achieving a series of unbroken successes in Vienna, her private anxieties pressed upon her with ever-increasing severity. The apparent improvement in Schumann's health had been but transitory. He had steadily lost ground since the spring of 1855, and before the winter had well come to an end the physicians were unable to conceal from themselves that his case was hopeless. The afflicted wife was sustained for the fulfilment of her duties by the best accounts that the situation admitted of, but she was obliged, on her return from Vienna, to relinquish all immediate hope of an interview with her husband, whom she had not seen since the hour before the catastrophe of 1854. Nor could she allow herself the solace of remaining near him. She was now sole bread-winner for the family, and a group of young children depended on her exertions. She had entered into engagements for the London season, and after a very short interval of rest, started on April 7 for England.

For Brahms, bound as he was by the closest ties of affection and gratitude to Schumann and his family, it was impossible, under the melancholy trend of events, to remain quietly at his studies in Hamburg. There was some idea of removing the patient from Endenich; at all events, it would be a satisfaction to obtain the opinion of fresh experts on brain disease; and Johannes undertook to make personal inquiries of certain eminent doctors, and to send his report as soon as possible to England. On April 15 Frau Schumann wrote from London to Dietrich, who had in the summer been appointed Wasielewski's successor as music-director at Bonn:

"DEAR HERR DIETRICH,
     "I enclose a long letter from Gisela von Arnim. Will you give it to Johannes on his return? I must again thank you and Professor Jahn very fervently for the sympathy which you show Johannes in his undertaking; it is a comfort to me that he does not stand alone, it would be too hard for him. Of myself I have little satisfactory to relate. In spirit I am always in Germany. I played yesterday at the Philharmonic with a bleeding heart. I had a letter from Johannes in the morning, in which I read hopelessness between the lines as regards my beloved hus-

band, although he had tried in all affection to tell me everything as gently as possible. Whence the power to play came to me I do not know; I could do nothing at home, and yet in the evening things went.

"Think sometimes kindly of your

"CLARA SCHUMANN.

"I really think the enclosed letter is worth consideration. Johannes will certainly show it to you and Professor Jahn. I have just heard something about cold-water treatment for brain disease, which makes me very anxious to try it for my husband. Please tell Johannes I will write about it to-morrow."

All was in vain, however. Schumann was already in an advanced stage of the disease which, technically described under different learned names, according to its many varieties, is known to the layman as softening of the brain. Anyone who has watched the powers of friend or acquaintance gradually succumbing to this most cruel of all maladies is familiar with the general course of the symptoms. Minute particulars need not be described. Enough that Johannes, permitted to see Schumann again after an interval of more than a year, had been unutterably shocked, and had felt that the time had arrived when it was his duty to prepare Frau Schumann for the worst. As gently as possible he allowed her, as she expresses it, to read between the lines that no change of treatment could alter the inevitable. All the doctors were agreed in opinion; none, therefore, was attempted.

The concert so pathetically referred to in the letter quoted above was the Philharmonic concert at the Hanover Square Rooms of April 14, the occasion of Frau Schumann's first appearance in England. Could any incident of fiction be more heart-rending in its pathos than this occurrence of real life—this picture of the sensitive, highly-strung woman, whose nerves were habitually in a state of strained tension, obliged to force herself, for the sake of her children's existence, to step for the first time on to a London concert

platform, a sea of unknown faces before her, her kith and
kin far away, a few hours after she had accepted the certainty of her passionately loved husband's tragic doom?
No wonder she could "do nothing" before the concert.
Those who knew her best can understand how it was that,
after all, "things went." Her début in England was
made with Beethoven's E flat Concerto and Mendelssohn's
"Variations Sérieuses," and things went with a brilliant
success that was but an augury of events to follow.

Through the remainder of April, and throughout May
and June, did this great artist work incessantly, going in
desolation of spirit from triumph to triumph; and some of
Schumann's shorter compositions which were encored by the
public became something more than tolerated, even by the
conservative press, for the sake of her perfect playing of
them. Her numerous concert-journeys through the British
Islands extended as far as Dublin. Amongst the most important of her London appearances were those at the
Musical Union (John Ella's) concerts and at her own three
recitals. At the second of these, which took place on June
17, she imitated her own precedent at Vienna, and introduced Brahms' name for the first time to an English public.
The entire selection belongs so peculiarly to the events and
period occupying our attention that it may interest the reader
to have the complete programme:

Variations (Eroïca) - - - -	*Beethoven*
Two Diversions, Op. 17, from Suite de	
Pièces, Op. 24, No. 1 - - -	*Sterndale Bennett.*
Variations on a theme from the "Bunten	
Blättern" - - - - -	*Clara Schumann.*
(a) Saraband and Gavotte in the style	
of Bach - - - - -	*Johannes Brahms.*
(b) Clavierstück in A major - -	*Scarlatti.*
"Carnaval" - - - -	*Schumann.*

The Brahms Gavotte was enthusiastically applauded, but
Frau Schumann, having regard to the performance of the
"Carnaval" still before her, refused the encore. At the

close of the recital, however, she returned to the piano in response to continued demonstrations, and repeated the composition. Her performances were given on a pianoforte by Erard, whose instruments were preferred at that date by all the great pianists of Europe. A magnificent "grand" was presented by the house to Frau Schumann at the close of her London season, and despatched to her residence in Düsseldorf. It continued to be her favourite instrument for private use until 1867, when, reappearing in England after an absence of two years, she used a Broadwood pianoforte. On her departure a Broadwood concert-grand was sent to her house near Baden-Baden by Messrs. John Broadwood and Sons. Some years later, when the author was intimate at Frau Schumann's residence, the Broadwood pianoforte stood in the drawing-room, the Erard in the dining-room. On the former Frau Schumann and Brahms often played duets after afternoon coffee; on the latter Johannes—always "Johannes" to his old friend—played one evening after supper several numbers of the third and fourth books of the Hungarian Dances, not yet published, not yet books, his eyes flashing fire the while.

Brahms gave up all idea of returning to Hamburg for the present. Duty and inclination alike prompted him to remain in Schumann's neighbourhood, and the fact of Dietrich's residence at Bonn gave him additional satisfaction in resolving to pass the summer on the Rhine. It was at this time that he made the personal acquaintance of the poet Claus Groth, who was staying at Bonn to be near Otto Jahn; and the musical festival of the year (May 11-13) marked the beginning of his intimacy with the great singer Julius Stockhausen, who, making his first appearance on the Rhine, was heard in the part of Elijah in Mendelssohn's oratorio, in "Alexander's Feast," in an aria by Boieldieu, and in songs by Schubert, Mendelssohn and Schumann.

Stockhausen had been a pupil of Manuel Garcia in Paris and London, and was well known to the musical public and the private artistic circles of both cities before he became a celebrity in Austria and Germany.

"His delivery of opera and oratorio music," says Sir George Grove*—"his favourite pieces from 'Euryanthe,' 'Jean de Paris,' 'Le Chaperon Rouge,' and 'Le Philtre'; or the part of Elijah, or certain special airs of Bach—was superb in taste, feeling, and execution; but it was the Lieder of Schubert and Schumann that most peculiarly suited him, and these he delivered in a truly remarkable way. The rich beauty of the voice, the nobility of the style, the perfect phrasing, the intimate sympathy, not least, the intelligible way in which the words were given—in itself one of his greatest claims to distinction—all combined to make his singing of songs a wonderful event. Those who have heard him sing Schubert's 'Nachtstück,' 'Wanderer,' 'Memnon,' or the 'Harper's Songs,' or Schumann's 'Frühlingsnacht' or 'Fluthenreicher Ebro,' or the 'Löwenbraut,' will corroborate all that has been said. But perhaps his highest achievement was the part of Dr. Marianus in the third part of Schumann's 'Faust,' in which his delivery of 'Hier ist die Aussicht frei,' with just as much of acting as the concert-room will admit, and no more, was one of the most touching and remarkable things ever witnessed."

Cordial relations were so quickly established between Stockhausen and Brahms that before the close of the month they had given two concerts together—one on the 27th, in the "yellow room of the casino" at Cologne; the other on the 29th, in the hall of the Lesegesellschaft at Bonn. Stockhausen's performances, accompanied in each instance by Brahms, created a furore on both occasions. Brahms' solos —consisting on the 27th of Bach's Chromatic Fantasia and Beethoven's C minor Variations, and on the 29th of Beethoven's E flat Variations, Clara Schumann's Romance, a Schubert Impromptu, and the great Bach Fugue in A minor, to be found in vol. iii of the Leipzig Society's edition— were coldly received. This is not to be wondered at. During the half-century which has elapsed since these con-

---

* Grove's "Dictionary of Music and Musicians."

certs took place musical taste has passed through more than
one revolution; it is, however, questionable whether at any
time within the interval a pianist, of whatever qualifications, not already accepted into the prime affections of the
public, could have successfully courted its favour beside the
attraction of a really great singer in full possession of his
powers, whose selections included a number of the most
fascinating lyrics of Schubert, Mendelssohn and Schumann.
One of the Cologne critics, at all events, was satisfied with
the pianist. It is rather surprising to read, in the *Nieder-
rheinische Musik Zeitung*, that Herr Johannes Brahms
played his two solos on the 27th "with such purity, clearness, musical ripeness, and artistic repose, that his performances gave true pleasure."

Brahms' temperament was not really suited, however, to
the career of a virtuoso, nor had the obscure circumstances
of his youth fitted him for it. He generally felt too nerv-
ously self-conscious when before the public to have a chance
of gaining its entire confidence, and was too dependent on
his mood to be able to throw himself at all times completely
out upon his audience and compel their sympathy. The
achievement of striking and lasting success as a performer
involves a concentration of the best energies of body and
mind upon this career, whilst the attainment of real greatness as a composer means the devotion of a life to the end.
No illustration of these truths could be more apt than the
contrasted careers of Brahms and Joachim. Whatever
Joachim's natural creative faculty may have been, his
boundless success as an interpreter was fatal to its development. The divergence of the paths pursued by the two
friends resulted not altogether, or perhaps chiefly, from
variety of musical endowment, but largely from the radical
differences in their characters and circumstances. From
early childhood Joachim never appeared on a platform without exciting, not only the admiration, but the personal love
of his audience. His successes were their delight. They
rejoiced to see him, to applaud him, recall him, shout at

him. The scenes familiar to the memory of three generations of London concert-goers were samples of the everyday incidents of his life in all countries and towns where he appeared. Why? It is impossible altogether to explain such phenomena, even by the word "genius." Joachim followed his destiny. His career was unparalleled in the history of musical executive art. It began when he was eight; it closed only a few weeks before his death at the age of seventy-six. All possibility of his achieving greatness as a composer—notwithstanding that he produced one or two important works—was excluded by the time he had reached the age of fourteen.

The mistress of Brahms' absorbing passion, on the other hand, was from first to last his creative art, to which all else remained secondary. He never swerved by a hair's-breadth from his devotion, but accepted poverty, disappointment, loneliness, and failure in the eyes of the world, with all the strong faith that was in him, for the sake of this, his true love. He was never drawn by inclination to his virtuoso career, to which he submitted only as a necessity, discarding it as soon as circumstances allowed. He was seldom able to disclose the infinite possibilities of his playing under circumstances in which he was not at ease; and though he possessed a great technique which he could easily have developed into something phenomenal, and which, as it was, enabled him to excite an audience now and again by sounding and dramatic performances of Bach's organ compositions and other imposing works, yet the more distinctive beauties of his style were too subtle for the appreciation of a mixed body of listeners. His imagination of effects of tone was, to quote Schumann's article, quite original, and this was even more strikingly displayed in later years, when he conducted one or other of his orchestral works. His playing even of such a trifle as Gluck's Gavotte in A, arranged for Frau Schumann in 1871, which the author more than once heard, was full of unsought graces that were the immediate reflection of his delicate spirit. His performance of this little piece, and his conception of many works of the great masters, together with his whole style of playing, differed *in toto* from Frau Schumann's. The two artists admired each other's qualities. Frau Schumann courted Brahms' criticisms, and has, on some occasions, quoted to the author his sayings as to the reading of certain of Beethoven's sonatas, declaring she felt them to be right. Nevertheless, her temperament would never have allowed her to carry out these suggestions in actual public performance, and she was better fitted by temperament than Brahms for the interpretation, to the large public, of the masterpieces of musical art.

The author has been carried by this digression, which is the result of her personal intercourse with these great musicians, to a date many years later than that reached by the narrative. Its insertion here may, however, be of advantage to the reader by preparing him to expect that Brahms' career as a pianist, though not without success, was attended by few brilliant triumphs.

On June 8, the forty-sixth anniversary of Schumann's birthday, Johannes again went to Endenich, accompanied on the walk from Bonn by Jahn, Dietrich, Groth, and Hermann Deiters, another notable acquaintance of this summer. He looked very serious on rejoining his companions, though he said that Schumann had recognised and seemed pleased to see him. The end was, indeed, not far off. The mists that had so long been gathering around the lofty spirit of the master continued to close him into ever-increasing darkness. Bad news attended Frau Schumann's return from England early in July, and on the 23rd of the month she was summoned by a telegraphic despatch to Endenich. The doctors had persevered throughout the sad illness in their refusal to sanction her desire for a meeting with her husband, and even now the longed-for interview was again deferred. Fresh symptoms appeared before her arrival and she was obliged to return to Düsseldorf to live through four more days of agonising suspense. She went again to Bonn

on Sunday, July 27, there to await the end and, the same
evening, after nearly two and a half years of separation,
passed with Johannes into the solemn chamber of death.
Schumann was lying quietly with closed eyes as she entered,
but opened them presently on the figure kneeling at his bed-
side, and it became evident after a few moments that he
knew his wife. His power of speech was almost gone, but
a look of recognition passed over his countenance, a tender
word was half distinguishable, and suddenly, with a last
accession of strength, he was able to place one of his arms
round her. Those faint looks of love, that last embrace,
dwelt in Frau Schumann's memory as an ever-present solace
during the forty years of her widowhood and, in spite of
her many sorrows, the radiance was never dimmed that had
been shed over her spirit once and for all by the enchantment
of an early, ideal happiness.

Schumann lingered yet a day or two, becoming weaker
hour by hour, as his wife and young friend watched at his
side. Once at least on Monday it was apparent that he
felt the solace of his wife's touch as she tenderly moistened
his lips with a few drops of wine. He passed quietly away
at four o'clock on Tuesday afternoon, July 29, and Frau
Schumann, returning from a short interval of repose at her
hotel, accompanied by Brahms and by Joachim, who had
taken immediate train to Bonn on receiving a hopeless report, learned that her husband's sufferings were over for
ever.

Two days more, and on Thursday, July 31, in the stillness of a balmy summer evening, the mortal remains of the
master were laid to rest in the cemetery of Bonn. The funeral
was arranged with touching simplicity. A pleasant spot
had been chosen by the city, some plantain-trees planted
by the grave. The coffin, borne from Endenich by the choristers of the Concordia, was immediately preceded by the
three chief mourners—Brahms, who carried a laurel wreath,
Joachim and Dietrich. Following the body came the clergy-
man, Pastor Wiesemann, and the Mayor of Bonn, and at

an appointed spot in the city a long string of musicians and music lovers joined the procession, which passed on foot through the streets accompanied by a band of brass instruments playing one and another of the most solemnly beautiful of the old German chorales. At the graveside Brahms stepped forward and placed the wife's wreath upon the coffin, bare of other floral decorations. Frau Schumann herself stood a little apart from the mourners, following the service unobserved. A short address was delivered by Pastor Wiesemann, then came a sacred part-song by the choristers, a chorale, a few simple words spoken by Ferdinand Hiller, the last farewell of friends throwing earth upon the coffin, and all was over.*

On the anguish of the widow looking out despairingly to the future of her lonely life, who yet might not despair because of the little ones clinging to her side, on the steadfast loyalty of the affectionate friends in whose sympathy she had found, and continued to find, support, it is unnecessary to dwell; they are matter of history. Rather let the chapter be closed in silent remembrance of the departed master and of the group of his loved ones who lamented together in the sacred presence of an irreparable grief.

---

* Partly taken from the account written at the time for the *Neue Zeitschrift*, by Ferdinand Hiller.

CHAPTER VIII.

1856-1858.

FRAU SCHUMANN returned to Düsseldorf the day after the
funeral, accompanied by Brahms and Joachim. There were
certain things to be done, the performance of which she
desired to entrust to the two young musicians who had been
so near the master's heart. Together they set in order the
papers left by the deceased composer, wrote necessary
letters, and made plans for the immediate future. Joachim
writes on August 2 to Liszt:

"Frau Schumann returned here yesterday; the presence
of her children and of Brahms, whom Schumann loved like
a son, comforts the noble lady, who appears to me, in her
deep grief, a lofty example of God-given strength. I shall
remain here for some days."

Johannes had taken over some lessons which Frau Schumann had arranged to give, on her return from England,
to Fräulein von Meysenbug, daughter of the late Minister
and sister of the then Hofmarschall at the Court of Lippe-
Detmold, and by so doing had added four people to the list
of his friends: his pupil, her mother and sister—all settled
for a few weeks in Düsseldorf—and her young nephew Carl,
who came from Detmold to visit his relations.

"On the occasion of one of the lessons," says Freiherr
von Meysenbug,* "I first saw and heard the almost boyish-
looking, shy, and socially awkward young artist, who
played to us Schubert's 'Moment Musical' in F minor. His
rendering of the piece made an indelible impression on me."

The boy's admiration led later on to a fast alliance
between Brahms and Carl. The ladies, on their part,
became enthusiastic in their admiration of the young musician, and on the termination of the lessons, which could not
long be continued on account of the sad circumstances of the
moment, they invited him to stay with them in the spring at
Detmold, with a view to his appearance at Court.

It was felt that the all-important necessaries for Frau
Schumann were rest and good air. Since the crisis of her
husband's malady in February, 1854, followed after a few
months by the birth of her youngest son, she had enjoyed
but little repose, and since the autumn of 1855 practically
none. During November and December of that year she
travelled, as we have seen, in Germany, giving concerts with
Joachim in Leipzig, Berlin, Danzig, Berlin again, Rostock,
and many other towns. At home for Christmas, she gave
her first concert in Vienna on January 7, which was followed
by five others, the last taking place on March 3. Travelling
meanwhile, she combined her engagements in the Austrian
capital with performances at Prague and other cities. Returning early in March by way of Leipzig, she was at home
about a fortnight, and on April 7 started for England, to
remain until the second week of July. We have seen to
what she returned, and may well understand that she
seemed to Joachim and Brahms "an example of God-given
strength." It was now decided that she should go to
Switzerland, and that Johannes' sister should accompany
her. Elise Brahms was not artistic, and had little education. She had suffered all her life from bad headaches, and
the constitutional tendency had been aggravated by her

---

* "Aus Johannes Brahms' Jugendtagen," by Carl, Hreiherr von
Meysenbug (*Neues Wiener Tagblatt*, April 3 and 4, 1902).

employment of plain sewing, carried on at home or in the
houses of her clients. She was not pretty, but her single
personal attraction being an abundance of light-brown hair
which grew to a great length, but she was simple, unselfish
and kind; she was the sister of Johannes; and Frau Schumann hoped that a respite from her confined life, in the fine
air and scenery, might do her good. The whole party—
Frau Schumann with some of her children, Elise, and
Johannes—set off together as soon as the necessary arrangements could be made, accompanied on the first part of their
journey by Joachim, and proceeded by short stages to
Gersau, on the Lake of Lucerne, where they settled down
for several weeks. The time was spent in quiet walks and
excursions, with some amount of music and a few meetings
with close friends, and the return was made in the same
leisurely way, with ten days' stay at Heidelberg. The holiday had its effect, and the beginning of October found the
three musicians prepared to take up the ordinary duties of
life. Frau Schumann began to practise for her concert-
season, Joachim was at his post at Hanover, and Johannes
about to return to his home in Hamburg, to apply himself to
the occupations which had been interrupted by the events
of the past six months. He appeared at Otten's concert of
the 25th of the month with Beethoven's G major Concerto,
and this time with immense success. "The concerto was
played with such fire and élan as to excite enthusiastic
demonstration." Some special outward circumstance or
inner mood probably stirred him on this occasion. His performance was so powerful that it is still vividly remembered,
with its effect upon the audience. His appearance on
November 22 at a Philharmonic concert chiefly devoted to
Schumann's works awakened no enthusiasm. He played
the master's Pianoforte Concerto, and the indifference with
which his performance was received was the more marked
by contrast with the stormy applause that followed
Joachim's playing of Schumann's Violin Fantasia and of
Bach's Chaconne.

It was, however, a joy to Brahms to have his friend with him for a day or two, and a convenient opportunity was welcomed by both young musicians for the leisurely trial of the quartet by Johannes that had been examined by Joachim in the spring of the year. "Ich möchte nicht wagen von Anderungen zu sprechen bevor ich's nochmals gehört, ordentlich gehört!" Joachim had written in April. No record is to be found of the result of the rehearsal, which took place in the dwelling of Brahms' friend, Grädener, a musician of Hamburg, except such as is furnished by the subsequent history of the quartet. The work, in spite of its great imaginative power, proved somewhat of an *enfant terrible* to the composer. It was tried again in Hanover early in 1857, no doubt with such alterations as had been suggested by the experience of the Hamburg rehearsal. After this date there is no more news of it for many years.*

The season 1856-7 was passed uneventfully by Brahms in the studies and other occupations already described, varied by an occasional journey. He may be said to have had at this time at least three possible homes in addition to that of his parents in Hamburg. He knew himself to be sure of a welcome at any moment, not only in Düsseldorf and Hanover but also in Göttingen, where Grimm, lately married to Fräulein Philippine Ritmüller, daughter of the head of the pianoforte firm of that name, was rapidly making a position for himself as the centre of a circle of energetic music-lovers. Moved partly, perhaps, by this

---

* Compare Brahms' "Briefwechsel," Vol. V, No. 6, 93, 94, 116; and Vol. IV, No. XXX.

In the absence of the specific reason on which it is based, it is impossible to endorse the suggestion of the editor of the Brahms-Joachim "Briefwechsel" that the quartet tried in Hamburg was one of the pair Opp. 25 and 26.

The same remark applies to the editor's footnote on Brahms's letter, No. XXX of the Brahms-Grimm "Briefwechsel."

For further elucidation of this point see footnote to p. 265 of this biography.

friend's enthusiastic affection for the symphony movements
of 1854, yet convinced, as we have seen, of his present in-
capacity for the successful completion of a purely orchestral
work in large form, Johannes had conceived the idea of re-
arranging portions of his composition as a pianoforte concerto. The changes of structure involved in the plan
proved, however, to be far from easy of satisfactory accomplishment and occupied much of the composer's time during
two years. The movements were repeatedly sent to Hanover for Joachim's inspection, and returned with his
suggestions; for his time, sympathy, musicianship, and
knowledge of the orchestra, were placed, with unfailing
generosity, at Brahms' disposal during all the years of
ripening experience that led up to the composer's maturity.
The immediate fortunes of the work after it was at length
completed will be related in due course.

The invitation of the von Meysenbugs having been duly
renewed and accepted, the young musician paid a short visit
to Detmold at Whitsuntide. Arriving at the little town one
pleasant afternoon, the last stage of his journey having been
made by post, he was met by his pupil and her nephew Carl,
and brought by them to Frau von Meysenbug's house. The
article of the Vienna *Neues Tagblatt* already referred to,
by Freiherr von Meysenbug, the "Carl," or "Charles," as
he was generally called, of 1857, gives a pleasant account of
the visit :

"I can still see the young fellow standing in silent embarrassment in the old Excellency's drawing-room, not quite
knowing how to begin a conversation with the ladies, who
were still practically strangers to him. Just then—it was
about four o'clock—a princely carriage drove through the
quiet street, in which were seated the three sisters of the
reigning Prince on their way to dine with their brother at
the palace. The ladies were accustomed to look up, as they
passed, to the windows of my relations, and my aunt, seeing the carriage coming, said, 'I will just nod to the
Princess (Friederike) that Herr Brahms is come.' Upon this
Brahms broke silence with the words, 'Do they live close

by, then, like everyone else?' evidently thinking that the
sign was to be given to an opposite window. This set the
conversation going till I showed Brahms his room."

The same evening Charles reappeared with his parents
and Concertmeister Bargheer, of the Detmold court orchestra, a fine player, pupil of Spohr and Joachim, and
already an acquaintance of Brahms. The Hofmarschall
wished to hear the new-comer as a preliminary to his appearance at Court, and listened to most convincing
performances of a thundering prelude and fugue of Bach
and of Beethoven's C sharp minor Sonata, Op. 27. An orchestral court concert was arranged, at which Johannes
played his favourite Beethoven Concerto in G major and
took part in a performance of Schubert's "Forellen"
Quintet with Concertmeister Bargheer, viola-player Schulze,
violoncellist Julius Schmidt, all soloists of the court orchestra, and a bassist, member of the same body. His success was unequivocal, and he appeared with Bargheer at an
assembly of musicians and their friends held after the concert at the chief confectioner's, in rollicking boyish spirits.
Capellmeister Kiel, on the other hand, who looked rather
askance at a probable future favourite at Court, assumed
airs of even unusual importance. He was at present, he
said, setting one of the Psalms as a chorus; he often composed Biblical texts, but was sometimes puzzled by the
Scriptural expressions. For instance, "To the chief musician on the Gittith." "Pray, can you inform me what a
Gittith was?" solemnly to the young hero of the evening.
"Probably a pretty Jewish girl," returned Brahms, with a
serious air—an answer which procured him a suspicious look
over the spectacles of the old musician, and enraptured
Charles, who, supposed by his parents to be in bed, had
found means of his own to join the party. The entertainment having been prolonged until dawn, the more ardent
spirits of the gathering proposed a walk to a neighbouring
height to see the sun rise, and Brahms and Charles strode
off together, leading the way. Their enthusiasm survived

that of their companions, who gradually dropped off; and overcome by weariness as they reached the beginning of the last steep climb, they turned into the garden of a restaurant hard by, where Charles dropped on to the corner seat of an arbour bench, and Brahms, stretching himself out at full length with his head on his companion's knee, immediately went soundly to sleep.

"Just as I, too, was giving way to fatigue," continues Freiherr von Meysenbug, "a fine brown spaniel came sniffing at Brahms' face, and he suddenly jumped up, roused by the dog's cold nose. Meanwhile the house had awakened, we drank some hastily-prepared coffee, satisfied our healthy young appetites with delicious country black bread and golden-yellow butter, and trotted back to the little town. We both presented rather a questionable appearance in the streets, which were already astir, especially so the small Brahms in dress-coat, crumpled and disarranged white necktie, and crush-hat on one side. Paying a passing visit to the faithless Bargheer, whom we disturbed in his morning slumbers, we next set out for my grandmother's dwelling. There—oh, horror!—we suddenly came upon my aunt setting out for her morning walk. A distant look of righteous indignation travelled up and down the two night-enthusiasts, for Brahms' attire betrayed but too clearly that he had not been back since the previous evening. A stormy atmosphere prevailed during the day in the house of the hospitable ladies, who were not only unused to visits from men, but could never have imagined that the ideal artist would commit himself to such extravagances. I was severely censured by grandmother and aunts as the harebrained youth who had led the honoured guest astray. Brahms left the next day, not having been very warmly pressed to prolong his visit! He had, however, given such satisfaction in high quarters that his return in the autumn for a long stay in Detmold was definitely arranged. He was to give lessons to the Princess, play at Court, and conduct an amateur choral society, which, by invitation of the Prince, held its weekly meetings at the castle, and to which His Serene Highness, together with his brothers and sisters, belonged as regular members."

Brahms, who could now look forward to the autumn without anxiety as to his finances, and who appreciated in anticipation the advantages he would derive as a composer from his position as conductor of a choral society and from constant association with a standing orchestra, met Frau Schumann on her return from England, where she had again passed the London season, in happy mood. Any regret he may have felt at resigning his freedom of action for a few months by a binding engagement was mitigated by the fact that his association with Düsseldorf must in any case shortly be severed. Frau Schumann had made up her mind that she would best serve her own happiness and the interests of her family by settling near her mother in Berlin, and was to take up her residence there in September, in readiness for the concert season and for the more advantageous opportunity of working as a teacher in the Prussian capital, by which she hoped to supplement her income. Born September 13, 1819, the great pianist, now not quite thirty-eight, was in the zenith of her powers, and, with the probability of a long career before her, it is not surprising that she should have resolved to begin a new chapter of life away from the town that was chiefly associated in her mind with painful recollections. The summer vacation was passed by her on the Rhine in the more or less constant society of Brahms, Joachim, and Grimm, and a memorial of a few specially pleasant days at St. Goarshausen is in existence in the shape of a copy, in her handwriting, of Brahms' Variations, Op. 21, No. 2. On the outside page is written:

"Ungarische Variationen von Johannes. Herrn Julius Otto Grimm, zur Erinnerung an die Tage in St. Goarshausen. August, 1857. Clara Schumann."*

It was at this moment that Joachim resolved on a step which contributed not a little to inflame the party feeling animating the younger disciples of the New-German school. That they had felt increasingly aggrieved by the position taken up by him since the crisis of Schumann's illness, by

---

* In the possession of Fräulein Marie Grimm.

his thoroughgoing association of his name and influence with
the art of the master and his wife, by his intimacy with
Brahms, and by his passive attitude towards Liszt's Symphonic Poems, may be read in letters of the period.
Bülow, whose correspondence up to the middle of 1854
contains repeated affectionate references to Joachim, to
whom he was immensely attached, wrote to Liszt in reference to the numerous concert journeys of 1855 undertaken
with Frau Schumann :

  "Joachim and the statue of which he is making himself
the pedestal are not coming here till the beginning of next
month.   I am afraid we shall have difficulty in recognising
each other, for we are at work in completely opposite
directions."

Perhaps their secret conviction of Joachim's artistic sincerity added to the disappointment of the Weimarites,
which undoubtedly increased during the two following
years, though his dislike of the Symphonic Poems was only
to be guessed by his silence about them.   On the publication of the works in 1857, however, with a somewhat pre-
tentious preface, the embarrassment he felt from the
consciousness that he would be unable to live up to the de-
sires of his quondam associates, stimulated beyond a doubt
by the sympathy of Johannes, who fully shared his sentiments, induced him to pen a letter to Liszt in which he
made full confession of his apostasy.   The intense pain
which the writing of it caused him, attached as he was to
everything about Liszt excepting his compositions, may be
read in every line of the epistle, which is dated August 27,
1857.

  " . . . . But of what use would it be if I were to delay
any longer saying plainly what I feel?   My passivity
towards your works could not but reveal it to you, who are
accustomed to be treated with enthusiasm, and who regard
me as capable of true, active friendship.   I will not, therefore, longer conceal what, as I confess, your manly soul
had the right to demand of me sooner.   I am entirely with-

out sensibility for your music; it contradicts everything upon which my powers have been nourished since early youth from the spirits of our great ones. If it were conceivable that I could ever be robbed, that I must renounce what I have learned to love and reverence in their works, what I feel as music, your tones would be no help to me in the vast, annihilating desert. How, then, could I associate myself with the object of those who, under the banner of your name and in the belief (I speak of the conscientious among them) that they are bound to make themselves responsible for con-temporary justice towards artistic achievement, make it the aim of life to spread the acceptance of your works by every means at their command? . . . ''

These lines were written when Joachim was twenty-six. That they were wrung from him by the strength of his artistic convictions is clear, and it is certain that they were entirely characteristic of the writer at the time. It is probable that Brahms, if he had been called upon to com-pose the letter, would have expressed himself differently; but then, he would not, under similar circumstances, have felt the same amount of pain. An element in his great in-fluence over his friends, and one which he encouraged through life by deliberate training, was to accept the in-evitable with philosophy, and to look on the bright side of things; and his natural elasticity of temperament would have enabled him, had circumstances demanded of him the sacrifice of a friendship, to yield it with little outward flinching. It is difficult for the present generation, for whom the artistic party questions of half a century ago have little beyond historic interest, to judge of the position of those for whom they were a burning personal topic; but it is certain that Joachim's letter to Liszt added fuel to a fire which raged violently through the next succeeding years, and which occasioned the issue of a mass of controversial pamphlets and articles almost unreadable at the present day.

Liszt himself accepted the young musician's confession with generous dignity, and never allowed a disrespectful word to be uttered about Joachim in his presence. His first and only reply to the letter of 1857 was not made until nearly thirty years later. Joachim, arriving one year early in the eighties at Budapest to perform his great Variations for violin and orchestra, called on Liszt, who happened to be staying in the same hotel with himself. The two artists had not met for many years, and the pleasure felt by each at the accidental rencontre reminded them of the tie of affection that had formerly united them. It turned out that Liszt had already made himself acquainted with the variations, and he proposed now to attend the rehearsal in order to hear the composer's performance of them, saying: "As you do not like my music, dear Joachim, I feel that I must admire yours in double measure."

By the end of September Brahms found himself once more in Detmold. The terms of his engagement, which extended through the last three months of the year, included free rooms and living, and he was lodged in the hotel Stadt Frankfurt, a comfortable inn, since enlarged and modernised, exactly opposite the castle enclosure—close, therefore, to the scene of his duties. The difficulty of procuring a piano in the little town was got over by the loan of an old "grand" belonging to the Frau Hofmarschall that had been superseded in her drawing-room by one of later construction; and Brahms, relieved at having succeeded in obtaining something that had at least been good in its day, rewarded Charles for his suggestion that the instrument should be sent to the Stadt Frankfurt by promising him right of entrance to all practices and performances that he might hold in his room with Bargheer, Schmidt, and others.

The daily life of our musician during the next three months was one very much after his own heart. His mornings were sacred to work. Bargheer joined him at the Stadt Frankfurt for early dinner, and the afternoons were generally passed in exercise in the crisp autumn air of the Teutoburger forest. There were games with Carl and his

16

younger brother Hermann; trials of strength with Bargheer, in which Brahms was invariably defeated; Sunday excur-sions with Bargheer, Carl, and others, which occupied the whole day and included an al-fresco luncheon carried from Detmold, to which Brahms was proud to be able sometimes to contribute an excellent bottle of Malvoisier. This he procured by dispensing with the half-bottle of ordinary wine daily provided with his dinner until he had covered the cost of the superior vintage to be shared with his friends. "He was as happy as a king at these times, he loved beautiful nature so much," says Julius Schmidt, who was occasionally one of the party.

His post as conductor of the choral society was at first particularly welcome, not only as giving him experience in a branch of musical activity which he had not practised since he stood, a boy of fifteen, at the head of his little society of teachers at Winsen, but as affording opportunity for the practical application and test of the studies to which he had been devoting special attention. He began his duties as conductor with the practice of short works by early and modern masters, and arranged some of his favourite folk-songs expressly for the use of the society. deriving from each rehearsal fresh insight into the art of writing for voices. There were frequent informal musical soirées at Court, which provided occasion for choral performances in the intervals between the instrumental works that formed the bulk of the programmes. These were played by Brahms, Bargheer, Schulze, Schmidt, and the splendid hornist, August Cordes, whose rich, mellow tone drew from Brahms enthusiastic expressions of admiration. Almost the entire répertoire of classical chamber music seems to have been gone through during this and succeeding seasons; all the duet sonatas and pianoforte trios and quartets, etc., of Bach, Mozart, Beethoven, Schubert, and Schumann, were played in turn. Brahms' Trio was performed several times, and it gave the young musician particular pleasure to execute, not only Beethoven's Horn

Sonata with Cordes, but Mozart's and Beethoven's quintets for pianoforte and wind with the soloists of the orchestra, who were one and all artists. The powers of the flutist are said to have been hardly less remarkable than those of Cordes.

The court violoncellist, Julius Schmidt, who in 1857 was a man in the early prime of life, has described to the author Brahms' appearance, on his coming to Detmold, as so delicate and refined as to be almost girlish; and this impression was strengthened by his voice, which was still of the high quality that has been frequently mentioned. Impatient of the remarks elicited by the peculiarity, he began at this time to practise a series of vocal gymnastics for the purpose of forcing his voice down, and was eventually successful in this aim.

When engaged in the performance of his duties, he was always quiet and serious, and would stand, before the commencement of a choir practice or a court concert, at the extreme end of the long room in which the functions took place, speaking to no one, perhaps looking through a piece of music or a letter. His duties in connection with the orchestral concerts were to play from time to time, and to conduct now and then. In the course of the successive autumns passed by him at Detmold, his performances included several of Mozart's and Beethoven's concertos, which were heard with especial delight; Schumann's Concerto; Mendelssohn's G minor and D minor Concertos; E flat Rondo and B minor Caprice; Chopin's E minor and Moscheles' G minor Concertos; and, with Bargheer and Schmidt, Beethoven's triple Concerto. Occasionally, as time went on, the Princess Friederike played a concerto, and on the occasion of a performance of Beethoven's Choral Fantasia the Frau Hofmarschall von Meysenbug undertook the pianoforte solo, whilst Brahms acted as conductor.

The young musician soon became a favourite at Court, not only on account of his musical genius, but also because of the general culture of his mind. He invariably seemed

at home on a topic of real interest, and able to contribute
something worth hearing at its discussion. "Whoever
wishes to play well must not only practise a great deal, but
read a great many books," was one of his favourite sayings, and the excellent public library of Detmold afforded
him good opportunity for indulging his literary tastes. On
the evenings that were free from duties, some of the musicians often dropped into Brahms' room to play, and the
performances generally went on until late into the night.

"And how Brahms loved the great masters! how he
played Haydn and Mozart! with what beauty of interpretation and delicate shading of tone! And then his trans-
posing!"

He would play a new composition by one or other of his
Detmold friends at sight in a transposed key without a
mistake, taking it at any interval suggested, and thinking
nothing of the feat. He even liked to play tricks on Court
Concertmeister Bargheer, and to lead off Mozart's duet
sonatas, which Prince Leopold was fond of hearing in
private, in transposed keys, in which Bargheer was obliged,
and luckily able, to follow.

"His score playing, too, was marvellous. Bach, Handel,
Haydn, Mozart, all seemed to flow naturally under his
fingers, and each point to come out, as it were, of itself.
Then, he was of such a noble character, such a good, kind
nature, and so loved children. . . ."

It must be added, however, that Schmidt, like most of
the Detmold musicians, whilst enthusiastically admiring
Brahms' gifts as an executant, regarded his compositions
with scepticism. The B major Trio was by no means a
favourite with himself or his colleagues—Bargheer always
excepted—and he thought the 'cello part most ungratefully
written for the instrument.

Enough has been said to make it evident that Brahms'
sojourn at Detmold was an unmitigated success, and before
his departure his re-engagement the following season had

come to be regarded as a matter of course. The Christmas festival, passed by him in the midst of the Hofmarschall's family party, was as bright and happy as can be imagined. Johannes became for the evening a child of the house, entering eagerly with the boys into the mystery of the hour preceding the great presentation of Christmas gifts, and ready to laugh heartily at the practical jokes of which he and others were made victims later in the evening. A few words written in an album given to Hermann are still treasured by their owner: "This was written in hearty friendship by your Johannes."

Two signs, contrasted one with the other, but both prophetic of things to come, are to be noted in January newspaper issues of 1858. One, which points to the swelling bitterness of feeling with which the Weimarites contemplated the compact phalanx of friends who may conveniently be termed the Schumann party, is contained in a reference to Rubinstein as composer, penned by Bülow in the *Neue Berliner Musikzeitung* of January 27:

"He [Rubinstein] knows his powers; he has tested his arms, and has therefore attained to a higher stage than the brooding Brahms."

The other is the record, in a paragraph of the *Signale*, of what was probably the début of Brahms' name in Italy. The distinguished pianist Alfred Jaell had included one of his compositions in the programmes of a lately-ended concert-tour through that country.

Leaving Detmold on January 1, Brahms, travelling by way of Hanover, where he enjoyed an hour's conversation at the railway station with Joachim, proceeded direct to Hamburg and was soon engrossed with his studies, compositions, and pupils. The question of the completion of the pianoforte concerto had become urgent. Again and again had the several movements of the work been despatched to Hanover and returned to the composer with Joachim's comments. Yet once more had Johannes, before

leaving Detmold, sent back the first movement with a request for his friend's opinion on fresh alterations. This
last petition remained unanswered for a week or two, but
was at length fulfilled in a most practical manner. Joachim
returned the manuscript, marked in pencil with his thorough
revision of the instrumentation, which Johannes was to keep
or reject at his pleasure, but no further interruption of the
copyist's task was to be countenanced. The writing out of
the parts of the entire work was to be completed without
more delay and the concerto tried on the first opportunity
at Hanover or Hamburg.

"I refrain from all further remarks on your concerto only
that I may not again delay the copying; but I am burning
with impatience for the undisturbed enjoyment, through
hearing, of the many beauties of the first order which have
delighted me on reading it. Let me know if you like what
I have done."*

Joachim's mandate helped matters considerably forward.
The composer braced himself to face the inevitable, and
actually announced in his next letter to his untiring adviser
that the parts would be ready in a few days, and that he
had, almost in spite of himself, accepted an engagement to
play the concerto at Otten's subscription concert of March
25, and would welcome the opportunity of a preliminary
rehearsal at Hanover before that date.

The work, however, was not to be heard immediately.
The concert engagement fell through because the publisher
Cranz, who owned the only adequate piano of which Hamburg could boast, refused the loan of it for the occasion;
and the young composer postponed the rehearsal of his work
in Hanover on successive pretexts, probably but various
spellings of the word "nervousness." Mortified by the
equanimity with which Otten received the news of the pianoforte difficulty, Brahms resolved to absent himself altogether
from the concert of March 25 even though Joseph was to

---

* Brahms-Joachim "Briefwechsel," No. 139.

take part in it, and went off to Berlin to greet Frau Schumann in her new home on her return from a concert-tour in Switzerland.   No doubt he derived encouragement from her sympathy on the completion of his great work, though her step-brother, Woldemar Bargiel, expressed but moderate appreciation of its merits.   Matters were brought to a crisis on March 28 by a telegram from Hanover.   Joachim had arranged to conduct a trial performance of the composition in two days' time at the end of a rehearsal for the next Hanover subscription concert.   He wished Johannes to join him immediately and hoped Frau Schumann would make it possible to be present on the occasion.   Thus it came about that after long anxiety and delay, Brahms' first completed orchestral work was heard privately for the first time on Tuesday, March 30, 1858, at Hanover.   Not only was Frau Schumann present, Grimm, too, had come to hear the beloved symphony movements in their new dress, and to dream of future triumphs in which Göttingen might participate; and Johannes, helped by the consciousness of his friends' sympathy, forgot his fears and rose to the demands of the hour.

"I think you must be pleased to hear," Frau Schumann wrote to Bargiel, "that the rehearsal went off splendidly to-day.   There was only time to play it through once, but it went almost without a mistake and quite roused the musicians.   If you had heard it to-day it would have seemed clear to you.   Almost everything sounded so fine; better even than Johannes, himself, had hoped or expected.

"The whole is wonderful, so rich and fervent, and has such unity!   Johannes was blissful and played the last movement *prestissimo* from sheer delight.   We took a walk afterwards; it was as though heaven had desired to lend special brightness to the day.   Johannes enjoyed it in full measure; I wish you could have seen his happiness."*

It was too late in the season to make immediate arrangements for a public performance of the concerto, but Brahms

* Litzmann III, 35.

returned to his parents' home with confident hope in his heart. The family moved again this year to a more commodious dwelling at 74, Fuhlentwiethe, still in the old quarter of Hamburg, but with good-sized rooms, which were always kept in beautiful order. The parlour was comfortably though plainly furnished, and decorated with ivy after the custom of the time. It had a large open fireplace with old-fashioned hobs on either side, which occasionally served in the summer as a refuge for cake-eating child-visitors, to the preservation of Fräulein Elise's spotless floor. The room set apart for Johannes, who, now as always, was responsible for a large share of the family expenses, afforded ample space for a sleeping sofa, washing-stand, piano, writing-table, and large bookcase, on the top of which stood a bust of Beethoven. Two or three small prints from good pictures decorated the walls, one of them being a representation of Leonardo da Vinci's "Last Supper." There was sufficient space in the dwelling for the accommodation of one or two boarders—a means of income to which Jakob and his wife had had recourse, as we have seen, in the early part of their married life.

A visit to Frau Schumann in April and May of nearly a month's duration and the enjoyment of her society in Hamburg for a few days in June, afforded Johannes some compensation for the loss of the constant daily companionship at certain seasons of the year that had been brought to a close by the removal of his friend's home from Düsseldorf to Berlin. He applied himself closely to work during the summer and in the general character of the composition on which he was chiefly engaged, we may perhaps perceive a reflection of the satisfaction caused him by some of the incidents of the spring and, not least, by the gratifying issue of his long struggle with the pianoforte concerto.

Inspired by the delight with which he had listened to the "cassation music," the serenades and divertimenti of Mozart, as performed by the Detmold orchestra, Johannes had set about writing something in the same style in the

form of an octet, bearing in mind the special qualifications
of Prince Leopold's band; and he soon became so engrossed
in his work as to be disinclined to yield to the persuasions
by which Grimm, in a letter of June 30, sought to persuade
him that he was called upon by every consideration of
health, work and duty to others, to spend the rest of the
summer at Göttingen. Satisfied at length, however, that
his friends, content to know him near them, would leave him
in undisturbed possession of his working hours, Johannes
wrote to Grimm to announce his coming and left Hamburg
at the end of July. It was understood at home that his
absence would be a long one. He would not, at any rate,
return before the beginning of the next year, after the close
of his Detmold season, and there was great uncertainty as
to what his future plans might be. It was a sad time for
Fräulein Friedchen Wagner, who had been his regular pupil
during all the months of his stay, and at her last lesson she
begged her master for some little souvenir, desiring that
it should be of a serious character to correspond with her
mood. She was not at home when he called to say good-
bye, however, and he left Hamburg apparently without a
sign. Too melancholy for some days to feel that she could
open her piano, her delight was the greater when at length,
resolving to go to work again, she found under the lid of
the instrument a manuscript in Brahms' hand, which bore
the inscription: "To Fräulein Fr. Wagner, in kind remembrance. July, 1858." It was the organ prelude to the
chorale, "O Traurigkeit, O Herzeleid," which was published with a fugue, in 1881, in a supplement of a number
of the *Musikalisches Wochenblatt.*

Brahms' stay in Göttingen proved memorable in more
than one respect. Frau Schumann, after drinking the
waters at Wiesbaden, took up her residence with five of her
children in the Grimms' house; Johannes lodged close by;
Bargiel, with whom Brahms had become intimate in Berlin,

---

* "Brahms in Hamburg," by Professor Walter Hübbe.

and Bargheer joined the party, and about six weeks were
passed in work and play that were almost equally delightful.   Brahms was left to himself, by general understanding,
during the morning hours, and the serenade advanced so
rapidly that he was able to announce the work to his deeply
interested friends while their circle was still intact.   Immediate arrangements were made for its rehearsal;
Johannes, himself, Grimm, Bargiel, Bargheer, all set to
copy out the parts; Grimm got together the necessary musicians and the work was tried before an audience of friends,
under the composer's direction.   This was the first performance in its original form—an octet for string and wind instruments in three movements—of the Serenade in D major
published later on as Op. 11.*

Grimm and his wife were inexpressibly touched by the
beautiful and rare relation in which Johannes stood to Frau
Schumann.   "He was to her as a careful friend, a loving
and protecting son."   She was, indeed, the centre of the
party, and the chief thought of all the younger musicians
gathered about her.   Johannes was a famous playfellow for
her little ones, proposing all sorts of romping games for
them, in which the elders willingly joined.   As for music,
they had their own share in that, too.   One can imagine
them cowering quiet in their hiding-places as they heard the
approaching voice of the seeker :

Wil-le, wil-le, will, Der Mann ist kom - men ;
Did-dle, did-dle dee, There's some-one com - ing ;

the demands of the four-year-old Felix for another ride on
somebody's knee, in spite of the answer :

---

* For the information that the Serenade in D major was originally composed as an octet for solo instruments, the author is indebted
to some unpublished notes on his acquaintance with Brahms written
by Concertmeister Bargheer.

Ull Mann will ri - - - den, wull hat er kein Pferd;
He would go ri - - - ding, but no horse had he;

the efforts of the small Eugénie to keep the dust out of her
eyes just a little longer, though

Die Blü-me-lein sie schla-fen schon,
The flow-er-ets are sleep-ing,

These and other songs which were sung by Johannes with
and to Frau Schumann's children at Göttingen this summer
were published anonymously by Rieter-Biedermann at the
end of the year as "Children's Folk-songs, with added accompaniment, dedicated to the children of Robert and Clara
Schumann."

About the middle of September the party broke up. The
children returned to Berlin; their mother went to visit an
old friend at Düsseldorf; others were called away by their
respective affairs; and only Johannes, who had his own particular reasons at the moment for thinking Göttingen the
most delightful place in the world, remained behind with
the Grimms. Nothing could have been more opportune
under these circumstances than a note received by Brahms
which announced Joachim's return from England and his
wish to join his friend, wherever he might be, during the
brief remainder of the holiday season. His attendance at
Göttingen was commanded forthwith and Brahms, never
sure of the value of a new work of his own until he had possessed himself of Joseph's opinion of its merits, lost no time
in playing the Serenade movements to his companion, who
received them with approval tempered with reserve. There
was definite reason for the composer's anxiety on this occasion. His inexperience in the art of instrumentation had
again been betrayed by the rehearsal of the Serenade, and

Frau Schumann had declared her belief that no alteration less drastic than its rearrangement for full orchestra would avail for the realisation in performance of the attractive ideas of the composition. Joachim, however, questioned by Johannes, withheld his opinion on this and other points until he should have had opportunity for quiet study of the score, which he took with him to Hanover at the close of the month; and Brahms, who left Göttingen in his friend's company to return to the duties of his post in Detmold, destroyed the parts in the conviction that, as then written, they would be of no further use to him.

With the approach of autumn, the desirability became pressing of arranging for a public performance of the pianoforte concerto, and in the course of October the following paragraph, for which the enthusiasm of Frau Schumann may have been indirectly responsible, appeared in the *Signale*.

"We hear that since the arrival of J. Brahms in Detmold a few weeks ago there has been an animated musical life there, of which the young artist is the centre. Brahms will remain in Detmold until the end of the year, and it is hoped that some of his compositions may be brought to a hearing. He has completed amongst other things, a pianoforte concerto, the great beauties of which have been reported to us."

The same journal notices concerts given by Frau Schumann in Düsseldorf and elsewhere, at which she played arrangements by Brahms for two hands on the pianoforte, of a selection of Hungarian Dances, "that called forth a veritable storm of applause." This unanswerable statement should effectually dispose of the fable which has obtained considerable credence amongst the musical laity, that the "Hungarian Dance" arrangements were the outcome of impressions derived during Brahms' residence in Vienna. As has been shown in an earlier chapter, he owed his first acquaintance with the melodies to the playing of Reményi.

The hope expressed in the *Signale*, that the new works might be performed at Detmold, was only partially ful-

filled.   As we have seen, Brahms was not seriously accepted
as a composer by the musicians there—one of them only
excepted—and Capellmeister Kiel regarded his compositions with peculiar jealousy and mistrust.   So far as can be
ascertained, the D minor Concerto was not even tried at
Detmold.   The ultimate result of the successful rehearsal at
Hanover in March was, however, that Joachim, in spite of
some official opposition, carried through his wish that it
should be put down for a first performance at one of the
Hanover subscription court concerts, choosing for date January 22, 1859, when Johannes would be free from duties;
and that through the influence of Court Concertmeister
David arrangements were made for its second performance
a few days later at Leipzig Gewandhaus concert of
January 27.

As to the serenade, Joachim found himself completely in
accord with Frau Schumann's high opinion of its musical
value, but was still unwilling to judge prematurely on the
question of the scoring :

"The last movement is, in its way, as happy as the first,"
he wrote, "and the trio charming also, only sometimes unfortunately instrumented, especially too difficult for the
violins.   You played the last movement so carelessly in
Göttingen that I could form no opinion about it; here everything is clear to me. . . . Whether you should really set the
serenade for orchestra or leave it as it is with the addition,
perhaps, of a horn or an oboe, I cannot decide without
hearing it."*

Meanwhile Brahms was making progress with still newer
compositions.   Until a comparatively late period of his
career, his method of working in some respects resembled
that of Beethoven.   We have seen that he was in the habit,
as a boy, of putting his thoughts down as they occurred to
him.   Later on he was accustomed to keep several large
compositions on hand at once, allowing his ideas to expand

---

* Brahms-Joachim " Briefwechsel," No. 155.

gradually; and he sometimes had a work by him for years before completing it in its final shape. The cases of the D minor Concerto, the C minor pianoforte Quartet, and the C minor Symphony, are well established instances in point, though Brahms took care that the process by which his works were developed should not, after his death, become public property, by destroying the vast majority of his sketches.*

Very soon after his departure from Göttingen he sent Grimm, with an urgent request for opinion and criticism, a packet of new MSS., one of which proved to be the completed first movement of a second serenade in A major, scored for small orchestra. The succeeding movements were not yet ready for inspection.

"How does it sound?   Shall I go on with it?" he asks.

"The movement is wonderful," replied Grimm, "and as warm as the beautiful summer months of the year. . . . I found no difficulty in reading the score, for after the first few bars I noticed that I was already acquainted with what follows. You must have played the movement incognito to me some time in the summer, though I do not remember where or when."†

The many important claims on the composer's time which were to be fulfilled during the next few months prevented the immediate completion of the second serenade, the history of which will be resumed in a later chapter.

Carl von Meysenbug was not long able this season to enjoy the evening music which was more than ever an institution at the Stadt, Frankfurt. He departed before the end of October to enter upon the life of a university student at Göttingen, where he soon found himself at home with the congenial friends of Grimm's circle.

---

* The few sketches which Brahms allowed to survive him are preserved in the library of the Gesellschaft der Musikfreunde in Vienna.

† Br.: Grimm "Briefwechsel," No. XLIV.

N.B.—The footnote to the preceding letter is an obvious editorial *lapsus.*

"You will see," Johannes said to him as they parted,
"how surprised you will be after your admiration of the
stiff court ladies here when you become acquainted with the
pretty, fresh, lively daughters of the professors."

These words were significant. The age of twenty-five is
suitable to romance, and Brahms was at this time in love.
That he had passed through the earliest years of manhood
without any serious *affaire de cœur* is to be explained by the
circumstances in which he had been placed. The prosecution of a noble ambition which involved unremitting application to work occupied one half of his energies, whilst
his affections had been absorbed by family ties, by a dear
companionship, and by his love for two people to whom he
looked up with unbounded reverence. A calmer period had
succeeded the exciting course of past events, and he now
had leisure to think of himself. His intercourse with the
charming young people who frequented the Grimms' house,
and the contemplation of his friend's great happiness in his
wedded life, had awakened in him a feeling of loneliness,
and he thought much of Fräulein Agathe, daughter of Professor von Siebold, of Göttingen University, and Frau
Philippine's most intimate friend. Agathe was handsome,
lively, cultivated and gifted with a fine voice; and she sang
Brahms' songs with especial sympathy, particularly when he
played the accompaniments. A memorial of the friendship
that sprang up between the pair during the two summer
months of their acquaintance is preserved in the correspondence that passed between Detmold and Göttingen in
the autumn of the year, which points clearly to the conclusion that the Grimms encouraged the intimacy in the
natural hope that it might lead to a nearer relationship.
After his return to Detmold Johannes constantly exchanged
letters with Agathe, whom he addressed by her christian
name, through these mutual friends; composed songs for her
which she copied and sang, and constantly spoke in affectionate terms of his "Kleeblatt" in which poetic figure
Agathe was associated with Grimm and his wife. Amongst

the manuscripts sent in the autumn of 1858 for Grimm's inspection, was a "Brautgesang" (Bridal Song), set for soprano solo and women's chorus, to a poem by Uhland, and Brahms replied to Grimm's critical suggestions on the work :

"So a poor composer sits sadly alone in his room and makes himself dizzy with matters which do not concern him, and so a critic sits down between two beautiful ladies and— I would rather not complete the picture."

The friendship was pursued with ardour during a week's visit to Göttingen, for which Brahms found time on his departure from Detmold at the opening of the New Year, but the very confident rumour that prevailed amongst their acquaintances of the impending, or even accomplished, betrothal of Brahms and Agathe proved a tale without an ending. As the binding words remained unspoken, Grimm thought it right to interpose and, after reminding Brahms of his precarious position in the world, told him that he was in duty bound to make himself clear of his intentions one way or the other, and to shape his course accordingly. It can surprise no one who has grasped the key to the young composer's character and aims that his decision, which caused a temporary rupture of his friendly relations with the Grimms, should have led him away from marriage. Now and afterwards he liked the society of charming girls and perhaps thought it no harm to enjoy the pleasure of a special friendship without going beyond the consideration of the hour; but it may safely be assumed that he would not, at the outset of his career, have risked the sacrifice of his artistic aims by accepting binding responsibilities, even had his worldly prospects been much more certain than they were. He resolutely put away the visions of happiness with which he had dallied for a time and turned cheerfully to confront the future in undivided allegiance to the art that was to maintain supreme sway over his affections till the end of his life. That the remembrance of Agathe, who married happily in the course of time, remained treasured in

BRAHMS AND JOACHIM.

some corner of his heart as the years rolled onward, will seem certain to those who have had opportunity to appreciate the tenacity of his memory for old friendships. Several of the songs published later on by Brahms were the immediate result of his intimacy with Agathe; notably " Die Liebende schreibt" (Op. 47, No. 5); "Schmeiden u. Meiden" (Op. 19, No. 2); " In der Ferne " (Op. 19, No. 3); whilst in the last verse—in B major—of the exquisite "Ewige Liebe" (Op. 43, No. 1) is to be found a survival, crystallised and transfigured, of one of the melodies of the "Brautgesang." This work, if any conclusion may be drawn from the composer's own remarks and those of his friends to whom it was shown, was not one of Brahms' happiest efforts, and it remained unpublished.

CHAPTER IX.

1859.

First public performances of the Pianoforte Concerto in Hanover, Leipzig, and Hamburg—Brahms, Joachim and Stockhausen appear together in Hamburg—First public performance of the Serenade in D major—Ladies' Choir—Fräulein Friedchen Wagner—Compositions for women's chorus.

IT is not difficult to realise something of the mingled feelings of hope and anxiety that must have filled the mind of Johannes on his arrival in Hanover on January 8, 1859. If the first chapter of his career had closed in triumphant fashion with the extraordinary series of events that followed his first little concert-journey, the second chapter can only be regarded as an intermezzo which was spent in quiet preparation for what was to succeed it. The prelude of his artistic life had been successfully completed in 1853; the main action was to begin with the performances in Hanover and Leipzig in the opening month of 1859. Brahms was almost extravagantly self-critical, but he must have felt encouraged when he recalled the substantial success of his début as a composer at Leipzig immediately after the appearance of Schumann's famous article; and the joy of the trial performance of his concerto at Hanover less than a year ago was still bright within his heart. Such recollections, combined with the enthusiasm of his best friends, may well have raised his hopes high.

The concerto was heard at Hanover on January 22 in the

presence of the entire court circle and under the most favourable artistic conditions. Joachim conducted the orchestra,
Johannes played the solo, and it would be hard to say which
of the two young musicians was the more interested in the
occasion, but though the composer was honoured with a
recall, the actual result of the performance was that the
public was wearied and the musicians puzzled.

"The work had no great success with the public," reported the Hanover correspondent of the *Signale* ten days
later, "but"—and we seem to read the promptings of a
Joachim in the following words—"it aroused the decided
respect and sympathy of the best musicians for the gifted
artist."

"The work, with all its serious striving, its rejection of
triviality, its skilled instrumentation, seemed difficult to
understand, even dry, and in parts eminently fatiguing,"
said another critic;* "nevertheless Brahms gave the impression of being a really sterling musician, and it was con-
ceded without reservation that he is not merely a virtuoso,
but a great artist of pianoforte-playing."

Johannes had to leave almost immediately for Leipzig,
and he started from Hanover without knowing more about
the impression produced there by his concerto than could be
gathered from the politeness of the audience and the enthusiasm of his friend, but that his frame of mind was not
despondent may be inferred from a paragraph which appeared in the *Signale* immediately after his arrival.

"Herr Johannes Brahms is here, and will play his Concerto at the Gewandhaus concert of the 27th. He thinks of
remaining the rest of the winter at Leipzig."

It is necessary to remind the reader what kind of audience
it was for whose acceptance our young composer was now
about to submit his work. Leipzig still occupied the position of musical capital of Europe to which it had been raised

---

* Dr. Georg Fischer's "Opern und Concerte im Hoftheater zu
Hannover bis 1866."

by the genius of Mendelssohn. By the most influential of its artistic circles, the premature death of this fascinating master (1809-1847) was still deplored as an almost recent event. Most of his old friends were living, and, in virtue of their former personal association with him, looked upon themselves as competent judges of all later aspirants to fame. It is a matter of daily experience that the uninformed satellites of a man of genius are arrogant in proportion to their ignorance, and that even professional adepts of sincerity are apt to allow their horizon to be limited by their hero-worship. Musicians and amateurs, alike, of the Gewandhaus circle associated the idea of a concerto with the clear melody of Mozart and Beethoven, still, perhaps, regarding Beethoven as a little difficult to follow, with the attractive sparkle of Mendelssohn and with the opportunity for a display of the soloist's virtuosity afforded more or less by the works of all three masters. If asked to listen to a novelty, they expected that it should not be too unlike what they had heard before to be difficult to follow. Bernsdorf, newly appointed to succeed Brahms' friendly critic, Louis Köhler, on the staff of the conservative *Signale*, was himself a conservative of the most obstinate type, who was honestly convinced that the series of great masters had closed with Mendelssohn.

On the other hand, the New-Germans had by this time made considerable conquests in Leipzig, where they had established an important party organisation, and had, as we have seen in an earlier chapter, even been admitted on trial to the platform of the Gewandhaus. The *Neue Zeitschrift* was their organ, but they had supporters also amongst the journalists of the daily press, Ferdinand Gleich, of the *Leipziger Tagblatt*, being one of the principal. They were on the look-out for champions who would rally to their cause, and welcomed the unusual as such, though reserving their heartiest approval for the piquant, sounding, sensational, or even revolutionary.

To these two bodies of extremists our Johannes, with his

inexperience, his ideal aims, his genius, and his dislike of the sensational, was now to appeal. Had he been compelled at the moment to declare for either party, he certainly would not have chosen the side of revolution. But he was gifted with an imagination at once profound, original, and romantic. This sealed his fate with the men who considered themselves the modern representatives of classic art. The day after the concert he wrote to Joachim to announce —"a brilliant and decided failure."

"In the first place," he says, "it really went very well; I played much better than in Hanover, and the orchestra capitally. The first rehearsal aroused no feeling whatever, either in the musicians or hearers. No hearers came, however, to the second, and not a muscle moved on the countenance of either of the musicians. In the evening Cherubini's Elisa overture was given, and then an Ave Maria of his uninterestingly sung, so I hoped Pfund's (the drummer's) roll would come at the right time.* The first movement and the second were heard without a sign. At the end three hands attempted to fall slowly one upon the other, upon which a quite audible hissing from all sides forbade such demonstrations. There is nothing else to write about the event, for no one has yet said a syllable to me about the work, David excepted, who was very kind. . . .

"This failure has made no impression at all upon me, and the slight feeling of disappointment and flatness disappeared when I heard Haydn's C minor Symphony and the Ruins of Athens. In spite of all this, the concerto will please some day when I have improved its construction, and a second shall sound different.

"I believe it is the best thing that could happen to me; it makes one pull one's thoughts together and raises one's spirit. . . . But the hissing was surely too much? . . .

"The faces here looked dreadfully insipid when I came from Hanover, and was accustomed to seeing yours. Monday (January 31) I am going to Hamburg. There is interesting church music here on Sunday, and in the evening Faust at Frau Frege's."†

---

* The concerto opens with a long-continued roll of drums.

† Brahms-Joachim "Briefwechsel," p. 167.

The grimness of the young composer's disappointment may be read between these Spartan lines. But perhaps he has exaggerated his failure. Let us see what Bernsdorf has to say.

"It is sad but true; new works do not succeed in Leipzig. Again at the fourteenth Gewandhaus concert was a composition borne to the grave. This work, however, cannot give pleasure. Save its serious intention, it has nothing to offer but waste, barren dreariness truly disconsolate. Its invention is neither attractive nor agreeable. . . . And for more than three-quarters of an hour must one endure this rooting and rummaging, this dragging and drawing, this tearing and patching of phrases and flourishes! Not only must one take in this fermenting mass; one must also swallow a dessert of the shrillest dissonances and most unpleasant sounds. With deliberate intention, Herr Brahms has made the pianoforte part of his concerto as uninteresting as possible; it contains no effective treatment of the instrument, no new and ingenious passages, and wherever something appears which gives promise of effect, it is immediately crushed and suffocated by a thick crust of orchestral accompaniment. It must be observed, finally, that Herr Brahms' pianoforte technique does not satisfy the demands we have a right to make of a concert-player of the present day."

Nothing could be more representative than these lines, of the conscientious bigotry which almost always opposes what is really original, though it is expressed by Bernsdorf with exceptional coarseness. The narrowly orthodox antagonists of Brahms' art resembled those who had levelled their shafts against Beethoven and Schumann each in their day. The young composer fared differently at the hands of the progressists. The *Neue Zeitschrift* wrote:

"The appearance of Johannes Brahms with a new concerto was bound to attract our especial attention. In the first place, on account of the hopes entertained of an artist who had been introduced in a most exceptional manner, even before his first appearance, by the enthusiastic words of a revered master; and secondly, from the rarity of his subsequent public announcements and the retirement in which he has lived.

" Notwithstanding its undeniable want of outward effect, we regard the poetic contents of the concerto as an unmistakable sign of significant and original creative power; and, in face of the belittling criticisms of a certain portion of the public and press, we consider it our duty to insist on the admirable sides of the work, and to protest against the not very estimable manner in which judgment has been passed upon it."

Ferdinand Gleich writes:

" Who would or could ignore in this new work the tokens of an eminent creative endowment! We least of all who regard it as our duty to encourage young talent. Many doubts, however, suggested themselves as we listened to this concert-piece in large form. This work again suggests a condition of indefiniteness and fermentation, a wrestling for a method of expression commensurate with the ideas of the composer, which has indeed broken through the form of tradition, but has not yet constructed another sufficiently definite and rounded to satisfy the demands of the æsthetics of art. . . . The first movement, especially, gives us the impression of monstrosity; this was less the case with the two others, although even there we were not able, in spite of the beauties they contain, to feel real artistic enjoyment. Brahms places the orchestra, as far as is possible in a concert-piece, by the side of the obbligato instrument, and by so doing establishes himself as an artist who understands the requirements of the new era. The treatment of the orchestra shows a blooming fancy and the most vivid feeling for new and beautiful tone effects, although the composer has not yet sufficient command over his means to do justice to his intentions. The work was received calmly, not to say coldly, by the public; we, however, must acknowledge the eminent talent of the composer, of whom, though he is still too much absorbed in his *Sturm und Drang* period, it is not difficult to predict the accomplishment of something great."

Whether or not these two reviews were penned with a deliberate purpose—and a desire on the part of the supporters of the New-German school to identify Brahms with

their cause can hardly be regarded as either remarkable or
dishonourable—no trace is to be found in either of the in-
sincerity attributed by Kalbeck, in his Life of Brahms, to
the journalistic partisans of the Weimarites, and especially
to Brendel, editor of the *Zeitschrift* and friend of Liszt.
Their honesty of purpose, as well as their liberality of view,
has been vindicated by the fate which for many years attended the published concerto, and again we may place the
remarks of Hanslick, the avowed champion of classical art
and the enthusiastic admirer of the mature Brahms, beside
those published in the *Zeitschrift* of the fifties. Writing in
1888, he says:*

"Brahms began, like Schumann, in *Sturm und Drang*,
but he was much more daring and wild, more emancipated in
respect to form and modulation. The fermentation period
of his genius, which is generally supposed to have closed
with his Op. 10 (Ballades for pianoforte), should, perhaps,
be extended . . . does it not include the D minor Concerto,
with its wild genius?"

It has, indeed, taken nearly half a century to establish the
concerto in a secure position of public acceptance, and the
day, though now probably not far distant, has not even yet
arrived when it can be said to rank as a prime favourite
amongst compositions of its class with the large body of
music-lovers.

Conceived as part of a symphony, the first movement of
the work is symphonic in character, though, as Spitta has
pointed out, not in form. The desire attributed to the
composer by Ferdinand Gleich and by many others since,
to create a new form, to compose a symphonic work with a
pianoforte obbligato, did not exist. Brahms simply wished
to use what he had already written, and did not feel that
the time had come when he could successfully complete a
symphony. He rewrote his first two movements, therefore,
as we have noted, making room in them for a pianoforte

---

* " Musikalisches und Literarisches " : " Neuer Brahms Katalog."

solo, put away the third movement, and composed a new
finale. How successfully he accomplished his task is to-day
apparent to accustomed ears, for which the first movement,
though it contains slight deviations from traditional concerto form, has no moment of obscurity. The imagination
of this portion of the work is colossal. It has something
Miltonic in its character, and seems to suggest to the mind
issues more tremendous and universal than the tragedy of
Schumann's fate, with which it must be associated. No one
will assert that it contains what are termed "brilliant
pianoforte passages," the very existence of which is unthink-
able in a movement of such exalted poetic grandeur; but
that its performance brings due reward to capable inter-
preters has been proved by the enthusiasm of many a latter-
day audience. After all that has been said, the reader will
have no difficulty in understanding the fervent intensity of
mood which impelled the composition of the slow movement, or in realising something of the emotions which suggested the motto, *Benedictus qui venit in nomine Domini,*
written above it in the original manuscript which was presented to Joachim by Brahms. In the finale, the difficult
task of creating something which should relieve the tension
of feeling induced by the preceding movements, without
impairing the unity of the concerto as a whole, has been well
achieved. If it is somewhat more sombre in colour than the
usually accepted finale in rondo form, it is abundant in
vigour and impulse, whilst, on the other hand, though
written with a view to the concert-room, it never descends
towards the trivialities of mere outward glitter.

Much more might be said in explanation of the dubious
position so long occupied in the world of art by this great
work of genius. We must not, however, linger too long
over such interesting matters. It is enough to say that the
purpose expressed by Brahms in his letter to Joachim, of
"pulling his thoughts together," was literally carried out,
and that his development proceeded in the direction it had
already taken, which was the very opposite of that pursued

by the adherents of the New-German school. It consisted
in the still closer concentration of his powers within the
forms of tradition, and the rapidity with which he attained
to complete and free mastery over musical structure is
marked by the production—soon to be recorded—of the first
of the great series of *chefs-d'œuvre* of chamber music which
have set his name, in this particular domain of art, as high
as that of Beethoven himself.

Unrecognised by the public and misunderstood by the
academics of Leipzig, whose sympathies he seems particularly, though for many years vainly, to have desired to
gain, our young musician had now no choice but to return to
his home and pupils at Hamburg. If, however, he himself
felt at all despondent at the failure of his hopes, his friends
were determined about the future of his work. Prompted
and backed up by Joachim, Avé Lallement, who was a member of the Philharmonic committee, persuaded the directors
to engage composer and concerto for their concert of March
24. Joachim had written to Avé:

" DEAR FRIEND,
    " Nearer acquaintance with Brahms' concerto inspires
me with increasing love and respect. The most intelligent
people amongst the public and the orchestra (of Leipzig)
with whom I have spoken express a high opinion of Brahms
as a musician, and even those who do not like the concerto
are at one as to his eminent playing. I have never expected
anything else than that prejudice on the one hand, and, on
the other, astonishment at an individuality which surrenders
itself so unreservedly to the ideal as that of our friend,
should present some impediment to the brilliancy of his
success. A few places in the composition which, though
good in themselves, are too much spun out may also here
and there disturb one's enjoyment. Nevertheless, one may
say that the concerto has had a success honourable alike to
artists and public; the same in Hanover. Now let fault-
finders and malicious detractors gossip as they please—I
don't mind; we have done right. . . . Now do as you like

in Hamburg, but if you give the concerto at the Philharmonic I will come and conduct. That has long been settled."*

Nor was this all. While staying in January with Joachim, who was anxious to hear the effect of the D major Serenade in its original scoring, Johannes had recopied the parts of one movement of the work, which was tried at Hanover on January 23, the day after the important subscription concert. The ineffectiveness of the instrumentation, and especially the want of balance between strings and wind, could not be ignored by the two friends; but Joachim formed the opinion that with certain alterations in the distribution of the passages, the work might prove satisfactory in its original form, not indeed for solo instruments, but for what may best be described as a small orchestra. Brahms' first business on his return to Hamburg was to improve the parts of the work, the dimensions of which he had enlarged in the autumn by the addition of three short movements; and, on the conclusion of the negotiations with the Philharmonic committee for the performance of the D minor Concerto, it was decided between the composer and his friends that a soirée should be arranged which should be signalised by the introduction to the music lovers of Hamburg of the D major Serenade.

The Philharmonic concert of March 24 was made a musical event of unusual importance by the engagement of Joachim and of Stockhausen—his first appearance in Hamburg—and public interest was only increased by the advertisement of a musical soirée in the joint names of Brahms, Joachim and Stockhausen, for the 28th. That Johannes had taken heart again after his disappointments, and was looking forward with pleasure to the visits of his friends, is evident from a letter written by him a few days beforehand to the lady in waiting on the Princess Friederike of Lippe-Detmold.

---

* Moser's " Life of Joachim."

"VERY ESTEEMED, GRACIOUS FRÄULEIN,

"In the first place I beg you to express my most humble thanks to Her Serene Highness the Princess Friederike for the despatch of the new Bach work.

"How often this present will remind me in the most agreeable manner of Her Highness's kindness. You know how I love the divine master, and may imagine that his tones (so dreaded by you) are often heard here.

"I am glad that Her Serene Highness continues to work so industriously at her music, and only wish I could help her in some way.

"In the trio mentioned by you* the most simple way is that the left hand (which ceases playing) should help the poor right. For what embarrassment the mischievous arrogance of the composer is responsible!

"The day after to-morrow I play my pianoforte concerto here, and a few days later introduce other works at a concert of my own. Joachim and Stockhausen, who are coming for it, will make the days into real musical festivals.

"In spite of the great diversity of opinions expressed about my works, I have reason to be quite satisfied with my first attempts for orchestra, and I confidently hope that they will find friendly hearers in Detmold also.

"And I may venture to hope, above all, for later ripening and better swelling fruits . . . ."†

The Philharmonic committee had no reason to regret their arrangements. The attraction of the two great names filled their concert-room to suffocation. Every seat and every

---

* Brahms's Trio in B major.

† First published in Reimann's "Johannes Brahms." One of the Princess Friederike's Christmas presents to Brahms whilst he was her teacher consisted of the five volumes (1851-1855 inclusive) of the Leipzig Society's edition of Bach's works issued before he became a subscriber, and it would appear from the opening of the above-quoted letter that she made herself responsible for his subscription during the consecutive seasons of his visits to Detmold. It is interesting to read the traces of his movements furnished by the subscription list placed at the commencement of each volume. In 1856 his name appears as belonging to Düsseldorf; 1857-1864 inclusive, to Hamburg; and from 1865 onwards, to Vienna.

standing-place was occupied, and crowds were turned from the doors. Those who have witnessed similar scenes during —how many decades! can picture the excited expectancy that followed the performance of a Cherubini overture, the thunder of welcome at the first glimpse of Joachim, the never-ending applause and recalls at the conclusion of his first solo, Spohr's "Gesang-Scena," the sensation of Stockhausen's first appearance, the magnificent success of his performance of a great aria from his oratorio répertoire. Then a lull, the disappearance of Capellmeister Grund, the opening of the piano, the reappearance of Joachim, this time to take his stand at the conductor's desk, and the entrance of the slight, blonde young Hamburger, pale and nervous, but calm and self-controlled, almost happy in the support of his two friends.

On such an evening of enthusiasm, what public could have refused its tribute to the young fellow-citizen who came before them as a composer practically for the first time, with two heroes at his side to champion his cause? Johannes was really successful. "The concerto created an impression, and excited applause far beyond that of a mere *succès d'estime*," and the critic of the *Nachrichten* records the fact with the more satisfaction from its contrast with the result of the performance at the Leipzig Gewandhaus.

It would appear from the wording of the letter to Detmold quoted on a foregoing page that the concert of the 28th, advertised in the three names, was especially Brahms' undertaking. Ten years had elapsed since his performance of the Variations on a favourite waltz had passed unrecorded save in Marxsen's paper. Since that time he had given no concert in Hamburg, and the change in his prospects is well measured by the different circumstances of the occasions of 1849 and 1859. True that at the age of twenty-six he had achieved no popular success, that his concerto had effectually alienated from him the sympathies of the Leipzigers, and that the Weimarites, whilst encouraging his efforts, partially misunderstood his aims. Thorough-going belief in his art and its promise was more firmly established than ever as a leading principle of the inner Schumann circle, and this was itself gradually spreading. We give the full programme of March 28, as advertised in the *Hamburger Nachrichten*, which is interesting for many reasons:

1. Bach:	Sonata for Clavier and Violin.
2. Handel:	Aria from " The Messiah."
3. Tartini:	" Trillo del Diavolo."
4. Schubert:	Song, " Der Erlkönig."
5. Brahms:	Serenade for String and Wind Instruments.
6. Boieldieu:	Cavatina, " Fête du Village Voisin."
7. Schubert:	Rondeau Brilliant for Pianoforte and Violin.
8. Schubert, Schumann, etc.:	Songs (including " Der Nussbaum," " Mondnacht," " Widmung ").

There was good reason to be delighted with the material result of the undertaking. The large Wörmer hall was thronged. Brahms' artistic success was also assured in regard to his playing of the duet sonata and rondo with Joachim, and many of the musicians present appreciated his wonderful accompaniment of Stockhausen's songs. He was himself, moreover, satisfied with the reception of the Serenade that was conducted by Joachim.

" It really seemed to reach the audience yesterday. The applause continued until I showed myself on the platform. You would scarcely have known the Hamburgers,"

he wrote to Frau Schumann, whose engagements prevented her from going to Hamburg for the eventful week. Nevertheless, the press notices did not adventure beyond the safe limits of patronising encouragement, and the *Nachrichten* expressed the general professional sentiment of the time in the concluding sentence of its review:

" If Brahms will learn to say what is in his heart plainly and straightforwardly, and not go out of his way to cut strange capers, the public will endorse Schumann's hopes,

and the laity be able to understand what it is that professional musicians prize so highly in his works.''

Such contemporary criticism might well pass unnoticed if
it were not that, in spite of the wealth of beautiful material
and the fine workmanship contained in the serenade, only
one or two of its movements are occasionally heard in the
concert-rooms of the present day, whilst the composer's later
and more difficult orchestral works grow every year in the
favour of the public. The circumstance is to be chiefly explained by considerations similar to those we have already
applied to the first concerto. When Brahms wrote the work
he had not quite passed from his apprenticeship. Though
within sight of mastery, he had not achieved it. The Serenade in D is a serenade in the character of its ideas, but
not entirely so in the structure of its movements. The instrumental "serenata" (fair weather), a form which
flourished vigorously during the latter half of the eighteenth century, and was exhibited in its greatest perfection
by Mozart, was especially cultivated in an age when music
was dependent on the patron—the prince or nobleman who
kept his private band, and who delighted himself and his
friends by open-air performances in his park on fine summer
nights. It consisted of a longer or shorter series of movements—a march, an allegro, rondo, one or two andantes, a
couple of minuets, none of them developed to any great
length, and was composed for more or fewer solo instruments according to circumstances. Brahms, fascinated by
the performances of the Detmold wind players, probably
began his work with the intention of composing a serenade
pur et simple; but his interest in the art of thematic development outran his discretion, and, by over-elaborating one of
its movements, he injured the balance of his composition
and introduced into it a character of complexity foreign to
the nature of its form. The Serenade in D consists of an
allegro molto, scherzo, adagio non troppo, minuets 1 and 2,
scherzo, rondo. Some of the six movements, irresistible
from their grace, daintiness, or romance, delight the public

when performed as separate numbers, but the length of the opening movement and the somewhat mechanical development of its middle section may perhaps prove in the future, as they have done in the past, obstacles to the frequent performance of the entire work. Traces of the young musician's studies are to be found in the well-known reminiscences of Beethoven and Haydn in the second scherzo.

The few years immediately succeeding Brahms' second return from Detmold must be regarded as forming another turning-point in his career. They witnessed the close of his *Sturm und Drang* period and his complete transformation into a master. They are remarkable not only on account of the appearance of a number of short choral works which, perfect in themselves, lead directly to the splendid achievements of later years in the same domain, to the German Requiem, the Schicksalslied, the Triumphlied, but they form a period of actual magnificent fruition. To them is to be referred the inauguration of those chamber-music works of Brahms which stand in the forefront of the finest compositions of their kind, and the appearance of a classic for pianoforte unsurpassed by any other of its form, the Variations and Fugue on a theme by Handel. This portion of our composer's life belongs especially to his native city, though it is certain that the difficult conditions of his home life supplied some counterweight to the influences of patriotic sentiment and family affection which made him desire to settle in Hamburg permanently. That he was not at once accepted as a great composer by his fellow-citizens should not be a matter of surprise. It has too often been forgotten by Brahms' partisans that his development as a creator was not precocious. The list of Mendelssohn's compositions when he was a boy of sixteen is bewildering in its length and variety; at the same age the most important of Johannes' achievements was presumably the set of Variations on a favourite waltz. Schubert's career was cut short in his thirty-second year; Mozart died at thirty-five. Brahms at the age of twenty-six had not completed any large work which can be regarded as entirely representative of his mature powers, and had introduced but few compositions either to the public or his friends. There were, however, those among the musicians of Hamburg who, belonging to the increasing circle of his personal acquaintances, believed in his creative genius with the enthusiasm of absolute conviction, and as a pianist, though not regarded as a phenomenal performer, he was generally accepted as an artist of first rank.

Brahms' regard for his pupil, Fräulein Friedchen Wagner, had led to his becoming intimate at her father's house, and here he frequently had opportunity of hearing some of the compositions and arrangements for voices which engaged much of his attention. Fräulein Friedchen, her sister Thusnelda, and the charming Fräulein Bertha Porubszky, from Vienna, who arrived in Hamburg to stay for a year with her aunt, Frau Auguste Brandt, were delighted to practise short works in two and three parts under his direction. Probably he hoped gradually to obtain a larger number of recruits for his purpose. Before long, however, accident led to his becoming the conductor of a quite considerable ladies' choir.

On May 19 the wedding of Pastor Sengelmann and Fräulein Jenny von Ahsen took place at St. Michael's Church. There was a large gathering of friends to witness the ceremony. Grädener, already mentioned as a friend of Brahms, who was an accomplished composer and the director of a singing school, conducted his pupils in the performance of a motet for female voices which he had written for the occasion, and Johannes, a very old acquaintance of the bride, accompanied on the organ. Pleased with the effect of Grädener's composition, Brahms expressed a wish to hear his own "Ave Maria" for female voices with accompaniment for organ, composed during his second visit to Detmold, under similar conditions of performance, and with the assistance of Fräulein Friedchen, who exerted herself to procure the requisite number of voices, a rehearsal was arranged. On Monday, June 6, twenty-eight ladies

18

assembled at the Wagners' house, and tried, not only the "Ave Maria," afterwards published as Op. 12, but the " O bone Jesu" and "Adoramus," now known as Op. 37, Nos. 1 and 2. Brahms was seized with a fit of nervousness whilst conducting, and Grädener, who was present amongst a few listeners, stepped forward to the rescue; but a second rehearsal on the following day went well, and the third trial in church with organ accompaniment was in every respect highly successful. The practices had been so enjoyable that, with the concurrence of Grädener, it was arranged that the ladies, most of whom were pupils of the singing school, should assemble every Monday morning to practise with Brahms; and the society thus founded, which soon increased to forty members, became a source of delight to all who were associated with it. The meetings were held during the first season at the Wagners' house in the Pastorenstrasse; later on they took place at several members' houses in turn. Each young lady used to sing from a small oblong manuscript book, into which she copied her parts, and several of these volumes are still in existence. After the business of the morning was over, the conductor usually played to his young disciples and admirers, who soon learned to look upon his performances as not the least memorable part of the weekly programme. Writing in the course of the summer to Fräulein von Meysenbug, Brahms says:

" . . . I am here, and shall probably remain until I go to Detmold. Some very pleasant pupils detain me, and, strangely enough, a ladies' society that sings under my direction; till now only what I compose for it. The clear silver tones please me exceedingly, and in the church with the organ the ladies' voices sound quite charming."*

The season closed on September 19 with a performance at St. Peter's Church before an invited audience. Some of the "Marienlieder" (afterwards Op. 22) and the 13th Psalm (Op. 27) were included in the programme. The mem-

---

* "Aus Johannes Brahms' Jugendtagen," by Hermann Freiherr von Meysenbug (*Neues Wiener Tagblatt*, May, 1901).

bers of the choir appeared attired in black to denote their
grief at the approaching departure of their conductor, and
sent him, afterwards, a silver inkstand buried beneath
flowers as a mark of their appreciation of his labours. This
Brahms acknowledged from Detmold in the following official
letter to Fräulein Friedchen, his energetic helper in the
founding of the choir:

"DETMOLD, end of Sept., 1859.

"ESTEEMED FRÄULEIN,
      "Nothing more agreeable than to be so pleasantly
obliged to write a letter as I am now.
      "I think constantly of the glad surprise with which I
perceived the inkstand, the remembrance from the ladies'
choir, under its charming covering of flowers.
      "I have done so little to deserve it that I should be
ashamed were it not that I hope to write much more for you;
and I shall certainly hear finer tones sounding around me as
I look at the valued and beautiful present on my writing-
table. Pray express to all whom you can reach my hearty
greeting and thanks.
      "I have seldom had a more agreeable pleasure, and our
meetings will remain one of my most welcome and favourite
recollections.
      "But not, I hope, till later years!
      "With best greetings to you and yours,
                  "Your
                        "heartily sincere
                        JOHS. BRAHMS."*

That the composer did not forget his maidens during his
season at Detmold appears from another letter to Fräulein
Wagner written a couple of months later:

"Dec., 1859.

"ESTEEMED FRÄULEIN,
      "Here are some new songs for your little singing re-
public. I hope they may assist in keeping it together. If
I can help towards this end pray command me.
      "Kindest greetings to you and yours.
                  "Most sincerely,
                  "JOHS. BRAHMS."*

* First published, with an account of the Ladies' Choir, in Hübbe's
"Brahms in Hamburg."

Acquaintance with the charming circumstances which
stimulated Brahms to the writing of most of his published
choruses for women's voices gives an additional interest to
the study of these beautiful compositions, which undoubtedly take their place amongst the most fascinating
works of their class. Those with sacred texts, all evident
fruits of the composer's studies in the strict style of part-
writing, show, nevertheless, considerable variety of character. The "Ave Maria," with accompaniment for
orchestra or organ, Op. 12, first sung by, though not composed for, the ladies' choir, is animated by a gentle, childlike, devotional spirit appropriate to a prayer addressed by
a group of tender girls to the Virgin Mother of Christ.
The 13th Psalm, with accompaniment for organ or pianoforte, Op. 27, composed expressly for the choir and tried
for the first time on August 29, 1859, strikes at once a more
solemn note, with its three opening cries to the Lord; and
the mourning plaint of the writer is reproduced in tones
whose fervent pleading is not impaired by the clear simplicity of style in which the music is conceived. The Three
Sacred Choruses, without accompaniment, Op. 37, are alike
beautiful, whilst varying in character. The "Adoramus"
and "Regina Cœli" (Nos. 2 and 3), written throughout in
canon, are fine examples of learned facility; and the last-
named, the bright "Regina Cœli," for soprano and alto
soli and four-part women's chorus, is an entirely captivating
composition.

The secular pieces—the Songs with accompaniment for
horns and harp, Op. 17, and the Songs and Romances to
be sung *a capella*, Op. 44—most of them composed at Hamburg in the summer of 1859, though fairly well known,
should be heard oftener than they are. The dainty charm
of such little works as the "Minnelied" and the "Bar-
carole," to name only two of the most effective from Op. 44,
gives welcome refreshment in a miscellaneous choral concert,
and never fails to captivate an audience.

In our rapid survey of some of the works which are to be

associated with Brahms' Ladies' Choir, we have only taken
account of those that were actually published in the form
required by the nature of the society. Many settings and
arrangements are to be found, in the little oblong manuscript books, of songs which have become known to the
world amongst the composer's settings for a single voice or
for mixed choir. The canons Nos. 1, 2, 8, 10, 11, 12, of
Op. 113 were sung at the society's meetings. The "Regina
Cœli," on the other hand, was not included in the ladies'
répertoire.*

---

* Hübbe.

CHAPTER X.

1859-1861.

Third season at Detmold—" Ave Maria " and " Begräbnissgesang "
performed in Hamburg and Göttingen—Second Serenade, first performed in Hamburg—Lower Rhine Festival—Summer at Bonn—
Music at Herr Kyllmann's—Variations on an original theme first
performed in Leipzig by Frau Schumann—" Marienlieder "—
First public performance of Sextet in B flat in Hanover.

BRAHMS found himself more than ever in request amongst
the general circle of Detmold society during the autumn of
1859. He had become the fashion. It was the thing to
have lessons from him, and his presence gave distinction to
a gathering. The very circumstance of his popularity, however, caused some friction between himself and his acquaintances. He disliked to waste his time, as he considered it,
in mere society, and, when occasionally induced to attend a
party against his will, gave his hosts cause to regret their
pertinacity. If not silent the whole evening, he would
amuse himself by exercising his talent for caustic speech.
Carl von Meysenbug, when at home, jealous for his friend's
credit, often called Johannes privately to account for his perversity, but was always silenced by the unanswerable reply,
" Bah! that is all humbug!" (Pimpkram).

The young musician's relations with the princely family
remained undisturbed, and his musical gifts were, on the
whole, fairly appreciated by the entire court circle, though
he was not regarded personally with unanimous favour by
those who did not know him well. Carl's mother, the Frau
Hofmarschall, took a few lessons from him to please her

friends at the castle, and once accepted his offer to play duets with her; but no subsequent invitation could induce her to repeat this performance. "The good fellow should not have behaved as he did that once; I cannot put up with it," she wrote to Carl. Something in Brahms' manner—independence, artistic self-consciousness, or whatever else it may be called—repelled her; and, in view of the fact that she was not the first person whom he had offended in a similar way, since the time when he had visited as a youth at the Japhas' house in Hamburg, it may fairly be assumed that Her Excellency had justifiable grounds for the reserved attitude she maintained towards him.

It is, indeed, certain that Brahms, during his third season at Detmold, began to grow impatient of his position there. His lessons to the Princess, who was really musical and made rapid progress, continued to give him genuine pleasure, but he chafed at the constant demands on his time arising from his fixed duties, and the rigid etiquette observed at the Court of a very small capital gave him a distaste for his work as conductor of the choral society. The circle of Serene Highnesses, Excellencies, and their friends, did not furnish sufficient voices for the adequate rendering of two or three oratorios and cantatas by Handel and Bach which he selected for practice during his second and third seasons; and, with Prince Leopold's permission, he supplemented them by persuading some of the townspeople to become members. His sense of the ridiculous was strongly excited by the rules of conduct prescribed for these not very willing assistants, who were not even permitted to make an obeisance to the Serenities, and scarcely ventured to lift their eyes from the music whilst in their august presence. There were some good performances of great works, however, and Bach's cantata "Ich hatte viel Bekümmerniss" was given four times; but the difficulty of procuring tenors continued serious, and the entire circumstances of the meetings made Brahms feel increasing desire to be relieved from the necessity of attending them.

Of his own choral compositions, besides the "Ave Maria," the "Begräbnissgesang," for mixed chorus and wind, published later on as Op. 13, was practised during the season. It is strange that this fine work, composed at Detmold during the autumn of 1858 to a sixteenth century text by Michael Weisse, the editor of the first German church hymn book, is not better known. Intended as a song for the graveside, it would be out of place in an ordinary miscellaneous programme, but is well adapted for performance at a Good Friday concert, or as a church anthem in Passion Week. Like all Brahms' sacred compositions of the time it gives evidence of the strong impression he had derived from his exhaustive study of the mediæval church composers; and the music, austere in its simplicity, is characterised by uncompromising fidelity to the almost grimly severe spirit of the words. It was heard, together with the "Ave Maria," for the first time in public, at Grädener's Academy concert of December 2, and Brahms, who obtained leave to go to Hamburg for the occasion, appeared the same evening with Schumann's pianoforte concerto. A day's visit to Hanover on his way back brought about the renewal of his relations with Grimm whom Joachim had invited to meet him, and Grimm soon afterwards obtained the manuscripts of the two choral works for practice by his society, of which Carl von Meysenbug was an enthusiastic member.

"As Grimm was distributing the parts of the 'Ave Maria' and the 'Begräbnissgesang' at one of the practices," says the Freiherr von Meysenbug, "my neighbour, a glib University student with the experience of several terms behind him, said to me in a surprised tone : 'Brahms! who is that?' 'Oh, some old ecclesiastic of Palestrina's time,' I replied— a piece of information which he accepted and passed on."

The compositions were given under Grimm's direction at the society's concert of January 19, 1860. There is little doubt that Philipp Spitta, author of the exhaustive biography of Sebastian Bach, whose essay "Zur Musik" should be read by all earnest students of Brahms' music,

took part in the performance of the "Begräbnissgesang."
His friendship with the composer dates from this period
when he was a student of the Göttingen University and one
of the intimates of Grimm's circle.

The Serenade in D major was heard for the second and
last time as set for "strings and wind" at one of the Detmold court concerts of the season 1859. The composer soon
afterwards rejected this form as a mere "Zwittergestalt."
Adopting Frau Schumann's original suggestion, he re-
arranged the work for large orchestra and was rewarded for
his effort by Joachim's very warm congratulations on the
success of his instrumentation.

The tradition once current that an early version of the
Pianoforte Quartet in G minor was tried in Detmold has
been practically destroyed by the publication of the several
volumes of Brahms' correspondence.*

It will be convenient to add here that the invitation to
revisit Detmold on the same terms as before was finally
refused by Brahms in a letter to the Hofmarschall dated
from Hamburg, August, 1860:

---

* The evidence of Litzmann's "Clara Schumann," Vol. VIII, and
of the Brahms "Briefwechsel," IV and V (Grimm and Joachim) shows.
that Brahms, during many years of his career, invariably submitted a
new movement, or series of movements, on completion, first for the
opinion of Frau Schumann or Grimm, and then for that of Joachim.
It has already been explained (p. 203) that the quartet composed in
1856 is identified by one of Joachim's letters as an early version of
the work in C minor published twenty years later. No published
letter, however, suggests the existence of a second quartet, or part.
of one, until in July and September, 1861, respectively, Frau Schumann and Joachim write about movements, evidently new to them,
with which we are familiar as belonging to the Quartets, Opp. 25
and 26. The inference is that though one or more movements of
these works may have been sketched at the time of Brahms's connection with Detmold, no portion of either had advanced sufficiently to
be shown, much less rehearsed, during that period. In the author's.
opinion the whole internal evidence of the two works is indicative of
the place which they actually occupy in the catalogue of Brahms'
compositions of chamber music.

" After renewed consideration, I must beg to express to
His Serene Highness the Prince my regret that I shall not be
able to visit Detmold in the winter. I have to add to the
causes of this decision which I have already had the honour
to communicate, that I shall be much occupied this autumn
with the publication of my works, with revising the proofs
of some, and preparing others for the engraver. On this
account alone, therefore, I must decide to stay here during
the winter. I particularly desire to express my regret to the
Princess Friederike that I shall be unable to enjoy her progress in playing and her great sympathy for music. . . ."*

The post of conductor to the court orchestra, which became
vacant on Kiel's retirement with a pension in 1864, and
which might probably under other circumstances have been
offered for the acceptance or refusal of Brahms, passed to
Bargheer, who retained it until 1876, when Prince Leopold's
death put an end to the musical activity of Detmold.

Brahms was able to give his friends a good account of
himself at the end of the year. Before leaving Detmold he
sent Joachim the completed second Serenade in A major,
the first movement of which had aroused Grimm's enthusiasm in the autumn of 1858, scored for small orchestra (wind,
violas, 'celli and basses); and despatched part of a sextet
for strings in B flat to Göttingen. Grimm again failed
signally in the task of fault finding so frequently urged upon
him by Johannes, and could only write of the two new movements in terms of wonder and delight. The serenade was
tried privately in Hanover.

"I have tried my second serenade in Hanover," wrote
Johannes on January 17, 1860, to Frau Schumann,
" Joachim thought it was satisfactory and sounded well.
What have I not in him?"

The work was performed for the first time in public under
the composer's direction at the Hamburg Philharmonic concert of February 10. On the same occasion Joachim
transported the audience by his performances of Beethoven's

---

* " Aus Brahms' Jugendtagen." See footnote on p. 216.

Concerto and Tartini's " Trillo del Diavolo," and Johannes had a great success as pianist with Schumann's Concerto.

The second serenade was considered easier to understand than its elder sister, and was received with comparative favour, though not with enthusiasm. To the ears of the present generation the work appears limpidly clear, and it is difficult to realise that it was ever accounted otherwise. In it we have a *chef-d'œuvre* which displays our musician passed finally from his transition stage and standing out clearly as a master in definite possession both of aim and method. Unmistakably he has taken his footing on the basis of tradition, and creates with the freedom of self-control within the forms consecrated by the works of Haydn, Mozart, and Beethoven, no longer betrayed by immaturity into anything that could be misconstrued as the intentional discursiveness of rhapsody. The work is impregnated with a breath as fragrant as the spirit of Schubert's muse, and, though perhaps not fully representative of the very powerful individuality now associated with the name of Brahms, bears the distinct impress of his mind, and could have been written by no other composer. Each of the five movements is a gem of the first water. Each has a character of its own, which yet combines with every other to make the serenade a perfect example of a developed form of garden music, night music. Graceful romance, tender playfulness, lively frolic, just the stirring of the deeper emotions, all the gentler phases of poetic sentiment, are suggested in turn by its lovely melodies.

Why is this masterpiece so seldom heard?
Appropriately called a serenade from the character of its

ideas, and even from the structure of its movements, which, whilst fully developed, are all quite clear, balanced and symmetrical each in itself and as part of a whole, and indicate the composer's perfect fulfilment of his intention, the length of the work again approaches that of a symphony. It must be borne in mind that to a general audience the name "serenade" as applied to instrumental music does not now suggest any particular class of composition, the times and customs which produced this form having long since passed away; whilst it is customary to associate with the word "symphony" a suggestion of the more strenuous emotions of human existence. Thus, the ordinary concertgoer who listens to Brahms' work is puzzled as to what he ought to expect, and his uncertainty interferes with his enjoyment.

Another drawback, under modern concert conditions, to the general appreciation of the beautiful Serenade in A major is the absence of violins from the score. It hardly needs pointing out that the, so to say, muted tone of the combination of instruments employed by the composer would be ideal in the surroundings proper to the performance of the "serenade" as originally so called—palpitating summer heat, deep-blue, starlit sky, flitting to and fro of gallant and graceful forms—but in the prosaic atmosphere of a modern concert-room the bright tone of the violins cannot, perhaps, be safely dispensed with throughout the length of so long a work. It consists of an allegro moderato, scherzo, quasi minuetto with trio, rondo. It may still be hoped, however, that the serenade may be revived, and take its place in the répertoire of our concert societies.

We have lingered so long over the two serenades that a bare mention must suffice of the performance of the first in D major—the first performance in the second and final rearrangement of the score—by command of King George at the Hanover subscription concert of March 3 under Joachim's direction, nor need we dwell upon the fact that it was received with indifference by audience and critics. It is time

to glance again at the party conflicts of the day, and especially to note the activity of the disciples of Weimar, whose
partisanship, as the reader may remember, had been stimulated to violence by the candid admissions of Joachim's
letter to Liszt quoted on p. 223.

"The Weimarites continue their uproar," reported
Johannes in the summer of 1859 to Joachim in England,
"my fingers often itch to do battle, to begin to write anti-
Liszt. But I ! . . . It would be glorious, however, if you
were to remain in Germany in the summer, to compose wonderfully and to strike these people dead with a few flying
shots, whilst I sat near you and helped write music . . . "*

To put the matter, so far as our narrative is concerned
with it, as shortly as possible, Brahms, who had been longing to enter the fray as an active combatant, now induced
Joachim to join him in drawing up a manifesto for signature by musicians of their way of thinking, and subsequent
publication. An obstacle to the fulfilment of the plan presented itself in the impossibility of obtaining unanimity of
opinion as to the suitable wording of the document, and
part of the difficulty seems to have arisen from Brahms'
desire to differentiate between the works of Berlioz and
Wagner on the one hand, and Liszt's "productions" on
the other. Before these preliminaries had been satisfactorily
arranged, however, accident settled the matter. By a mischance that has never been explained, a version of the manifesto which was presumably going round for signature,
found its way, with only four names attached, into the
Echo, a journal of Berlin. It ran as follows:

"The undersigned have long followed with regret the proceedings of a certain party whose organ is Brendel's *Zeitschrift für Musik*. The said *Zeitschrift* unceasingly pro-
mulgates the theory that the most prominent striving
musicians are in accord with the aims represented in its

---

* Brahms-Joachim, No. 178.

pages, that they recognise in the compositions of the leaders of the new school works of artistic value, and that the contention for and against the so-called Music of the Future has been finally fought out, especially in North Germany, and decided in its favour. The undersigned regard it as their duty to protest against such a distortion of fact, and declare, at least for their own part, that they do not acknowledge the principles avowed by the *Zeitschrift*, and that they can only lament and condemn the productions of the leaders and pupils of the so-called New-German school, which on the one hand apply those principles practically, and on the other necessitate the constant setting up of new and unheard-of theories which are contrary to the very nature of music.

"JOHANNES BRAHMS.
"JULIUS OTTO GRIMM.
"JOSEPH JOACHIM.
"BERNARD SCHOLZ."

A few days later the answer appeared in the *Zeitschrift* of May 4, in the shape of a parody written, not in a very formidable style of wit, by C. F. Weitzmann:

"DREAD MR. EDITOR,

"All is *out!* — — I learn that a political coup has been carried *out*, the entire new world rooted *out* stump and branch, and Weimar and Leipzig, especially, struck *out* of the musical map of the world. To compass this end, a widely *out*reaching letter was thought *out* and sent *out* to the chosen-*out* faithful of all lands, in which strongly *out*spoken protest was made against the increasing epidemic of the Music of the Future. Amongst the select of the *out*worthies [paragons] are to be reckoned several *out*siders whose names, however, the modern historian of art has not been able to find *out*. Nevertheless, should the avalanche of signatures widen *out* sufficiently, the storm will break *out* suddenly. Although the strictest secrecy has been enjoined upon the chosen-*out* by the hatchers-*out* of this musico-tragic *out*-and-*out*er, I have succeeded in obtaining sight of the original, and I am glad, dread Mr. Editor, to be able to communicate to you, in what follows, the contents of this aptly conceived state paper—I remain, yours most truly,

"CROSSING-SWEEPER."

" PUBLIC PROTEST.

" The undersigned desire to play first fiddle for once, and
therefore protest against everything which stands in the way
of their coming aloft, including, especially, the increasing
influence of the musical tendency described by Dr. Brendel
as the New-German school, and in short against the whole
spirit of the new music. After the annihilation of these,
to them very unpleasant things, they offer to all who are of
their own mind the immediate prospect of a brotherly association for the advancement of monotonous and tiresome music.

"(Signed) J. FIDDLER.   HANS NEWPATH.   SLIPPERMAN.
" PACKE.   DICK TOM AND HARRY.
" Office of the Music of the Future."

Bülow, writing from Berlin to Louis Köhler, says:

" The manifesto of the Hanoverians has not made the
least sensation here. They have not even sufficient wit
mixed with their malice to have done the thing in good style,
and to have launched it at a well-chosen time, such as the
beginning or end of the season."

It must be said here that Brendel was sincere in his views,
whether or not they commend themselves to us, and that he
had an exceptional power of appreciating the ideas put
forth by the leaders of the new school. Equally certain is
it that the antipathy felt by Joachim and Brahms for Liszt's
compositions proceeded from no feeling of malice or personal
animosity, but from the most sincere conviction. Joachim's
confession to Liszt had been wrung from him by the necessity of escape from a false position. The extraordinary
importance attached by the musical parties of the day to his
alliance is well illustrated by Wagner's bitter words:

"With the defection of a hitherto warm friend, a great
violinist, the violent agitation broke out against the generous
Franz Liszt that prepared for him, at length, the disappointment and embitterment which caused him to abandon his
endeavours to establish Weimar as a town devoted to the
furtherance of music."[*]

---

* Reprint of Wagner's pamphlet, " Das Judenthum in der Musik."

The baselessness, and even folly, of such a statement is
self-evident.

With regard to Brahms particularly, though such works
as Liszt's Symphonic Poems and Dante Symphony were
abominations to him, he always cherished a profound
respect for the powers of Wagner though the artistic principles by which they were guided were not those of his own
musical faith. His allegiance, like that of Joachim, was
wholly given to the masters of classical art, to whom he had
paid homage from childhood, and it was one of the ironies
of fate that he should have been widely supposed, during
many years, to belong to the New-German party, and that
he was handled more tenderly by the *Zeitschrift* than the
Signale. By Brendel himself, indeed, who from the year
1859 onwards worked earnestly to effect a reconciliation
between the contending musical parties, Schumann's young
hero was treated fairly, and even generously, and a steady
Brahms propaganda was practised in years to come by the
fraternity of the Allgemeiner Deutscher Musikverein, a
society founded by Brendel in 1861 for the furtherance of
his pacific aim.

Our composer, who had been betrayed into polemic partly
by loyalty to his convictions and partly by his exuberant
vitality, was not by temperament a party man any more
than his friend, and was to be removed before very long
from the immediate scene of party strife. For the future he
took the wiser course of holding himself aloof from the
contentions of the day, issuing no other manifestoes than
such as were constituted by his works, and never allowing
himself to be tempted into answering the many printed
attacks that were levelled at him. Henceforth he lived his
life, and wrote his works, and followed his faith, leaving
the question of the false or the true to the decision of time.
Who shall yet say what will be the final judgment of this
supreme arbiter of all such matters?

Johannes was again settled in his parents' home during the spring of 1860, but his thoughts were busy with many plans for the future. He longed to extend his travels, and the desire to see Vienna was stirring forcibly within him. He played his Concerto and some numbers of Schumann's *Kreisleriana* at Otten's concert of April 20; but the concerto was very badly accompanied, and once more proved a complete failure. The critic of the *Nachrichten* confesses his inability to understand the work, "which is recognised so warmly by the musicians of the newest tendency," and elects to say nothing about it.

The young musician's greatest pleasure was derived from his singing society of girls, who resumed with ardour their practices under his direction. He placed it this season on a more formal footing by drawing up a set of rules, signature to which was made a condition of membership. The document, headed "Avertimento," is playfully worded in a bygone style of formality, and after a short prelude, in which is set forth, amongst other things, that the practices are to be held only during spring and summer, five laws are laid down, the first two of which enjoin punctual attendance.

"Pro primo, it is to be remarked that the members of the Ladies' Choir must be *there*.

"By which is to be understood that they must oblige themselves to be *there*.

"Pro secundo, it is to be observed that the members of the Ladies' Choir must be there.

"By which is meant, they must be there precisely at the appointed time. . . ."

Absentees and late-comers were to be fined in various amounts, according to various degrees of delinquency, and the money collected given to "begging people," "and it is to be desired that it may surfeit no one."

The fourth rule relates to the careful preservation of the music entrusted to the care of the "virtuous and honour-

able ladies," which was not to be used outside the society,
and the fifth, to the admission of listeners under conditions.
The whole concludes :

"I remain in deepest devotion
and veneration of the Ladies' Choir their most assiduous
ready-writer and steady time-beater

"JOHANNES KREISLER JUN.
(*alias* BRAHMS).

"Given on Monday,
"The 30th of the month of April,
A.D. 1860."

Amongst the signatures is that of Frau Schumann who,
with her eldest daughter Marie, passed a few weeks of the
spring in Hamburg and regularly attended the Monday
choir practices during her stay. We shall have occasion to
mention the name of the great artist more than once again
in interesting connection with the sisterhood of singers, who
were not a little proud of the right given them, by her signature, to claim her as an honorary colleague.*

Notwithstanding the stringent rules as to punctuality of
attendance inserted in this formal document, the meetings
were seriously interrupted during the season, and by the
absence of no less a person than the director himself.
Johannes could in no case, especially in his present restless
mood, have remained away from the Rhine Festival of the
year (Düsseldorf, May 27-29). Schumann's B flat Symphony was to be performed, Hiller to conduct, Joachim to
play the Hungarian Concerto and a Beethoven Romance,
and Stockhausen to sing selections by Boieldieu, Schubert,
Schumann, and Hiller. Frau Schumann was to attend the
concerts, and expected to meet many intimate friends at
Düsseldorf, amongst them being Dietrich and his bride, a
lady long known to the circle as Clara Sohn, daughter of
the painter and professor at the Art Academy. Brahms

---

* The rules, first published by Professor Walter Hübbe in his
"Brahms in Hamburg," are given entire in Appendix No. II.

therefore accompanied Frau Schumann and her daughter when they left Hamburg for Düsseldorf on May 24, and the occasion of the festival proved no less enjoyable than those similar ones which have been referred to in our pages. A new feature at one or more of the private reunions that took place in the intervals of the concerts was the singing of quartets, under Brahms' direction, by four members of the Ladies' Choir who had come to the Festival : the sisters Fräulein Betty and Fräulein Marie Völckers, Fräulein Laura Garbe, and—Frau Schumann herself. She, indeed, it was who proposed to her hostess, Fräulein Leser, that the Dietrichs, Joachim, Stockhausen, and a few others, should be invited to listen to what proved a delightful performance.

Under the circumstances, it cannot be regarded as surprising that Brahms did not immediately return to Hamburg after the festival, but made one of a party that proceeded to Bonn, where he remained with his companions till towards the middle of August.

" The spring had set in gloriously," says Dietrich, who, as the reader will remember, had been settled for some years in the city. " There is something enchanting in such a spring on the Rhine. The pink blossoming woods of fruit-trees, the numerous whitethorn hedges on the banks of the river, the voices of nightingales in the light, warm nights, the fine outlines of the Siebengebirge in the distance; what excursions we were induced to make! It was a happy, sunny time rich also in artistic enjoyment.

" For Brahms, after six years' long silence, had brought with him a number of splendid compositions. There were the two serenades, the Ave Maria, the Begräbnissgesang, Songs and Romances, and the Concerto in D minor.

" He had employed his retirement in the most earnest studies; he had composed, amongst other things, a Mass in canon form, which, however, has not been printed.

" We met frequently at the Kyllmanns' hospitable and artistic house for performances of chamber music and the enjoyment of Stockhausen's splendid singing.

" The artists came also often and gladly to our young home, and before we parted they were present with us at the baptism of our first child. Brahms, Joachim, and Heinrich von Sahr were the sponsors."*

Herr Kyllmann's house in Coblenzstrasse, with its beautiful garden situated on the Rhine bank and commanding a view of the Siebengebirge, was the scene of many noteworthy reunions that gave equal pleasure to the famous guests and the art-loving, art-appreciating family, who were proud to entertain them. One party which took place early in June, during the week that Frau Schumann was able to remain amongst her friends, must be recorded in detail, for the musical performances included a string quartet played by Joachim, David, Otto von Königslow (for many years concertmeister of the Gürzenich subscription concerts, Cologne), and the excellent 'cellist Christian Reimers; Schumann's Quintet, by the same artists, with Frau Schumann as pianist; and songs sung by Stockhausen to Frau Schumann's accompaniment—amongst them Schumann's "Mondnacht" and "Frühlingsnacht." Otto Jahn, who was present to enjoy the music, brought with him his friend Dr. Becker, just arrived from England on his resignation of his post of private secretary to the Prince Consort, and Brahms must be counted with them amongst the listeners. He retired to the sofa of an inner drawing-room, and was not to be induced to perform, though Frau Schumann herself came to request him to do so, and Joachim followed with his persuasive "Oh, Johannes, do play!" Johannes, as is abundantly evident, was no diplomatist. He often felt it easier to know himself misunderstood than to overcome his nervous shrinking from the ordeal of sitting down to play before a mixed party of listeners.

The nearly two months passed at Bonn, during which

---

* This pleasant description is given entire, as containing a substantially accurate account of Brahms' artistic progress, though Dietrich, writing after the lapse of many years, has overlooked the fact that the works referred to had already been performed in public from the manuscripts.

Johannes and Joachim lodged respectively at 29 and 27, Meckenheimerstrasse, proved of importance in Brahms' career. It was at this time that he made the acquaintance of Herr Fritz Simrock, a young man about his own age, junior partner in the well-known publishing house of N. Simrock at Bonn, and destined, as the later head of the firm after the removal to Berlin, to usher into the world the great majority of the composer's works. Between Fritz Simrock and Brahms a cordial understanding gradually established itself; the publisher's dealings with the musician were from the first considerate and generous, and when Brahms' fortunes became flourishing, it was Simrock who was his confidant and adviser in business matters. As an earnest of the future, the Serenade in A, Op. 16, was published by the firm before the close of the year, the Serenade in D, Op. 11, being issued in the autumn by Breitkopf and Härtel. The Pianoforte Concerto, refused by this firm, was accepted by Rieter-Biedermann, together with the "Ave Maria," Begräbnissgesang, and the Lieder und Romanzen (Op. 14), all of which were published the following year.*

"I am very glad to see Johannes' things for orchestra in print before me at last," wrote Joachim to Avé Lallement. "Now the *Signale* and other superficial papers may abuse them as they please. We have done right. They will continue to smile on with their beautiful motifs long after the clumsy fault-finders have been silenced."

The meetings of the ladies' choral society were recommenced on Brahms' return to Hamburg in July. Fräulein Porubszky, with whom he had been on terms of lively friendship during her year of membership, which had seen him a frequent visitor at her aunt's house in the Bockmannstrasse, had now returned to Vienna, where the reader will presently renew her acquaintance as Frau Faber. The

---

* A revised edition of the second serenade was published by Simrock in 1875.

members of the choir were, however, one and all thorough-going admirers of their conductor, and amongst the houses open for the holding of the practices, two at which he became intimate, must be particularly mentioned—those of Herr Völckers and his two daughters at Hamm, and of the Hallier family at Eppendorf, both at that time country suburbs of Hamburg.

The large Eppendorf garden was the scene of many a pleasant gathering of the singers; now and again they performed there before an invited audience of friends. Hübbe tells of an open-air evening party, with an illumination, vocal contributions by the choir, which were conducted by the director from the branch of a tree, and fireworks in the intervals. The Halliers lived in town during the winter, and Brahms often dropped in to their informal Wednesday evenings, which were attended by the artists and art-lovers of Hamburg. He was good-natured about playing in this familiar, sociable circle, and would perform one thing after another, unless particularly interested in conversation, when no entreaty could get him to the piano. As his Detmold friends had found out, he formed definite opinions on most current topics of interest, and did not hesitate to avow them, or to confess the unorthodoxy of his religious views. He went constantly also to Avé Lallement's house, where a few men used to meet regularly to read Shakespeare and other authors, and found time to attend lectures on art history and to study Latin under Dr. Emil Hallier, and history under Professor Ægidi of the Academic Gymnasium.

The autumn of this year was signalised by the appearance of the String Sextet in B flat, the first of Brahms' important compositions to attain general popularity. Completed in September, it was at once approved by Joachim, who introduced it to the music lovers of Hanover at his quartet concert of October 20; and it was partly owing to his enthusiastic appreciation that the composition was so quickly and widely received into public favour.

It would be beside the mark to discuss, in a narrative

which has no technical aim, the musical characteristics of a
work that has become so entirely familiar as this one, which
has long since taken its place among the few classics that
attract an audience on their own merits, apart from the consideration of whether a public favourite is to lead their
performance. It may, however, be remarked that the String
Sextet in B flat is a work to which neither "if" nor "but"
can be attached. Both in beauty and variety of idea and
in spontaneous clearness of development, it is without flaw,
and these qualities combine with the fineness of its propor-
tions, perfectly conceived and perfectly wrought out, to
place it with few rivals amongst the greatest examples of
chamber music. Fresh, happy, and ingenuous, the mastery
it displays over the art which conceals art may be compared
with that of Mozart himself. With it opens the great series
of works of its class which reveals the powerful individuality
of Brahms in all its moods, and includes the first and second
Pianoforte Quartets, the Pianoforte Quintet, the second
String Sextet, and the Horn Trio—works which, in the
author's opinion, were not surpassed even during later
periods of the composer's magnificent activity in this
domain.

Frau Schumann, Joachim, and Johannes met in November
at Leipzig, the two last-named artists to assist actively on
the 26th of the month at the annual Pension-Fund concert
of the Gewandhaus, which was given under the direction of
Carl Reinecke, the lately appointed successor to Julius
Rietz. Both Johannes and Joachim appeared as composers
—Brahms conducted the second public performance of the
second serenade; Joachim played his Hungarian concerto
which, completed in the autumn of 1859, had been heard for
the first time at one of the Hanover subscription concerts in
the spring of the year.

"The serenade is a wonderfully poetic piece," wrote Frau
Clara, who heard the work for the first and second times at
the rehearsal and concert. "I could have embraced
Johannes for producing such a work. But how my heart

bled at its cold reception . . . and Joachim's Hungarian
concerto created a furore. . . . This gave me the warmest
pleasure, but I suffered under the feelings of joy and regret
for my two dearest friends. I was relieved to some extent
on the morning of the 27th, when Johannes' sextet was very
beautifully played in the conservatoire by Joachim and made
a decided impression.

"In the afternoon Johannes and I played (I insisted on
his doing it, under the pretext that Livia (Frege) had not
heard it) the serenade to Schleinitz. I knew that it must
please on the piano and this was so. Schleinitz said he had
no idea there was so much warmth in the piece, the orchestra
had played it so miserably.

"By Schleinitz's special desire Johannes and I played the
second serenade in the conservatoire, as the pupils had only
heard it once at the rehearsal. It again made the best impression on everyone. Rudorff was quite enchanted with it,
which pleased me particularly as I have had such difficulty
in getting him to appreciate Johannes' things."*

But scant interest was manifested by the critics of the
Leipzig press in the two new works. The daily papers left
the concert of the 25th unnoticed; the *Zeitschrift* dismissed
it with a few dubious sentences—perhaps not ungenerous
treatment under the circumstances—and the *Signale*, candid
as ever, declared the serenade to be a terribly monotonous
work which showed the composer's poverty of invention,
together with his despairing attempts to appear learned.
Joachim's concerto was pronounced decidedly richer in invention than his friend's work, but rather monotonous also,
and certainly very much too long.

Frau Schumann, nothing dismayed by these discourage-
ments, introduced at her concert of December 8, given in the
small hall of the Gewandhaus, Brahms' very beautiful
Variations on an original theme, which, though hardly
suitable for general concert performance, should be much
better known than they are. They show the composer in one
of his Bach-Beethoven-Brahms moods, by which is here

---

* Litzmann III, p. 89.

meant his learned and profoundly serious vein touched with exquisite tenderness. The theme, in three-four time, has about it, nevertheless, something of the pace of a grave march, and the opening variations are tender reflections on a solemn idea. In the eighth and ninth we have the imposing tramp of pomp, whilst the eleventh and last breathes forth tones of mysterious spirituality which subdue the mind of the listener as to some passing divine influence.

These Variations composed in 1856, the earlier set on a Hungarian melody (Op. 21, Nos. 1 and 2), and the three Duets for Soprano and Contralto, Op. 20, were published by Simrock in 1861.

The fact that Brahms' sextet was placed in the programme of the Hafner-Lee concert announced for January 4 affords evidence that the composer was gradually penetrating with his works to the heart of musical life in his native city, though he may not have enjoyed the particular favour of its public. The Quartet-Entertainments of these artists were among the regularly recurring artistic events of Hamburg, and enjoyed unfailing support. Hafner, a Viennese by birth and a Schubert enthusiast, had found a second home in the northern city, and was accounted its first violinist; and in the 'cellist Lee he had a sympathetic colleague. He was not, however, destined to lead the sextet. His sudden illness caused the postponement of the concert, and his death followed. The work was played in Hamburg from the manuscript by his successor in the enterprise, John Böie, with Honroth, Breyther, Kayser, Wiemann and Lee, and with immediate success. The impression made was so great that the work was repeated three times within the following few weeks by the same concert party.

CHAPTER XI.

1861-1862.

Concert season in Hamburg—Frau Denninghoff-Giesemann—Brahms at Hamm—Herr Völckers and his daughters—Dietrich's visit to Brahms—Music at the Halliers' and Wagners'—First public performance of the G minor Quartet—Brahms at Oldenburg—Second Serenade performed in New York—The first and second Pianoforte Quartets—"Magelone Romances"—First public performances of the Handel Variations and Fugue in Hamburg and Leipzig by Frau Schumann—Brahms' departure for Vienna.

FRAU SCHUMANN, Joachim and Stockhausen visited Hamburg repeatedly during the year 1861, and all made much of Johannes. Both Joachim and Brahms assisted at Frau Schumann's concert of January 15. Brahms took part in the performance of Schumann's beautiful Andante and Variations for two pianofortes, and conducted the Ladies' Choir, to the great delight of the members, in their singing of several of his part-songs. The first part of the programme included "Es tönt ein voller Harfenklang," "Komm herbei Tod," and "Der Gärtner," from the set with horns and harp accompaniment, Op. 17; the second part the "Minnelied" and "Der Bräutigam" (from Op. 44) and "Song from Fingal" (from Op. 17)—all performed from manuscript. The three artists were heard again the next evening at a soirée in Altona when the part-songs were repeated. On the 22nd of the month Frau Schumann and Brahms appeared together at a concert in the Logensaal

Valentinskamp, with Bach's C major Concerto and Mozart's
Sonata, both for two pianofortes.

Frau Schumann and her daughter Marie were, during this
somewhat prolonged visit, the guests of the Halliers, who
understood the necessities involved by the strain of the great
artist's arduous life, and allowed her perfect freedom of
action. Johannes visited his old friend every day, dining
privately with her and her daughter at an hour that suited
their convenience; and on a few free evenings there was
glorious music in the Halliers' drawing-room before a few
intimate acquaintances.

On March 8 Brahms played Beethoven's triple Concerto
with David and Davidoff at the Philharmonic concert, and
a few weeks later the Begräbnissgesang was performed
under his direction at a Hafner memorial concert arranged
by Grädener, and made a profound impression.

"The composer has realised the solemn spirit of mourning
with extraordinary insight. As part of a funeral ceremony,
the effect of the work would be quite overpowering," wrote
one of the critics.

Joachim and Stockhausen came in April for the Philharmonic concert of the 16th, and the brilliant season closed
with Stockhausen's and Brahms' soirées on the 19th, 27th
and 30th of the month. At the first two concerts, at
Hamburg and Altona respectively, the entire series of
Schubert's "Schöne Müllerin" was given; and at the last—
who can imagine a more enthralling feast of sound than the
performance of Beethoven's melting love-songs, "To the
Distant Beloved," the very thought of which brings tears to
the eyes, sung by Stockhausen to the accompaniment of
Brahms, followed by our composer's lovely second Serenade,
and this by Schumann's "Poet's Love-Songs." Happy
Hamburgers, happy Stockhausen, happy Brahms, to have
shared such delights together! Will their like ever come
again? Strangely enough, they lead in the course of our
story, as by natural transition, to the record of a visit paid

to Brahms in the second week of July by a very early friend
of his and of the reader. Lischen Giesemann had not met
her old playmate since she had bidden him God-speed at
the commencement of his concert-journey with Reményi
early in 1853. During the years immediately following
what proved to be his final departure from Winsen, she had
occasionally visited her dear "aunt" Brahms, but, never
finding Johannes at home, had been obliged to content herself by rejoicing with his mother over the letters he
constantly sent to his parents from Düsseldorf, Hanover,
etc. She was now a happy newly married wife, but the
memory of the old child-life remained like the warmth of
sunshine in her heart, and having ascertained that her now
celebrated hero was living at home again, she determined
to go with her husband to see him. As ill-luck would have
it, Johannes had gone out for the day when Herr and Frau
Denninghoff made their call in the Fuhlentwiethe, but his
mother, overjoyed to see her young friend again after a long
separation, offered such consolation as was in her power by
showing her his room. How many remembrances crowded
upon Lischen's mind as she entered it! The practices with
Reményi, the teacher's choral society, the dances at Hoopte,
the story of the beautiful Magelone and her knight Peter.
Lischen found herself standing near the piano—and what
did she see there? Some manuscript songs, apparently
newly composed, stood on the music desk, which bore the
name of the beautiful Magelone herself in Brahms' handwriting! It almost seemed like a waking dream to the
young wife, and the manuscript appeared to her as a link
by which the past would be carried into the future. Nor
was she mistaken. Brahms' "Magelone Romances" have
become world-famous, and wherever they are heard the
delight which stirred the heart of the youthful Johannes as
he and Lischen sat together in the pleasant Winsen fields
eagerly devouring the old story from Aaron Löwenherz's
purloined volume lives also. Lischen was not again to meet
her old friend, but she never forgot either him or his music,

and he, too, kept a faithful memory for the old pleasant
time. Writing to her twenty years later, when at the height
of his fame, he said:

" The remembrance of your parents' house is one of the
dearest that I possess; all the kindness and love that were
shown me, all the youthful pleasure and happiness that I
enjoyed there, live secure in my heart with the image of your
good father and the glad grateful memory of you all."

Lischen's daughter inherited her mother's voice, and was
endowed with fine musical gifts; and when Agnes came to
the right age, Frau Denninghoff sent her to be trained as a
singer at the Royal Music School of Berlin, of which, as
everyone knows, Joachim was director from the time of its
foundation. Joachim invited Agnes to his house one evening
to meet Brahms, who, coming forward to greet her, said it
was as though her mother were again standing before him.
He sent her a selection of his songs, and in due time she
became a successful singer, appearing in public under a
pseudonym, and the wife of a distinguished musician.

Lischen saw only the first four numbers of the " Magelone " song-cycle, which had, by a strange coincidence, just
been completed at the time of her visit; the fifth and sixth
were not composed until May, 1862.* These six songs were
published by Rieter-Biedermann in 1865, with 'the title
" Romanzen aus L. Tieck's Magelone," and a dedication
to Stockhausen; and there can be no doubt that the immediate incitement to their composition is to be traced to our
composer's association with this great singer in the performance of the song-cycles of Beethoven, Schubert and Schumann. The remaining nine songs of Brahms' series were not
published until 1868, and the exact date of their composition
has not been ascertained.

"I am living most delightfully in the country, half an
hour from town," wrote Brahms, pressing Dietrich to pay

---

* Max Kalbeck, p. 438.

him a visit; "you would be surprised to find how pleasantly one can live here. Perhaps I can take you in, and at any rate my room at my parents' in Hamburg is quite at your service. In short, I hope you will be comfortable."

He was established for the summer at Hamm in the pleasant country house of Frau Dr. Rösing, aunt of the two girls, the Fräulein Betty and Marie Völckers, already mentioned as members of the choir. Here a large airy room with a balcony, on the first floor, had been allotted him, that had been the billiard room of the house when it was inhabited by Herr Völckers and his family. This gentleman now lived next door with his two daughters in a charming old fashioned habitation built, cottage-wise, with a thatched roof and but two floors, and possessing a spacious apartment on the ground floor that had been frequently used for the choir practices. Both houses had pleasant gardens separated only by a green hedge, and close by, the spreading branches of fine old trees provided shelter for the many nightingales that built their nests in the quiet spot. Brahms' room was cheerful for a considerable part of the day, with the sunlight that shone through the outside greenery and the tinted panes of the open windows, and in it he could enjoy his favourite early morning hours of work with the added relish of feeling that they were but the prelude to days of quiet refreshment. He was intimate with all the branches of his hostess's family, from Herr Völckers, who had been a good public singer of his day, down to his gifted little granddaughter Minna (now Mrs. Edward Stone), one of the young composer's very favourite and most devoted pianoforte pupils; and that he passed a considerable portion of his time this summer in the society of the two girls next door —Betty and Marie Völckers—will astonish none of our readers. He went in and out their house as he liked, and frequently joined them as they sat in their garden with work or books, or chatting with their friends, Fräulein Reuter and Fräulein Laura Garbe, whom they often invited. Johannes would stroll in with his cigar or cigarette, and take a seat near the group, silent or talkative according to his inclination. By and by he would sing a note or two of a well known melody, begin to beat time, and the garden would be glad with the sound of four fresh young voices swelling and dying together in the charming harmonies of a favourite part-song. He often spent the evening with the young ladies and their father, gladly accepting their informal hospitality, and would play to them after supper until late into the night, sometimes performing duets with Fräulein Marie, who was his pupil on the pianoforte.

"I may say with pride that he was happy in our little house," said Frau Professor Böie (Fräulein Marie Völckers) to the author; "his playing was a great delight to our old father. His behaviour to old people was touchingly thoughtful and kind."

Dietrich, who had lately accepted the post of court capellmeister to the Grand Duke of Oldenburg, and was now quite a near neighbour, paid his promised visit to Hamburg in September.

"I occupied his very interesting room [at Hamburg], and was astonished at his comprehensive library, which he had gradually collected since early youth; it contained some remarkable old works.

"After breakfast in the morning I used to sit cosily with his dear old mother, who united true heart-culture with her plainness and simplicity; her Johannes was the inexhaustible subject of our lively conversations. The father generally left home early to follow his calling of bassist and music-teacher. I used to remain a little while with the dear people, and spent the rest of the day with Brahms in his charming country quarters, where we occupied ourselves with the detailed examination of his newest works."

The ladies' choir, which had served its purpose in the composer's course of self training, had been given up in the spring. Since that time Brahms had been devoting much of his energy to the completion of the two great works that were to follow the B flat Sextet in the domain of chamber music, and he no doubt made Dietrich acquainted with the

pianoforte quartets in G minor and A major, several movements of which had been sent to Frau Schumann in July.
The Handel variations, the manuscript of which bears the
date "September 61," must also be associated with the
composer's first summer in Hamm, and possibly Brahms
may have played his friend portions of a string quintet in
F minor which was about to pass from its embryonic stage
of growth. He does not seem to have confessed, however,
that he was listening again to the stirrings of an earlier
ambition, and Dietrich was probably as yet unaware that
Brahms, separated by six years of strenuous endeavour and
rapid result from the period of an earlier attempt, was once
more beginning to test his strength for the arduous flight
that should lead to the successful accomplishment of a
symphony.

The pianoforte quartets (Opp. 25 and 26) were sent at the
end of September—the G minor in its completed form; the
A major without the final movement—to Joachim, who took
rather serious exception to certain features of the first
movement of Op. 25. That the composer left the movement
essentially unaltered, however, will be evident to the
student who may compare the critical observations in
question with the published score of the work. Of the last
movement of the same quartet, the brilliant "Rondo alla
Zingarese," written in friendly emulation of the finale of
Joachim's Hungarian Concerto, the famous violinist
declared in generous triumph: "In the last movement you
have outstripped me on my own territory by a considerable
track." It is not the business of our pages either to endorse
or contradict this statement, but it may be permissible to
remind the reader, that the increasing perfection of Brahms'
instrumental works of the period was in no small degree
furthered by the invaluable experience and self-forgetting
sympathy of his friend.*

---

* Compare Brahms-Joachim "Briefwechsel," No. 23i.
It is difficult to determine by comparison of Joachim's letter with
the published score of the Quartet in G minor precisely how far the

SILHOUETTE BY DR. BÖHLER.

Photograph by R. Lechner (Wilh. Müller), Vienna.

Several indications suggest that Brahms' thoughts were still turned longingly in the direction of Vienna; not as a permanent place of residence—at no time in his life, probably, did he so seriously contemplate settling in Hamburg as at the present—but he wished to see the city that had been the home of Haydn, Mozart, Beethoven and Schubert;

---

composer's own judgment ratified his friend's critical observations since some of the references in the letter to the pagination of the MS. are obscure. It is, however, clear that Brahms made no change in the outlines of the movement, and the study of its design shows that the existing proportion of the parts, in which both Frau Schumann and Joachim felt a want of symmetry is, in fact, essential to the fundamental plan of the work.

The movement is not to be regarded as an example of sonata form arranged with undeviating conformity to the lines of tradition, but as one amongst others of Brahms' compositions in which is exhibited a special characteristic of his art—freedom in the use of classical form. The first subject, derived from a motif of four diatonic notes arrests the attention of the listener by its strong, broad simplicity, and is well adapted for the purposes of the development section with a view to which it was no doubt constructed. The second subjects, primary and derived, in the minor and major modes of the dominant key D, are flowing and melodious. It was to the prolongation of this second part of the statement, and to what they felt as the resultant undue prominence of its key—features which would undoubtedly be objectionable in a movement constructed in strict sonata form—that the composer's friendly critics demurred. In the movement under consideration however, the prolongation is both required and compensated by the treatment of the development section. This opens with a full repetition, without ornamental variation, of the first subject of ten bars' length in its original key, a peculiarity which in itself shows the movement to have been deliberately designed in free form; and the first subject supplies, together with the bridge passage, nearly the whole material treated in the section. Want of space prevents any detailed allusion here to the many interesting features of the repetition section and of the imposing coda, both so constructed as to sustain the balance of the movement, which, as the author ventures to think, is a worthy opening to the whole glorious work. It may be pointed out, in conclusion, that the interest attaching to the immortal pair of quartets is, from the musician's point of view, considerably enhanced by the fact that in the two opening movements are presented fine examples of musical design in the one case in free, in the other case in strict, sonata form. A note in Frau

20

and the enthusiastic sympathy accorded to Frau Schumann
on each of her visits to the Austrian capital confirmed him in
a desire to try his luck with its music-loving public. He
knew his way had been prepared for him, and a good opportunity seemed likely to occur for his appearance there.
Joachim, who had enjoyed his customary unequivocal success during an Austrian concert tour on which he had been
engaged early in the year, was meditating another journey
to Vienna and would gladly have arranged it with Johannes
as a companion. Matters went no further, however, than
they had done previously. As in a former year, paragraphs
appeared in the *Signale* announcing that Brahms was about
to visit Vienna, but in the end he remained at home—partly,
no doubt, from motives of policy.

It was generally understood that Wilhelm Grund, who
had for many years conducted the Philharmonic concerts
and the Singakademie connected with them, must soon
retire. He had done good work in his day, but his day was
over. Musical conditions had changed; he was too old to
alter with them, and the Philharmonic performances had
long ceased to satisfy modern requirements. It was hoped
by Brahms' friends that the young genius of Hamburg
would succeed to the post, and Johannes himself may have
thought it wise to remain on the spot with such an important
issue imminent. The disappointment he felt at giving up
the desired journey was partially consoled by the knowledge

Schumann's diary, entered soon after Johannes had received the
quartets back from Hanover and five days before the first public
performance of Op. 25, may probably be accepted as Brahms' own
comment on the question :

"Hamburg. 11th November.

"Interesting talk with Johannes on form. How it is the older
masters who are perfect in their use of form, whilst modern compositions are confined within the most rigid small forms. He, himself,
emulates the older masters and especially admires Clementi's large,
free employment of form." Litzmann III, p. 111.

that Frau Schumann, with her daughter Julie, would be much in Hamburg during the autumn months.

He began his concert season on October 19 at Altona, and appeared at one of the Böie-Lee concerts later in the month, playing the Schumann Variations for two pianofortes with Frau Clara. On the 30th there was a music-party at the Halliers', which is charmingly described in a letter written a few days afterwards by Fräulein Julie Hallier:

"The guests were late in coming; it was half-past eight when they had all arrived; and who comes with Frau Schumann?—Our dear friend from Hanover, with his beaming face and delightful friendliness; the glorious Joachim. Everyone was taken by surprise, Frau Schumann and Brahms in the morning, we in the evening. Avé: 'My boy! where have you come from?' After the first excitement was over, Edward showed his Italian photographs. Brahms literally devoured them; he was very nice the whole evening, especially with Edward. He teased me about my punch, which I altered three times, he following it with anxious looks as the bowl disappeared through the door. Frau Schumann and Brahms played beautifully beyond imagination; three rondos by Schubert and two marches. The violin of course had not come; Joachim only arrived yesterday and is already gone again. At first Avé turned over, but he did it badly, so Brahms called Joachim. Avé: 'My dreadful cold; I cannot see properly.' He now stood behind and began to beat time. During the music the table was laid in the small room. It was rather narrow, but comfortable. All went well. We separated at half-past eleven."

A few days afterwards there was a similar gathering at the Wagners', when Frau Schumann performed with Brahms his duet arrangement of the second serenade.

"The best of all was a set of variations by Brahms on a theme by Handel," continues the letter—"another magnificent work! splendidly long—the stream of ideas flowing inexhaustibly! And the work was splendidly played, too, by himself. It seemed like a miracle; one could not take one's eyes from him. The composition is so difficult that none but great artists could attempt it."*

These words give some measure of the progress effected during the last half-century in the technique of pianoforte-playing, partly, indeed, through the demands made upon pianists by the compositions of Brahms himself. Lovers of his art who have learnt his particular technique, which demands of the player certain qualities of endurance and grip, do not find the performance of his works unduly fatiguing. The twenty-five variations, with the fugue that succeeds them, are now in the fingers of most good players, and would undoubtedly be often heard in the concert-room if it were not for the great length of the work. They show a melodious fertility and power of invention which is practically inexhaustible. Each variation or pair of variations presents some fresh idea, some striking change of fancy, figuration, rhythm, mood, to hold the listener's attention, whilst the entire long work is essentially based upon the simple harmonic progression of Handel's theme (to be found in the second collection of Harpsichord Pieces). The changes of key in Brahms' variations are restricted to the tonic minor (Nos. 5, 6, 13) and the relative minor (No. 21). The finale, the great free fugue which invariably "brings down" a house, is, with its grand and brilliant climax, to which extraordinary effect is imparted by an original employment of the dominant pedal point, a unique example of its kind.

If there ever were a young composer who had reason to be made happy from the outset of his career by the appreciation of the most eminent of his colleagues—appreciation sweeter than any other to the soul of the true artist—Brahms was he. At each of Frau Schumann's three appearances in Hamburg during this autumn, she performed a great work of his composition, two being introduced for the first time to the public. At her first concert, on November 16, she performed

---

* First published in Hübbe's "Brahms in Hamburg," pp. 42-4.

the G minor Pianoforte Quartet with Böie, Breyther and Lee for the first time in public, and on the same evening several of the composer's part-songs were sung under his direction by the former members of the Ladies' Choir; on the 3rd of the month she appeared as the champion of the unpopular concerto, playing it with especial pleasure, in association with Brahms as conductor, at the Philharmonic concert of that date; and on the 7th of the same month she brought forward the Handel Variations and Fugue at her second concert. These she repeated a week later at the Gewandhaus soirée of the 14th in Leipzig.

Not even the magnetic personality of Frau Schumann availed to awaken any show of enthusiasm for the concerto. The new works were more favourably received both in Hamburg and Leipzig, and the *Signale* itself bestowed a mild word or two upon some of the variations. It is easy, however, to read between the lines of the press notices that such encouragement as was awarded to the composer was mainly due to the personality of the performer. The B flat Sextet was given with fair success at the Gewandhaus Quartet concert of January 4 by David, Engelbert, Röntgen, Hermann, Hunger, Davidoff and Krummholtz.

Brahms passed the first two months of the new year in Joachim's society, making his headquarters at Hanover, and undertaking frequent short journeys with his friend. The two artists appeared together on January 20 at one of the Münster subscription concerts, of which Grimm, who had been called to Münster in 1860, was now the conductor; and on February 14 they gave a concert in Celle, a locality which the reader will remember as the scene of Johannes' transposition feat during the Reményi *tournée* of 1853. The A major Pianoforte Quartet was now finished, and was, with its companion in G minor, much appreciated in the private circles of Hanover, where both works were frequently played by Brahms with Joachim and his colleagues.

Brahms, answering an invitation from Dietrich received on the eve of his departure, says:

"DEAR FRIEND,

"I have been here for some time, and have your letter
forwarded from Hamburg. I go back to-morrow, and write
a few words in haste.

"I should much like to visit you and to make the acquaintance of those whom I know pleasantly by name, otherwise I would say no. I will come and see how long I can
afford to be idle.

"What shall I play? Beethoven or Mozart? C minor,
A major, or G major? Advise!

"And for the second—Schumann, Bach, or may I venture
upon some new variations of my own?

"You, of course, will conduct my serenade. We have
been playing my quartets a great deal here; I shall bring
them with me and shall be glad if you and others approve
of them.

"*A propos!* I must have an honorarium of 15 Louis-
d'ors [about £14], with the stipulation that if I should play
at Court I receive extra remuneration. I much need the
money; pro sec. my time is valuable to me, and I do not
willingly take concert engagements; if, however, this must
be, then the other must also."*

Dietrich had already had the pleasure of welcoming Frau
Schumann and Joachim to Oldenburg during this his first
season of activity there, and had worked well to prepare the
way for Brahms, so that the evening of March 14, the date
fixed for the composer's personal introduction to the concert-
going public, was awaited with keen interest. Arriving at
Dietrich's house a few days previously, Brahms found
himself surrounded by new friends, and had won the favour
of the musical élite of the town before his public appearance,
by playing several of his works in private circles. The
members of the orchestra, who assembled *en masse* on the
evening of the 13th, were excited to enthusiasm by his
performance of the new Handel Variations and Fugue, and

---

* Dietrich.

every condition that could ensure a sympathetic reception for the hero of the 14th was fulfilled.

The concert opened with the D major Serenade (Op. 11), conducted by Dietrich, who had the delight of finding that he had secured an adequate reception for his friend's orchestral work.

"The whole made the most satisfactory impression, and carried the hearers away more and more, especially from the fourth movement onwards, and at the close the applause reached a pitch of enthusiasm not hitherto experienced here. The members of the orchestra, who had been studying the serenade for some time, showed their concurrence in the general approval by a lively flourish." (*Oldenburger Zeitung.*)

No less satisfactory was the verdict of the audience on the performances of Beethoven's G major Concerto and Bach's Chromatic Fantasia, with which our composer came forward as pianist. His success was repeated at the chamber music concert of the 19th, when the sextet was performed by Court Concertmeister Engel and his colleagues. Both in public and private Brahms left endearing memories behind him.

"He was the most agreeable guest," says Dietrich, "always pleased, always good-humoured and satisfied, like a child with the children.

"He took the greatest pleasure in our happiness. He thought our modest lot enviable, and had his position then allowed him to establish a home of his own, perhaps this might have been the right moment, for he was attracted by a young girl who was often with us. One evening, when she and other guests had left, he said with quiet decision : 'She pleases me; I should like to marry her; such a girl would make me, too, happy.' He met many people at our house, and in small and large circles outside it, and everyone liked his earnest nature and his short and often humorous remarks."

It is pleasant to have to record here that a few weeks before the events now described, New York, distinguished, as we have seen, by Mason's timely performance of the

B major Trio in 1855, led the way a second time in connection with Brahms' career. In February, 1862, the first performance after publication of the second serenade took place there at a Philharmonic concert, and the occasion is doubly memorable as marking the earliest introduction of an orchestral work of Brahms to a public audience outside the cities of Hamburg, Hanover and Leipzig. This early appreciation of the composer's genius in America has proved to have been neither accidental nor transitory. It grew steadily year by year with the general growth of interest in musical art, and his works, great and small, were welcomed as they appeared, and performed—often, it must be said, from pirated editions in the earlier days—with ever-increasing success. It has been impossible to ascertain the exact dates of first American performances. New York, the earliest centre in the United States for the cultivation of Brahms' music, was emulated later on, especially by Boston; and the famous Symphony Orchestra of this city has, since its foundation in 1881, performed each of the four symphonies, in Boston and in the course of numerous concert tours, at an average of forty concerts; whilst the two overtures, the concertos, and other large works, have been given with corresponding frequency.

The chamber music has been a special feature in the programmes of several concert-parties resident in various parts of the United States. Of these, special mention should be made of the Kneisel String Quartet of Boston, whose performances, familiar not only to American, but also to some of the circles of European music-lovers, were warmly appreciated by Brahms himself.

In the spring of 1862, an artistic tour undertaken in France by Frau Schumann laid the foundation of Brahms' reputation in Paris, which, little to be noted during many years, has of late been rapidly increasing. That the great pianist. when introducing her husband's works, which were almost unknown to French audiences, had to confront the inevitable prejudice against what is new, explains the fact that

Brahms' name did not appear in the programmes of her concerts at the Salle Erard. The efforts she made in the cause of his art, however, amongst the inmost musical circle of her acquaintance created an impression that was not entirely fleeting.

The two first Pianoforte Quartets, now finally completed, and performed, as we have seen, during the winter of 1861-62—the earlier one in public, and both frequently in private—add two glorious works of chamber music to the series so brilliantly inaugurated by the Sextet in B flat. In their broadly-flowing themes, their magnificent wealth of original and contrasted melody, their consummate workmanship, their fresh, vigorous vitality, their enchanting romance, one seems to hear the bounding gladness of the artist-spirit which has attained freedom through submission to law, and revels in its emancipation. They are so rich in beauty, so transcendent in power, that the attempt to point out this or that particular detail for admiration results in bewilderment. The romantic intermezzo, the riotously brilliant Hungarian rondo, of the first; the graceful scherzo with its bold trio, of the second, and the adagio, with its atmosphere of mystery, lit up twice by the outbreak of passion that subsides again to the hushed expressiveness of the beginning and end; the opening allegro of either work— all are original, great, beautiful; but so is every portion of every movement of both quartets, and each movement proclaims—from Bach to Brahms. That Brahms' course of development proceeded ever further in the direction of concentration of thought and conciseness of structure cannot affect the value of the splendid achievements of his earlier period of maturity, and of these the two quartets stand amongst the greatest.

The sincerity of Brendel's efforts to conciliate the contending musical parties, and his desire to do justice to each, is strikingly proved by the appearance in his journal, in the course of several months of the year 1862, of a series of articles signed "D. A. S.," by Dr. Schübring, a distinguished musician and critic of the Schumann school. The first few numbers are devoted to sympathetic reviews of the works of Theodor Kirchner, Woldemar Bargiel, and others; and following these are five articles in which the whole of Brahms' published works are examined in detail. The composer's genius, his progress, his moods and his methods, are discussed with the skill of a scientific musician, the impartiality of a sound critic, and the affection of a personal and artistic friend. They are too technical for quotation here, but the last sentence of the concluding number may be given in well-deserved tribute to Brendel, who must have known what he was doing when he arranged for Dr. Schübring's contributions.

"The foregoing words may sound inflated, but stopped horns are of no use when it is desired to arouse the great public, which does not yet seem to comprehend in the least what a colossal genius, one quite of equal birth with Bach, Beethoven, and Schumann, is ripening in the young master of Hamburg."

The mediator's task is seldom a grateful one, and it appears probable that Dr. Brendel was reproached for his large-mindedness by some of the New-German party, with whom he had been so long intimately connected, as a half-apologetic explanation of his reasons for desiring the publication of the "Schumanniana," as the articles were entitled, appeared in a later number of the *Zeitschrift*.

It would be unsatisfactory to omit all mention of the first performance of a "Magelone Romance," though there is but little to record save the fact that Stockhausen sang the opening one, the "Keinen hat es noch gereut," from the manuscript, at the Philharmonic concert of April 4, as one of a group of songs by Brahms. It produced no impression whatever on the Hamburgers, who were only mystified. How many persons in the audience had read Tieck's poems? How many had ever heard anything about the adventures of Magelone and Peter? Without such knowledge, the first and second numbers of the cycle cannot be really appreciated. To those who are aware that the first is the song of a minstrel who incites a valiant young hero to journey to distant lands in quest of adventure, and the second the exultant shout of the joyful aspirant as he rides forth from his parents' home, resolved on doughty deeds, the music becomes living, and seems to breathe forth the very spirit of chivalry. The third, fourth, and some other of the songs, notably the ninth—the ravishing "Ruhe Süssliebchen"— are capable of telling a tale of their own, and give rich delight apart from their place in Tieck's version of the story; but the enjoyment even of these favourite and familiar songs is much heightened by an acquaintance with the incidents of the romance. Tieck's "Beautiful Magelone" is contained in his "Phantasus," a collection of tales published between 1812 and 1816, some of which have been made familiar to English readers by the translations of Hare, Froude and Carlyle. The "Magelone" story of the book is a modernised version of an old romance of chivalry, and, by introducing into it a number of songs, Tieck furnished the opportunity seized upon more than forty years later by Brahms, to which the world is indebted for some of the composer's most perfect inspirations.

To provide in this place the much needed clue to their connection with the events of the tale would cause too serious an interruption to our narrative. The author has therefore added, in Appendix I, an account of the romance and the incidence of Tieck's songs, which it is hoped may interest the reader and increase his love for the compositions.

Brahms continued to make Frau Dr. Rösing's house at Hamm his headquarters, and remained there during most of the spring and summer of 1862. Before going to Oldenburg in March, he had written to Dietrich: "It is delightful here in Hamm, and unless I look out of window at the bare trees I fancy summer is come, the sunlight plays in the room so gaily." Later it was: "It is blooming splendidly, and the trees are blossoming in Hamm, so that it is a joy." He occupied his leisure in similar agreeable pursuits to those of

the preceding year, and now in the springtime a double
choir of maidens and nightingales might often be heard by
the passer-by, carolling together as if in mutual emulation of
the others' song.   He begged, later on, for photographs of
his girls' quartet and of the two houses, and said that he
neither remembered nor saw before him a happier time than
that he had passed in Hamm.   The sisters met their fate in
due time.   Each married a distinguished violinist, and Concertmeister Otto von Königslow of Cologne and Professor
John Böie of Altona were amongst the most active admirers
of Brahms' art.   The composer remained on terms of intimacy
with the entire Völckers family, and never failed, when
occasionally staying at Hamburg during the later years of
his career, to visit both the Böies and the Stones.

Avé Lallement, who personally, perhaps, would gladly
have seen Johannes settled in Hamburg as conductor of the
Philharmonic, says, in a letter written in the early spring of
the year to Dr. Löwe of Zürich :

"We had the 'Matthew Passion' here under Grund;
Brahms also was delighted, in spite of the defective performance.   He thinks of going to Vienna in the autumn; then
I shall be quite alone, but thank God I have learnt to know
the man so well.   I have come a good piece forward through
him."

Brahms and Dietrich met at the Rhine Festival given this
year at Cologne (June 8-10), where they made the artistic
and personal acquaintance of Frau Louise Dustmann, court
chamber singer, and of the court opera, Vienna, whom
Brahms knew well in later years.   From Cologne they proceeded to Münster-am-Stein, taking lodgings together near
Frau Schumann, who was staying there with her family.
From Münster Dietrich wrote to his wife :

"The longer I am with Brahms, the more my affection
and esteem for him increase.   His nature is equally lovable,
cheerful, and deep.   He often teases the ladies, certainly,
by making jokes with a serious air which are frequently
taken in earnest, especially by Frau Schumann.   This leads

to comical and frequently dangerous arguments, in which I usually act as mediator, for Brahms is fond of strengthening such misunderstandings, in order to have the laugh on his side in the end. This to me attractive humorous trait is, I think, the reason why he is so often misunderstood. He can, however, be very quiet and serious if necessary."

Brahms had heralded his arrival by sending Frau Schumann a packet of new manuscripts, the last completed of which was a symphony movement. When he played this work to his friends in the course of his fortnight's stay at Münster-am-Stein, he introduced to them an early version of the first movement of his C minor Symphony, which was not finally completed until fourteen years later.

Frau Schumann received three movements of the string quintet in F minor (two violoncelli) mentioned earlier in the chapter, in August, and the completed work was sent to Joachim in September.

The Sextet in B flat, the Handel Variations, and the horns and harp Songs for women's chorus, were published this year by Simrock. Two works in the hands of Rieter-Biedermann—the Marienlieder for mixed chorus (Op. 22), composed in the autumn of 1859, and the Variations for Pianoforte Duet, Op. 23, finished in the summer of 1861, appeared early in 1863.*

The Marienlieder, seven in number, to be sung *a capella*, are not sacred compositions. They are settings of old texts founded upon some of the mediaeval legends that grew up around the history of the Virgin, and are delightfully fresh examples of the pure style of part-writing of which Brahms had made himself a master. In spite of the restricted means at the disposal of the composer who elects to forego, for the nonce, all but the few diatonic harmonies alone available in this style, there is a something about these attractive little pieces which allows Brahms' individuality to be distinctly felt. If, as is inevitable, they carry back the mind of the

---

* The Variations are dated 1866 in the published catalogue.

listener to the choral music of the sixteenth century, they recall the style of the early German, rather than of either of the Italian schools. Perhaps the most fascinating of the set is No. 2, entitled "Mary's Church-going." Mary, on her way to church, comes to a deep lake, and, finding a young boatman standing ready, requests him to ferry her over, promising him whatever he may like best in return. The boatman answers that he will do what she asks provided she will become his housewife; but Mary, replying that she will swim across rather than consent to the suggestion, jumps into the water. When she is half way to the other side, the church bells suddenly begin to ring, loudly, softly, all together. Mary, on her safe arrival, kneels on a stone in prayer, and the boatman's heart breaks. The first five verses are composed strophically (each like the other) for two sopranos, contralto and tenor, in E flat minor, and are marked *piano*. The bass enters with the sixth verse, composed in E flat major, and, whilst the whole choir bursts into a jubilant *forte*, keeps up a movement in concert, first with the tenor and then with the soprano, suggestive of bell-ringing. The concluding words return to the setting of the first five verses, and by this means the little composition is rounded into definite shape.

The Variations are amongst the most beautiful of Brahms' many fine achievements in this particular domain, and present for admiration conspicuous qualities of their own arising from the opportunities offered by their composition in duet form. The theme on which they are founded is that supposed by Schumann to have been brought to him in the night by angels a fortnight before his malady reached its crisis. The work is dedicated to Fräulein Julie Schumann, the master's third daughter.

And now, in a few weeks the period of Brahms' career which is to be especially associated with Hamburg, was to close. He would gladly have strengthened his ties with the city to which he was so proud to belong; and at this particular moment he had good reason for hoping that the day was not far distant which would find him settled there in a position that might ultimately secure him an income sufficient for his modest needs. He had been privately approached by his friend, Avé Lallement, of the Philharmonic committee, with reference to the proposed appointment of an assistant director to the society's Singverein, by which it was hoped to pave the way for the retirement of Grund from his post as conductor of the subscription concerts. As we shall see, however, his compatriots would have none of him. Twice in the coming years they passed him by, and when the time at length arrived in which they would willingly have proclaimed the world-famous composer as their own special prophet, his interests and affections had become too deeply rooted within the city that he made his second home to be capable of a second transplantation.

Brahms quitted Hamburg for his first visit to Vienna on September 8. That he expected to return speedily is evident from the lines sent by him to Dietrich on the eve of his departure :

" DEAR FRIEND,
        " I am leaving on Monday *for Vienna!* I look forward to it like a child.

" Of course I do not know how long I shall stay; we will leave it open, and I hope we may meet some time during the winter.

" The C minor Symphony is not ready; on the other hand, a string quintet (2 v.celli) in F minor is finished. I should like to send it you and hear what you have to say about it, and yet I prefer to take it with me.

" Herewith my Handel Variations; the Marienlieder are not yet here.

" Greet all the Oldenburg friends.

" Pray do not leave me quite without letters. You might address for the present to Haslinger, or to Wessely and Büsing.

" Heartiest farewell meanwhile, dear Albert, to you and your wife.

                              " Your JOHANNES."

"Father," said Brahms, looking slyly at his father as he said good-bye, "if things should be going badly with you, music is always the best consolation; go and study my old 'Saul'—you will find comfort there."

He had thickly interlarded the volume with bank-notes.*

It is highly interesting to possess a clear conception of Brahms' achievements as a composer, and, therewith, of his exact title to consideration at this important moment of his career. This will be best obtained by a glance at the list of the chief completed works with which he was to present himself in the city associated with the most hallowed memories of his art. His departure for Vienna is by no means to be regarded as coincident with the close of any one period of his creative activity, though it emphatically marks the end, not only of a chapter, but of the first book of his life.

LIST OF BRAHMS' CHIEF COMPLETED WORKS ON HIS
DEPARTURE FOR VIENNA.

Pianoforte Solos :	Op.
Three Sonatas	1, 2, 5.
Scherzo	4.
Variations on Schumann's theme in F sharp minor	9.
Ballades	10.
Variations on an original theme ...	21, No. 1.
Variations on a Hungarian song ...	21, No. 2.
Variations and Fugue on Handel's theme	24.
Pianoforte Duet :	
Variations on a theme by Schumann ...	23.
Pianoforte with Orchestra :	
Concerto in D minor	15.
Orchestral : Two Serenades	11, 16.

* Max Kalbeck, I, p. 477.

Chamber Music :   Op.
   Sextet in B flat for Strings   ...   ... 18.
   Trio in B major for Pianoforte and Strings 8.
   Quartet in G minor for Pianoforte and
      Strings ...   . 25.
   Quartet in A major for Pianoforte and
      Strings ...   . 26.

Songs :
   Five books (thirty-one songs)   ...   ... 3, 6, 7, 14, 19.
   " Magelone Romances " (first six)   ... 33.

Vocal Duets : two books   ...   . 20, 28.

Three Vocal Quartets   ...   . 31.

Women's Chorus :
   " Ave Maria "   ...   . 12.
   Part-songs   ...   . 17, 37.

Mixed Chorus :
   Begräbnissgesang   ...   . 13.
   Marienlieder   ...   . 22.
   The 13th Psalm   ...   . 27.
   Motets   ...   . 29.
   Sacred Song   ...   . 30.

The newly-finished String Quintet is not included in the
list, as the work was not published in this its first form. The
Hungarian Dances, as being arrangements, are also omitted.

21

APPENDICES.

I.

THE MAGELONE ROMANCES.

THE story of the Count Peter of Provence and the beautiful Magelone, Princess of Naples, which is associated with a well known ruin on the south coast of France, is said by Raynouard to have formed the subject of a poem written towards the close of the twelfth century by Bernhard de Trèves, Canon of Magelonne in Languedoc. It was adapted as a prose romance not later than the middle of the fourteenth, and printed in at least five different editions before the end of the fifteenth, century. Of these, rare copies are to be found in some of the famous libraries of England and the Continent. Two editions, copies of which are in the British Museum, were issued by Maître Guillaume Le Roy. With slight differences of spelling they begin :

"Au nom de notre seigneur ihesucrist, cy commēce listoyre du vaillant chevalier pierre filz du cōte de provēce et de la belle maguelonne fille du roy de naples."

The romance is constructed from the familiar elements of mediaeval fiction—chivalry, religion and love—and has been translated at various dates into almost every European language, Italian, Spanish, Portuguese, Russian, Norse, etc. It has been republished in German many times through the centuries since it was first done into that language (probably in 1483), and was included by G. O. Marbach in 1838 in his popular series of tales (Volksbücher). That it was this version of the story that found its way into Frau Löwenherz's library and was read by Johannes and Lischen is proved beyond doubt by its title, which is identical with that noted down by the present writer from the lips of Frau Denninghoff, the "Lischen" of our biography —"Geschichte der schönen Magelone und dem Ritter Peter mit den silbernen Schlüsseln"—and it seems probable that Marbach obtained his tale from an edition published in 1661 at Nürnburg : "Historia der schönen Magelona, eines Königs Tochter von Neaples, und einem Ritter, genannt Peter mit den silbernen Schlüsseln, eines Grafen Sohn aus Provincia." Of the many editions, fifteenth and up to the nineteenth century, to which the author has had access, no other contains in its title any mention of the silver keys.

Marbach's version is a fine one. Whilst he has modernised the old romance in certain respects, he has kept, not only to the main incidents of the tale, but to the quaint old dialogues which naïvely portray the characters of the manly-hearted but rather weak-minded Peter and the high spirited, self-willed, yet tender Magelone.

Tieck's version, published in 1812 in the first volume of the "Phantasus," differs considerably, especially in its particulars of the beginning and end of the romance, from the original details of the story. In making his alterations, the poet seems to have been chiefly concerned to eliminate the religious element from his narrative as far as possible, and to provide opportunity for the introduction of seventeen songs of which Brahms composed fifteen. The tale has suffered considerably in his hands. The general atmosphere of French mediaeval fiction, with its characteristic setting of sunrise and sunset, flowers and birds, and, in parts, the wording of the old romance, have, however, been preserved, and we may be grateful to Tieck for the poems which have placed us in possession of Brahms' beautiful song-cycle.

We propose to give an abridgment of his narrative up to a certain point and to summarise ensuing details, which become prolix and involved in all the versions. We shall insert only the first few lines of each song.

How a Strange Singer came to the Court of Provence.

A long time ago, a Count reigned in Provence whose beautiful and noble son grew up the joy of his parents. He was big and strong and his shining fair hair flowed round his neck and shaded his tender, youthful face. Then he was well proved in arms; no one in or beyond the land managed the lance and sword as he, so that he was admired by great and small, young and old, noble and simple. He was often absent-minded as though meditating on some secret desire, and many experienced people concluded that he must be in love, but none of them would awaken him from his thoughts, for they knew that love is like the vision of a dream, which is apt, if disturbed, to vanish and return to its dwelling in the ether and the golden mists of morning.

His father gave a great tournament to which many knights were invited. It was a wonder to see how the tender youth bore the best

22*

and strongest from their saddles. He was lauded by everyone, but no praise made him proud; indeed he sometimes felt ashamed at overcoming such great and worthy knights. Amongst the guests was a singer who had seen many lands; he was no knight, but he surpassed many nobles in insight and experience. He made friends with Peter and praised him uncommonly, but concluded his talk with these words: Sir Knight, if I might advise you, you should not remain here, but should see other places and other men, to improve your ideas and learn to associate the strange with the familiar. He took his lute and sang:

> No one yet hath rued the day
> When on charger mounting
> Youthful-strong he sped away,
> Pain nor peril counting, etc.

The youth listened to the song: when it was at an end, he remained awhile sunk in thought; then said: Yes, now I know what I want; many variegated pictures pass through my mind. No greater joy for a young knight than to ride through valley and over field. Here in the morning sunshine stands a stately castle, there over the meadow sounds the shepherd's shawn; a noble maiden flies by on a white palfrey. Oh, I wish I were already on my good horse. Heated by these new thoughts, he went at once to his mother's chamber where he found his father also. Peter immediately sank on one knee and made his request that his parents would allow him to travel and seek adventures: for, thus he concluded his speech, he who only stays at home keeps a narrow mind during his whole life, but by travel, one learns to associate the strange with the familiar; therefore do not refuse me your consent.

The old Count said: My son, your request appears to me unsuitable, for you are my only heir; if I should die in your absence, what would become of my land? But Peter kept to his request, whereat his mother began to weep and said to him: Dear, only son, you have never tasted trouble, and see only your beautiful hopes before you, but remember that if you depart, a thousand difficulties may confront you; you may be miserable and wish yourself back with us.

Peter remained humbly on his knees and answered: Beloved parents, I cannot help it. My only wish is to travel into the wide world, to experience pleasure and sorrow there and to return a known and honoured man. For this you travelled in your youth, my father, and brought home my mother from a strange land. Let me seek a like fortune, I beg for this with tears.

He took the lute and sang the song which he had heard from the minstrel, and at the end he wept bitterly. The parents were moved, especially the mother; she said: Well, I, for my part, will give you my blessing, dear son, for what you have said is true. The father also rose and blessed him, and Peter was glad from his heart that he had received his parents' consent.

Orders were given to prepare everything for his departure, and his mother sent for him to come to her privately. She gave him three precious rings and said: See, my son, I have kept these three precious rings carefully from my youth. Take them with you and treasure them, and if you find a maiden whom you love, and who is inclined towards you, you may give them to her. He gratefully kissed her hand, and the morning came on which he took leave.

How the Knight Peter departed from his Parents.

When Peter was ready to mount his horse, his father blessed him again and said: My son, may good fortune ever accompany you so that we may see you back again healthy and strong; think constantly of the precepts I have impressed upon your tender youth; seek good, and avoid evil, company; honour the laws of knighthood and never forget them, for they are the noblest thoughts of the noblest men in their best hours; always be loyal even though you may be deceived, for the touchstone of the brave is that though he may seldom meet honourable men, he remain true to himself. Farewell!

Peter rode away without attendance, for like many young knights, he wished to remain unknown. The sun had risen gloriously, and the fresh dew sparkled on the meadows. Peter was in cheerful spirits and spurred on his good horse so that it sprang boldly forward. An old song rang in his head and he sang it out loud:

> Yes! arrow on bow
> Shall swiftly be laid
> To humble the foe.
> The helpless to aid, etc.

He arrived, after many days' journey, at the famous city of Naples. He had heard much talk on his way of the king and his surpassingly beautiful daughter Magelone, so that he was very anxious to see her face to face. He dismounted at an inn to ask for news, and heard from the host that a distinguished knight, Sir Henry of Carpone, had come and that a splendid tournament was to be held in his honour. He learned also that entrance would be allowed to strangers who appeared equipped according to the laws of tourney. Peter at once resolved to be present to try his dexterity and strength.

PETER SEES THE BEAUTIFUL MAGELONE.

When the day of the tournament arrived, Peter put on his armour and betook himself to the lists. He had had two beautiful silver keys of uncommonly fine workmanship placed upon his helmet, and had caused his shield and the cover of his horse to be likewise ornamented with keys. This he did for the sake of his name and in honour of the Apostle Peter, whom he greatly loved. He had recommended himself to his care and protection from his youth and therefore chose this token, as he wished to remain unknown.

A herald rode forward and with sound of trumpet proclaimed the tournament that was opened to the honour of the beautiful Magelone. She herself sat on an elevated balcony and looked down on the assemblage of knights. Peter looked up but could not see her distinctly as she was too far off. . . . Peter opposed the knight in the lists and soon threw him from his horse, so that everyone marvelled at his strength; he did more, for in a short time he had emptied every saddle so that none remained to tilt against him. Then everyone desired to know the name of the strange knight, and the King of Naples himself sent his herald to learn it, but Peter humbly begged leave to remain unknown until he should have become worthy by his deeds to name himself, and this answer pleased the king.

It was not long before another tournament was held, and the beautiful Magelone secretly hoped that the knight with the silver keys might again be visible, for she loved him, but had as yet confided this to no one, since first love is despondent and holds itself a traitor. She grew red as Peter again entered the lists in his conspicuous armour. She gazed at him steadily, and he was victor in every contest; at length she felt no more surprise, for it seemed to her as though it could not be otherwise. At last the tournament was over. Peter had again won great praise and honour.

The king sent to invite him to his table; he sat opposite the princess and was amazed at her beauty. She constantly looked kindly at him, which caused him the greatest confusion. His talk pleased the king, and his noble and strong appearance astonished the attendants. In the hall he found opportunity to speak alone with the princess, and she invited him to come again often, upon which he took leave; she sent him away at length with another very kind glance.

Peter went through the streets as if intoxicated. He hurried into a beautiful garden and walked up and down with folded arms, now slowly, now quickly, without being able to understand how the hours passed. He heard nothing around him, for music within him drowned the whispering of the trees and the rippling murmur of the fountains. A thousand times he spoke the name Magelone and then was suddenly afraid that he had called it loudly through the garden. Towards evening a sweet music sounded, and now he sat down on the grass behind a bush and wept. It seemed to him as though heaven had for the first time displayed its beauty, and yet this feeling made him unhappy. He saw the grace of the princess floating on the silver waves; she appeared like sunrise in the darkening night, and the stars stood still, trees were quiet, and the winds hushed. Now the last accents of the music sounded, the trees rustled again and the fountains grew louder. Peter roused himself and softly sang the following song:

> Is it gladness that is ringing,
>   Is it sorrow, in my heart?
> Now a thousand flow'rs are springing
>   And all former joys depart, etc.

He was somewhat comforted and swore to win his love or to die. Late at night he returned to the inn, sat down in his room, and repeated every word the Princess had said to him. Now he thought he had reason to rejoice, then he was again troubled and in doubt. He wished to write to his father, but could only address Magelone, and then he reproached himself for his absence of mind in venturing to write to her whom he did not know. At length he lay down; slumber overcame him, and wonderful visions of love and flight, solitary forests and storms at sea, visited his chamber and covered the bare walls as with beautiful variegated hangings.

How the Knight sent Magelone a Message.

During the night Magelone was as restless as her unknown knight. She went often to the window and looked down thoughtfully into the garden. She listened to the rustling trees, looked at the stars mirrored in the sea, reproached the stranger because he was not standing before her window, then wept because she thought it impossible. When she closed her eyes she saw the tournament and the beloved unknown looking up with longing hope. Now she fed on these fancies, now she scolded herself. Towards morning she fell into a light slumber.

At last she resolved to confess her inclination to her beloved nurse. In a confidential evening hour she said to her : Dear nurse, something has for a long time been weighing upon me which almost crushes my heart; I must, at length, tell it you and you must help me with your motherly counsel, for I do not know any longer how to advise myself. The nurse answered : Confide in me, dear child; it is for this that I am older, and love you as a mother, that I may assist you to good purpose, for youth never knows how to help itself.

When the princess heard these words she became more courageous and confidential and said : Oh, Gertrude, have you observed the unknown knight with the silver keys? But of course you have, for he is the only one worth notice; all the others serve but to glorify him, to circle his head with the sunshine of fame. He is the one man, the most beautiful youth, the bravest hero. Since I saw him my eyes have become useless, for they now see only my thoughts in which he dwells in all his glory. If I only knew that he were of high race I would place all my hopes on him; but he cannot come from an unworthy house, who then could be called noble? Oh, answer, comfort me, dear nurse, and give me counsel.

When the nurse heard these words she was frightened and said : Dear child, I have long expected that you would confide to me who it is that you love of the nobles of this or another kingdom, for the highest of the land and even kings desire you. But why have you placed your inclination upon a stranger of whom no one knows whence he came? I tremble lest the King, your father, should observe your love. The princess became much agitated whilst the nurse was speaking, and when she ceased, vehemently reproached her for calling the knight who was so near her heart a stranger. . . . Oh, go and seek him, Gertrude, and find out his rank and his name. He will not keep them secret if I ask them, for I would keep no secrets from him.

When the morning came the nurse went to church to pray for guidance and perceived the knight also kneeling in devout prayer. When he rose, he approached and greeted her politely, for he had seen her at court. She gave him the princess's message and asked his name and his rank : because it did not become so noble a man to remain hidden.

Peter rejoiced, for he perceived that Magelone loved him. He begged leave to keep his name concealed a little longer, but ended his talk with the nurse by saying : Tell the Princess that I am of noble lineage, and that my ancestors are famed in history books. Meanwhile take this remembrance and let it be a little reward for your welcome message which has brought back hope to me.

He gave the nurse one of his rings and she was glad, because she knew from it that he must be of high descent. He modestly gave her, also, a leaf of parchment, saying he did so in the hope that the princess would read some words that he had written down in the sentiment of his love.

> Love drew near from distant places,
> No attendant in her train,
> Beckon'd me, nor called in vain,
> Held me fast in sweet embraces, etc.

The song touched Magelone deeply; it was like the echo of her own feeling. She persuaded the nurse to give her the ring in exchange for another trinket, and before going to rest at night she hung it by a chain of pearls to her neck. She dreamed of a garden, nightingales, music, love, and of another ring even more precious than the first. In the morning she told her dream to the nurse, who became thoughtful, for she saw that the happiness or unhappiness of the princess was fixed on the unknown knight.

How the Knight sent Magelone a Ring.

The nurse tried to see Peter again and found him in church. He went to her directly and asked after the princess. The nurse told him she had kept the ring and had read his words; she also mentioned Magelone's dream. Peter grew red with joy and said: Ah, dear nurse, tell her all I feel and that I must die of longing if I do not speak to her soon; if, however, I may talk with her face to face, I will reveal to her my rank and my name. All my desire is to win her for my wife. Give her this ring also and pray her to keep it as a little token.

The nurse hastened back to Magelone, who ran to meet her and asked for news. See, cried the princess, this is the ring I dreamed of. A leaf contained this song:

> Does pity so tender
> Tell love's sweet surrender?
> Oh, am I awake?
> The fountains are springing,
> The streams softly singing,
> And all for love's sake.

HOW THE KNIGHT RECEIVED ANOTHER MESSAGE FROM THE BEAUTIFUL MAGELONE

Peter again met the nurse in church. She asked him to swear to her his honourable intentions, and when he had taken his oath, promised to help him and the princess. She told Peter to prepare to go, to-morrow afternoon, through the secret garden gate to her room to see Magelone there, and ended by saying : I will leave you alone, that you may speak out your hearts to each other.

After telling him the hour at which he was to go through the gate, she left. Peter was distracted with joy, and it seemed to him that the time stood still until the evening hours. He sat up late at night without a light, looking at the clouds and stars, his heart beating violently. At length he slept. All the next morning he was unable to calm himself, so at last he took a lute and sang :

> Oh, how shall I measure
> The joy of our meeting?
> My spirit's wild beating
> Acclaimeth my soul's only treasure.

HOW PETER VISITED THE BEAUTIFUL MAGELONE.

When the nurse brought Peter to her room he trembled and was very frightened, and both he and Magelone were much confused. Magelone could scarcely help rising and going towards him. She controlled herself, however, and remained seated. The nurse left the room and Peter sank on one knee before the princess. Magelone gave him her beautiful hand and told him to rise and sit near her. Peter told the princess that all his life was consecrated to her. He gave her the third ring, which was the most precious of all, and in doing so kissed her hand. . . . Then she took a costly gold chain and hung it round his neck, and said : Herewith I take you as mine. Here she took the frightened knight in her arms and kissed him, and he returned the kiss and pressed her to his heart.

When they were obliged to part, Peter hastened at once to his room. He walked up and down with great strides and at length seized his instrument, kissed the strings and wept. Then he sang with great fervour :

Were they thine on which these lips were pressing,
  Thine the frankly-offered, tender kiss?
  Dwells in earthly living so much bliss?
Ha! what light and life were in thy sweet confessing,
All my senses tremble in its blessing! etc.

A Tournament in Honour of the Beautiful Magelone.

  The King of Naples much wished his daughter to be soon married to the knight, Henry of Carpone, who had now waited at Naples a long time for this purpose, and he proclaimed another tournament more splendid than any that had gone before it. Many famous knights came from Italy and France, and Peter was victor over all.

  When it was over he went to see Magelone; he had now visited her pretty often, and thought he would like to try her, so he said that he should now be obliged to leave her and go and be with his parents. Magelone wept very much, but as Peter persisted she at length gave way, and said: Go, then, I shall die. Peter rejoiced at this and told her he would not leave her.

  Magelone, however, became thoughtful, and after she had reflected for a while, said to the knight that her father would soon marry her to Sir Henry of Carpone, and that therefore it would, perhaps, be better for Peter to return to his father and mother and to take her with him. She desired him to have two good horses ready the next night at the garden gate: But let them be swift and strong, for if we were to be overtaken we should all be miserable.

  The youth heard the princess with joyful surprise. He said it would be best to take her to his parents, and that the horses should be ready. Magelone did not confide their intention even to the nurse for fear lest she should betray them.

  Peter took a walk through the town to bid farewell to the places near which he had so often wandered in his intoxication, and which he regarded as witnesses of his love. When he returned to his room he was moved to see his faithful lute on the table. Touched by his fingers, it had often expressed the feelings of his heart. He took it up again for the last time and sang:

        Dear strings, we are parting
          This night for evermore,
       'Tis time to be starting
          For the far-off blissful shore, etc.

How Magelone went away with the Knight.

When the night came it was very cloudy and the moonlight showed scantily through the darkness. Magelone said farewell to her favourite flowers as she went through the garden. She found Peter before the gate with three horses, one a palfrey with a light and easy step; the third was to carry provisions, so that they need not enter the inns.

The nurse missed the princess the next morning, and the king sent out many people to search, but all returned after some days without tidings.

Peter chose to ride towards the forests by the sea because they were quiet and lonely. He and Magelone rode on through the night and Magelone was happy. The forest was dark, but whenever they came to an open space she refreshed herself by gazing at Peter. In the morning there was a white mist and by and by the sun shone out. The horses neighed, the birds awoke and sang as they hopped from branch to branch, the happy larks flew upwards and sang from above into the red glimmering world.

Peter also sang cheerful songs. The two travellers saw in the glowing sky, in the brightness of the fresh forest, a reflection of their love. The sun mounted higher, and towards noon Magelone felt a great weariness. They dismounted, therefore, at a cool, shady place in the forest where there was a mound thickly covered with moss and tender grass. Here Peter sat down and spread out his mantle, and Magelone placed herself upon it, resting her head on the knight. She told Peter how happy she was, and begged him to sing to her, to mingle his voice with the birds, the trees, the brooks, in order that she might sleep a little : But wake me at the right time in order that we may soon arrive at the home of your dear parents. Peter smiled, watched her beautiful eyes close, and sang :

> Rest thee, sweet love, in the shadow
>   Of leafy, glimmering night;
> The grass rustles over the meadow,
> Refreshing and cool is the shadow,
>   And love holds thee in sight.
>   Sleep, lady mine,
>   Hush'd in woodland shrine,
>   Ever I am thine, etc.

Peter almost sang himself to sleep also. Then something roused him. He looked round and saw a number of beautiful, tender birds on the mound, and it pleased him that they came so near to Magelone. But a slight noise caused him to turn again, and he was startled to perceive a great black raven perched on the branch of the tree behind him; it seemed to him like a rough, coarse churl amongst noble knights.

He fancied that Magelone breathed with some uneasiness, and unlaced the neck of her dress. There he found a little red silk bag; it was new, and he was curious to know what was in it and turned it out. He was overjoyed to find that it contained his three precious rings, and quickly wrapped them up again and placed them beside him on the grass. But suddenly the raven flew down from the tree and carried away the bag, perhaps taking it for a piece of meat. Peter was frightened. Magelone might awaken and be displeased at losing her rings. He therefore folded his mantle and placed it carefully under her head, and then stood up to look for the raven. It flew away, and Peter followed and threw stones to make it drop the bag, but was unable to hit it. As it flew further and further he went after it, without noticing that he was already some distance from the spot where he had left Magelone sleeping, till presently he came to the sea. There was a pointed crag not far from the shore and the raven perched there, and Peter again threw stones. At last the bird dropped the bag and flew away screaming. Peter saw the bag floating in the sea close by and ran up and down to find something to help him into the water. He found an old weather-beaten boat left behind by fishermen as useless, and jumped into it and tried to steer towards the bag. Suddenly a strong wind blew from the land, the waves rose, and in spite of all Peter could do, the boat was carried past the crag and further and further from the shore. The bag was fast disappearing from sight; now it was only like a red spot in the distance, the land receded. Peter cried and lamented loudly, but without avail. His tones were echoed back mingled with the sound of the waves. He thought of Magelone sleeping in the wood, and wished to drown himself in his despair. Presently the sun shone out, and now he was seized with a terrible thirst which he was unable to quench. At length evening began to fall: Ah, dearest Magelone, he thought, how strangely have we been parted! The moon filled the world with golden twilight; stars appeared in heaven, and the firmament was mirrored in the waving water. All was still and only the waves splashed, and birds fluttered over him from time to time, filling the air with strange tones. At last Peter lay down in the boat and sang loudly:

> Foam on then in furious raging,
> Surround me, tempestuous waves,
> Relentless thy forces engaging,
> For death is the boon that love craves, etc.

The sequel may be summarised. Magelone, on awakening and finding herself alone, waits vainly for Peter's return, and at length, as night comes on, climbs a tree to be safe from the wild beasts which she fancies she hears in the distance. In the morning she loosens the horses which Peter had tied to a tree and lets them go their own way, and after a little while finds herself on the road to Rome, where she makes an exchange of dress with a passing pilgrim. Making her way first to Rome and thence to Genoa, she takes ship for Provence, where she thinks she may hear something of Peter. She is sheltered on her arrival there by a kind woman who talks to her about the good Count and Countess of Provence and of their great grief. They have heard nothing of their only son since his departure two years ago in quest of adventure. Magelone now knows that some sad mishap has befallen Peter, and that he had not intended to leave her. She resolves to remain unmarried, think of Peter, and dedicate her life to the service of God. The kind woman with whom she is staying tells her of a small island near "the port of the heathen," where all merchant ships and other vessels call in passing and where many poor and sick folk are to be found. Here she resolves to settle. She builds a small church, the altar of which is raised to the honour of St. Peter, and calls it the Church of St. Pierre de Maguelonne. The fame of her strict life and good deeds reaches the ears of the Count and Countess of Provence, who go to see her, and the countess, not knowing who she is, relates the history of her troubles. Magelone comforts her and inspires her with the hope that Peter will return. Some time afterwards the count's cook finds a small red bag in the belly of a great fish which he has cut open. He runs with it to the countess, who finds that it contains her three precious rings. This wonderful event convinces her that she will see her son again.

Tieck's version of Magelone's adventure is that, after untying the horses and wandering alone for some days till she comes to Provence, she finds shelter in a shepherd's hut, where she sings the song No. 11 of Brahms' cycle:

Not long enduring,
Light goes by;
The morning seeth
The chaplet dry
That yesterday blossomed
In splendour bright,
But drooped and withered
In gloom of night, etc.

Peter's adventures are various. Rousing himself from his despair on the morning after his separation from Magelone, he resolves to bear the anguish as well as the joy of life with manly courage. Soon a big pirate ship sails towards him. It is full of Moors and heathen who take him on board, and who, struck with his youth and glorious manhood, determine to carry him as a present to the Sultan of Babylon The Sultan is pleased with Peter and shows him high favour. He puts him in charge of a beautiful garden and lets him wait on him at table.

So far Tieck is faithful to the old story, only introducing the song (No. 12 of Brahms' work) which Peter sings as he walks in the garden thinking sadly of Magelone:

Are we, then, for ever parted?
Was our true love all in vain?
Why must we live broken-hearted?
Death were surely lesser pain, etc.

From this point the versions differ. In the mediaeval romance, Peter, who, though beloved by everyone in the Sultan's palace, and especially by the Sultan himself, is very unhappy, at length persuades his master to let him go and see his parents, and after adventures on the way, is recognised by Magelone in one of the beds of her hospital to which he has been brought almost lifeless.

Tieck, who does not localise the Sultan, introduces into the story his beautiful daughter Sulima, who falls violently in love with Peter and has him secretly introduced to her presence by a confidential slave. Peter, greatly surprised and embarrassed, is astonished at her beauty, but his heart holds fast to Magelone. He longs to see his native land again, to be amongst christians and with his parents. He often sees Sulima, who observes his unhappiness and one day offers to fly with him in a ship that is already standing in the harbour with sails filled. She will give him a sign for a certain evening; when he hears a little song he likes in the garden, he is to come and fetch her. Peter, after considering the proposal, decides to accept it. He believes Magelone to be dead, and thinks that he will thus be enabled to return to a christian land and to his parents.

On the appointed night he walks up and down the Sultan's garden by the shore. At length he sleeps, and dreams that Magelone is looking at him threateningly. On awaking, he walks up and down again, reproaching himself, and at last resolves to throw himself into a little boat and cast out to sea alone. It is a lovely summer night, a warm breeze is stirring, and Peter gives himself up to chance and the stars. Then he hears the sign. A zither sounds, and a sweet voice sings :

> Belovèd, where dwelleth
> Thy footstep this night?
> The nightingale telleth
> Its tale of delight, etc.

Peter's heart shrinks within him as he hears the song; it seems to call after him his weakness and vacillation. He rows more swiftly; love urges him backwards, love draws him onward. The music becomes fainter and fainter; now it is quite lost in the distance, and only the murmur of the waves and the stroke of the oar sound through the stillness.

Peter gathers heart when the sound of the song no longer reaches him, and lets the little vessel drift before the wind as he sits down and sings :

> Fresh courage on my spirit breaks
> And fading is my sadness ;
> New life within me reawakes
> Old longing and old gladness, etc.

Tieck preserves the further adventures of the romance, but brings the knight to Magelone as she sits spinning outside the door of the shepherd's hut. The song of their reunion is the fifteenth and last of Brahms' cycle :

> Faithful love long time endureth,
> Many an hour it doth survive,
> And from sorrow strength secureth,
> And from doubt doth faith derive.

II.

THE HAMBURG LADIES' CHOIR.*

Avertimento.

Sondern weilen es absolute dem Plaisire fördersam ist, wenn es fein ordentlich dabei einhergeht, als wird denen curieusen Gemüthern, so Mitglieder des sehr nuss- und lieblichen Frauenchors wünschen zu werden und zu bleiben jetzund kund und offenbar gethan, dass sie partoute die Clausuln und Puncti hiefolgenden Geschreibsels unter zu zeichnen haben ehe sie sich obgenannten Tituls erfreuen und an der musikalischen Erlustigung und Divertirung parte nehmen können.

Ich hätte zwaren schon längst damit unter der Bank herfür wischen sollen, alleine aberst dennoch, weilen der Frühling erst lieblich präambuliret und bis der Sommer finiret, gesungen werden dürfte, als möchte es noch an der Zeit sein dieses Opus an das Tageslicht zu stellen.

Pro primo wäre zu remarquiren dass die Mitglieder des Frauenchors da sein müssen.

Als wird verstanden : dass sie sich obligiren sollen, den Stehungen und Singungen der Societät regelmässig beizuwohnen.

So nun Jemand diesen Articul nicht gehörig observiret und, wo Gott für sei, der Fall passirete, dass Jemand wider jedes Decorum so fehlete, dass er während eines Exercitiums ganz fehlete :

soll gestraft werden mit einer Busse von 8 Schillingen H. C. [Hamburger Courant].

Pro secundo ist zu beachten, dass die Mitglieder des Frauenchors da sein müssen.

Als ist zu nehmen, sie sollen praecise zur anberaumeten Zeit da sein.

Wer nun hiewieder also sündiget, dass er das ganze Viertheil einer Stunde zu spät der Societät seine schuldige Reverentz und Aufwartung machet, soll um 2 Schillinge H. C. gestrafet werden.

| : Ihrer grossen Meriten um den Frauenchor wegen und in Betracht ihrer vermuthlich höchst mangelhaften und unglücklichen Complexion, soll nun hier für die nicht genug zu favorirende und adorirende Demoiselle Laura Garbe ein Abonnement hergestellt

---

* From " Brahms in Hamburg," by Walter Hübbe. See p. 274 of this narrative.

werden, wesmassen sie nicht jedesmal zu bezahlen braucht, sondern aber ihro am Schluss des Quartals eine moderirte Rechnung praesentiret wird : |

Pro tertio : Das einkommende Geld mag denen Bettelleuten gegeben werden und wird gewünscht dass Niemand davon gesättiget werden möge.

Pro quarto ist zu merken, dass die Musikalien grossentheils der Discretion der Dames anvertrauet sind. Derohalben sollen sie wie fremdes Eigenthum von den ehr- und tugendsamen Jungfrauen und Frauen in rechter Lieb und aller Hübschheit gehalten werden, auch in keinerlei Weise ausserhalb der Societät benüsset werden.

Pro quinto : Was nicht mit singen kann, das sehen wir als ein Neutrum an. Will heissen : Zuhörer werden geduldet indessen aber pro ordinario nicht beachtet, was Gestalt sonsten die rechte Nussbarkeit der Exercitia nicht beschaffet werden möchte.

Obgemeldeter gehörig specifizirter Erlass wird durch gegenwärtiges General-Rescript anjesso jeder männiglich public gemacht und soll in Würden gehalten werden, bis der Frauenchor seine Endschaft erreichet hat.

Solltest du nun nicht nur vor dich ohnverbrüchlich darob halten, sondern auch alles Ernstes daran sein, dass andere auf keinerlei Weise noch Wege darwider thun noch handeln mögen.

An dem beschiehet Unsere Meinung und erwarte dero gewünschte und wohlgewogene Approbation.

Der ich verharre in tiefter Devotion
und Veneration des Frauenchors allzeit dienstbeflissener
schreibfertiger und taktfester

Johannes Kreisler jun.
alias : Brahms.

Geben auf Montag
den 30 ten des Monats Aprili.
A. D. 1860.

Professor Hübbe adds :

"It must be said in explanation of the jesting note to section 2 that the Demoiselle Garbe mentioned in it was often prevented from being punctual, and that Brahms was unwilling to begin without her. The exception at first taken by her to the note in question was met most kindly by Frau Schumann, who pointed out that the special mention of her name in the highly important document would be the very means of securing its lasting fame.

"The 'begging people' of section 3 saw nothing, as I am told, of the money collected by the fines, which was used for other purposes —on one occasion for an excursion to Reinbeck.

"One of the ladies' copies still in existence bears the following signatures: Auguste Brandt, Bertha Porubszky, Laura Garbe, Marie Seebohm, Emilie Lentz, Clara Schumann, Julie Hallier, Marie Hallier, Ch. Avé Lallement, Friedchen Wagner, Thusnelde Wagner, M. Reuter, Betty Völckers, Marie Völckers, Henny Gabain, Marie Böhme, Francisca Meier, Camilla Meier, Susanne Schmaltz, Antonie Mertens (Emma Grädener)."

The metal badge which the members had to wear was no doubt adopted at this time (1860). It had the form of a trefoil clover leaf with a circle in the centre. This displayed a B upon red, and the three surrounding parts of the trefoil, the letters H. F. C. upon blue ground.

Music and Books published by Travis & Emery Music Bookshop:

Anon.: Hymnarium Sarisburiense, cum Rubricis et Notis Musicis.

Agricola, Johann Friedrich from Tosi: Anleitung zur Singkunst.

Bach, C.P.E.: edited W. Emery: Nekrolog or Obituary Notice of J.S. Bach.

Bateson, Naomi Judith: Alcock of Salisbury

Bathe, William: A Briefe Introduction to the Skill of Song

Bax, Arnold: Symphony #5, Arranged for Piano Four Hands by Walter Emery

Burney, Charles: The Present State of Music in France and Italy

Burney, Charles: The Present State of Music in Germany, The Netherlands ...

Burney, Charles: An Account of the Musical Performances ... Handel

Burney, Karl: Nachricht von Georg Friedrich Handel's Lebensumstanden.

Burns, Robert: The Caledonian Musical Museum ..The Best Scotch Songs. (1810)

Cobbett, W.W.: Cobbett's Cyclopedic Survey of Chamber Music. (2 vols.)

Corrette, Michel: Le Maitre de Clavecin

Crimp, Bryan: Dear Mr. Rosenthal ... Dear Mr. Gaisberg ...

Crimp, Bryan: Solo: The Biography of Solomon

d'Indy, Vincent: Beethoven: Biographie Critique

d'Indy, Vincent: Beethoven: A Critical Biography

d'Indy, Vincent: César Franck (in French)

Fischhof, Joseph: Versuch einer Geschichte des Clavierbaues. (Faksimile 1853).

Frescobaldi, Girolamo: D'Arie Musicali per Cantarsi. Primo & Secondo Libro.

Geminiani, Francesco: The Art of Playing the Violin.

Handel; Purcell; Boyce; Geene et al: Calliope or English Harmony: Volume First.

Häuser: Musikalisches Lexikon. 2 vols in one.

Hawkins, John: A General History of the Science and Practice of Music (5 vols.)

Herbert-Caesari, Edgar: The Science and Sensations of Vocal Tone

Herbert-Caesari, Edgar: Vocal Truth

Hopkins and Rimboult: The Organ. Its History and Construction.

Hunt, John: - see separate list of discographies at the end of these titles

Isaacs, Lewis: Hänsel and Gretel. A Guide to Humperdinck's Opera.

Isaacs, Lewis: Königskinder (Royal Children) A Guide to Humperdinck's Opera.

Kastner: Manuel Général de Musique Militaire

Lacassagne, M. l'Abbé Joseph : Traité Général des élémens du Chant.

Lascelles (née Catley), Anne: The Life of Miss Anne Catley.

Mainwaring, John: Memoirs of the Life of the Late George Frederic Handel

Malcolm, Alexander: A Treaty of Music: Speculative, Practical and Historical

Marx, Adolph Bernhard: Die Kunst des Gesanges, Theoretisch-Practisch

May, Florence: The Life of Brahms

May, Florence: The Girlhood Of Clara Schumann: Clara Wieck And Her Time.

Mellers, Wilfrid: Angels of the Night: Popular Female Singers of Our Time

Mellers, Wilfrid: Bach and the Dance of God

Mellers, Wilfrid: Beethoven and the Voice of God

Mellers, Wilfrid: Caliban Reborn - Renewal in Twentieth Century Music

Music and Books published by Travis & Emery Music Bookshop:

Mellers, Wilfrid: Darker Shade of Pale, A Backdrop to Bob Dylan
Mellers, Wilfrid: François Couperin and the French Classical Tradition
Mellers, Wilfrid: Harmonious Meeting
Mellers, Wilfrid: Le Jardin Retrouvé, The Music of Frederic Mompou
Mellers, Wilfrid: Music and Society, England and the European Tradition
Mellers, Wilfrid: Music in a New Found Land: ... ... American Music
Mellers, Wilfrid: Romanticism and the Twentieth Century (from 1800)
Mellers, Wilfrid: The Masks of Orpheus: ...... the Story of European Music.
Mellers, Wilfrid: The Sonata Principle (from c. 1750)
Mellers, Wilfrid: Vaughan Williams and the Vision of Albion
Panchianio, Cattuffio: Rutzvanscad Il Giovine
Pearce, Charles: Sims Reeves, Fifty Years of Music in England.
Playford, John: An Introduction to the Skill of Musick.
Purcell, Henry et al: Harmonia Sacra ... The First Book, (1726)
Purcell, Henry et al: Harmonia Sacra ... Book II (1726)
Quantz, Johann: Versuch einer Anweisung die Flöte trave rsiere zu spielen.
Rameau, Jean-Philippe: Code de Musique Pratique, ou Methodes.
Rastall, Richard: The Notation of Western Music.
Rimbault, Edward: The Pianoforte, Its Origins, Progress, and Construction.
Rousseau, Jean Jacques: Dictionnaire de Musique
Rubinstein, Anton : Guide to the proper use of the Pianoforte Pedals.
Sainsbury, John S.: Dictionary of Musicians. (1825). 2 vols.
Serré de Rieux, Jean de : Les dons des Enfans de Latone
Simpson, Christopher: A Compendium of Practical Musick in Five Parts
Spohr, Louis: Autobiography
Spohr, Louis: Grand Violin School
Tans'ur, William: A New Musical Grammar; or The Harmonical Spectator
Terry, Charles Sanford: Bach's Chorals – Parts 1, 2 and 3.
Terry, Charles Sanford: John Christian Bach
Terry, Charles Sanford: J.S. Bach's Original Hymn-Tunes for Congregational Use.
Terry, Charles Sanford: Four-Part Chorals of J.S. Bach. (German & English)
Terry, Charles Sanford: Joh. Seb. Bach, Cantata Texts, Sacred and Secular.
Terry, Charles Sanford: The Origins of the Family of Bach Musicians.
Tosi, Pierfrancesco: Opinioni de' Cantori Antichi, e Moderni
Tosi, Pierfrancesco: Observations on the Florid Song.
Van der Straeten, Edmund: History of the Violoncello, The Viol da Gamba ...
Van der Straeten, Edmund: History of the Violin, Its Ancestors... (2 vols.)
Walther, J. G. [Waltern]: Musicalisches Lexikon [Musikalisches Lexicon]
Zwirn, Gerald: Stranded Stories From The Operas

Travis & Emery Music Bookshop
17 Cecil Court, London, WC2N 4EZ, United Kingdom.
Tel. (+44) 20 7240 2129
© Travis & Emery 2009

Discographies by Travis & Emery:

Discographies by John Hunt.

1987: 978-1-906857-14-1: From Adam to Webern: the Recordings of von Karajan.

1991: 978-0-951026-83-0: 3 Italian Conductors and 7 Viennese Sopranos: 10 Discographies: Arturo Toscanini, Guido Cantelli, Carlo Maria Giulini, Elisabeth Schwarzkopf, Irmgard Seefried, Elisabeth Gruemmer, Sena Jurinac, Hilde Gueden, Lisa Della Casa, Rita Streich.

1992: 978-0-951026-85-4: Mid-Century Conductors and More Viennese Singers: 10 Discographies: Karl Boehm, Victor De Sabata, Hans Knappertsbusch, Tullio Serafin, Clemens Krauss, Anton Dermota, Leonie Rysanek, Eberhard Waechter, Maria Reining, Erich Kunz.

1993: 978-0-951026-87-8: More 20th Century Conductors: 7 Discographies: Eugen Jochum, Ferenc Fricsay, Carl Schuricht, Felix Weingartner, Josef Krips, Otto Klemperer, Erich Kleiber.

1994: 978-0-951026-88-5: Giants of the Keyboard: 6 Discographies: Wilhelm Kempff, Walter Gieseking, Edwin Fischer, Clara Haskil, Wilhelm Backhaus, Artur Schnabel.

1994: 978-0-951026-89-2: Six Wagnerian Sopranos: 6 Discographies: Frieda Leider, Kirsten Flagstad, Astrid Varnay, Martha Moedl, Birgit Nilsson, Gwyneth Jones.

1995: 978-0-952582-70-0: Musical Knights: 6 Discographies: Henry Wood, Thomas Beecham, Adrian Boult, John Barbirolli, Reginald Goodall, Malcolm Sargent.

1995: 978-0-952582-71-7: A Notable Quartet: 4 Discographies: Gundula Janowitz, Christa Ludwig, Nicolai Gedda, Dietrich Fischer-Dieskau.

1996: 978-0-952582-75-5: Leopold Stokowski (1882-1977): Discography and Concert Register

1996: 978-0-952582-76-2: Makers of the Philharmonia: 11 Discographies: Alceo Galliera, Walter Susskind, Paul Kletzki, Nicolai Malko, Issay Dobrowen, Lovro Von Matacic, Efrem Kurtz, Otto Ackermann, Anatole Fistoulari, George Weldon, Robert Irving.

1996: 978-0-952582-72-4: The Post-War German Tradition: 5 Discographies: Rudolf Kempe, Joseph Keilberth, Wolfgang Sawallisch, Rafael Kubelik, Andre Cluytens.

1996: 978-0-952582-73-1: Teachers and Pupils: 7 Discographies: Elisabeth Schwarzkopf, Maria Ivoguen, Maria Cebotari, Meta Seinemeyer, Ljuba Welitsch, Rita Streich, Erna Berger.

1996: 978-0-952582-75-5: Leopold Stokowski: Discography and Concert Listing.

1996: 978-0-952582-76-2: Makers of the Philharmonia: 11 Discographies Alceo Galliera, Walter Susskind, Paul Kletzki, Nicolai Malko, Issay Dobrowen, Lovro Von Matacic, Efrem Kurtz, Otto Ackermann, Anatole Fistoulari, George Weldon, Robert Irving.

1996: 978-0-952582-77-9: Tenors in a Lyric Tradition: 3 Discographies: Peter Anders, Walther Ludwig, Fritz Wunderlich.

1997: 978-0-952582-78-6: The Lyric Baritone: 5 Discographies: Hans Reinmar, Gerhard Huesch, Josef Metternich, Hermann Uhde, Eberhard Waechter.

1997: 978-0-952582-79-3: Hungarians in Exile: 3 Discographies: Fritz Reiner, Antal Dorati, George Szell.

1997: 978-1-901395-00-6: The Art of the Diva: 3 Discographies: Claudia Muzio, Maria Callas, Magda Olivero.

1997: 978-1-901395-01-3: Metropolitan Sopranos: 4 Discographies: Rosa Ponselle, Eleanor Steber, Zinka Milanov, Leontyne Price.

1997: 978-1-901395-02-0: Back From The Shadows: 4 Discographies: Willem Mengelberg, Dimitri Mitropoulos, Hermann Abendroth, Eduard Van Beinum.

1997: 978-1-901395-03-7: More Musical Knights: 4 Discographies: Hamilton Harty, Charles Mackerras, Simon Rattle, John Pritchard.

1998: 978-1-901395-95-2: More Giants of the Keyboard: 5 Discographies: Claudio Arrau, Gyorgy Cziffra, Vladimir Horowitz, Dinu Lipatti, Artur Rubinstein.

1998: 978-1-901395-94-5: Conductors On The Yellow Label: 8 Discographies: Fritz Lehmann, Ferdinand Leitner, Ferenc Fricsay, Eugen Jochum, Leopold Ludwig, Artur Rother, Franz Konwitschny, Igor Markevitch.
1998: 978-1-901395-96-9: Mezzo and Contraltos: 5 Discographies: Janet Baker, Margarete Klose, Kathleen Ferrier, Giulietta Simionato, Elisabeth Hoengen.
1999: 978-1-901395-97-6: The Furtwaengler Sound Sixth Edition: Discography and Concert Listing.
1999: 978-1-901395-98-3: The Great Dictators: 3 Discographies: Evgeny Mravinsky, Artur Rodzinski, Sergiu Celibidache.
1999: 978-1-901395-99-0: Sviatoslav Richter: Pianist of the Century: Discography.
2000: 978-1-901395-04-4: Philharmonic Autocrat 1: Discography of: Herbert Von Karajan [Third Edition].
2000: 978-1-901395-05-1: Wiener Philharmoniker 1 - Vienna Philharmonic and Vienna State Opera Orchestras: Discography Part 1 1905-1954.
2000: 978-1-901395-06-8: Wiener Philharmoniker 2 - Vienna Philharmonic and Vienna State Opera Orchestras: Discography Part 2 1954-1989.
2001: 978-1-901395-07-5: Gramophone Stalwarts: 3 Separate Discographies: Bruno Walter, Erich Leinsdorf, Georg Solti.
2001: 978-1-901395-08-2: Singers of the Third Reich: 5 Discographies: Helge Roswaenge, Tiana Lemnitz, Franz Voelker, Maria Mueller, Max Lorenz.
2001: 978-1-901395-09-9: Philharmonic Autocrat 2: Concert Register of Herbert Von Karajan Second Edition.
2002: 978-1-901395-10-5: Sächsische Staatskapelle Dresden: Complete Discography.
2002: 978-1-901395-11-2: Carlo Maria Giulini: Discography and Concert Register.
2002: 978-1-901395-12-9: Pianists For The Connoisseur: 6 Discographies: Arturo Benedetti Michelangeli, Alfred Cortot, Alexis Weissenberg, Clifford Curzon, Solomon, Elly Ney.
2003: 978-1-901395-14-3: Singers on the Yellow Label: 7 Discographies: Maria Stader, Elfriede Troetschel, Annelies Kupper, Wolfgang Windgassen, Ernst Haefliger, Josef Greindl, Kim Borg.
2003: 978-1-901395-15-0: A Gallic Trio: 3 Discographies: Charles Muench, Paul Paray, Pierre Monteux.
2004: 978-1-901395-16-7: Antal Dorati 1906-1988: Discography and Concert Register.
2004: 978-1-901395-17-4: Columbia 33CX Label Discography.
2004: 978-1-901395-18-1: Great Violinists: 3 Discographies: David Oistrakh, Wolfgang Schneiderhan, Arthur Grumiaux.
2006: 978-1-901395-19-8: Leopold Stokowski: Second Edition of the Discography.
2006: 978-1-901395-20-4: Wagner Im Festspielhaus: Discography of the Bayreuth Festival.
2006: 978-1-901395-21-1: Her Master's Voice: Concert Register and Discography of Dame Elisabeth Schwarzkopf [Third Edition].
2007: 978-1-901395-22-8: Hans Knappertsbusch: Kna: Concert Register and Discography of Hans Knappertsbusch, 1888-1965. Second Edition.
2008: 978-1-901395-23-5: Philips Minigroove: Second Extended Version of the European Discography.
2009: 978-1-901395-24-2: American Classics: The Discographies of Leonard Bernstein and Eugene Ormandy.
2010: 978-1-901395-25-9: Dirigenten der DDR: Conductors of the German Democratic Republic

Discography by Stephen J. Pettitt, edited by John Hunt:

1987: 978-1-906857-16-5: Philharmonia Orchestra: Complete Discography 1945-1987

Available from: Travis & Emery at 17 Cecil Court, London, UK. (+44) 20 7 240 2129. email on sales@travis-and-emery.com .